Trading Futures

FOR

DUMMIES®

by Joe Duarte, MD

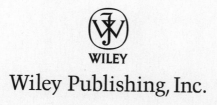

Wiley Publishing, Inc.

Trading Futures For Dummies®

Published by
Wiley Publishing, Inc.
111 River St.
Hoboken, NJ 07030-5774
www.wiley.com

Copyright © 2008 by Wiley Publishing, Inc., Indianapolis, Indiana

Published by Wiley Publishing, Inc., Indianapolis, Indiana

Published simultaneously in Canada

For general information on our other products and services, please contact our Customer Care Department within the U.S. at 800-762-2974, outside the U.S. at 317-572-3993, or fax 317-572-4002.

For technical support, please visit www.wiley.com/techsupport.

Wiley also publishes its books in a variety of electronic formats. Some content that appears in print may not be available in electronic books.

Library of Congress Control Number: 2008929124

ISBN: 978-0-470-28722-4

Manufactured in the United States of America

10 9 8 7 6 5 4 3 2 1

WILEY

Trading Futures For Dummies®

Cheat Sheet

Rules to Keep You Sane in the Futures Markets

- Trust in Chaos Theory to set the market's rhythm and in policymakers to make mistakes.
- Avoid undercapitalization and pay attention to money management.
- Be patient when setting up trades.
- Believe in the charts and the markets, not the talking heads.
- Diversification is protection.
- Set realistic goals.
- Remember that bragging is a sign of trouble.
- Have low expectations.

Essential Economic Reports to Monitor as a Futures Trader

- The monthly employment report
- The Consumer Price Index
- The Producer Price Index
- ISM and regional purchasing manager's reports
- The Beige Book from the Federal Reserve
- Housing Starts
- Index of Leading Economic Indicators
- Gross Domestic Product
- Oil Supply Data

Making Sense of Technical Analysis

Technical analysis, discussed in Chapters 7 and 8, can be intimidating. These tips should help.

- Charting isn't meant to replace fundamental analysis. Charts are meant to complement and enhance it, enabling you to make better decisions.
- Understanding the fundamentals of supply and demand in your particular segment of the market is necessary for you to be able to trade futures based on charted technical signals. Knowing the fundamentals and the technical analysis makes investing your hard-earned money easier.
- Becoming familiar with more than one set of indicators and combining them gives you more than one perspective from which to view the markets. Narrow-minded traders don't go too far.
- Learning the basics of following moving averages, identifying trend reversals, and drawing trend lines is important. But you should also add new layers of analysis, such as moving average crossover systems, Fibonnacci retracements, and other more sophisticated techniques as you gain more experience.
- Continuing to expand your knowledge of technical analysis is important. You can do so by reading books as well as magazines like *Technical Analysis of Stocks and Commodities* and *Active Trader*, which are excellent sources of interesting articles. *Investor's Business Daily,* either the print or the digital version of the paper on its Web site, is a chart reader's paradise for stock and futures traders.
- Exercising care to avoid clutter in your charts, even as you become more sophisticated in your approach to trading futures, is advantageous. The simpler your charts, the better the picture you get and the better your decisions will be.

For Dummies: Bestselling Book Series for Beginners

Trading Futures For Dummies®

Essential Requirements of an Online Charting Service

- **Accessibility:** The service needs to be available to you virtually anywhere, either online or by the use of a convenient online interface.
- **Support:** Make sure the service provides both a toll-free telephone number to call for support and online support.
- **Charting tools:** The charts provided by your charting service must be easy-to-read and user-friendly. You shouldn't have to punch five or ten keys or toggle your mouse for ten minutes while trying to make your chart look right.
- **Real-time quotes:** Trading futures without real-time quotes is a sure path down the road to ruin.
- **Live charts:** If you're going to trade, you need access to *live charts* that actually change with every tick (up or down movement) of the market.
- **Time-frame analysis:** Make sure your charting service enables you to produce intraday charts. You want to be able to look at different time frames simultaneously.
- **Multiple indicators:** Make sure your service lets you plot price charts and multiple indicators at the same time.

Three Reasons to Consider Using Candlestick Charts

- **Trends are easier to spot.** For example, a sea of rising green (or white), meaning a large grouping of bullish candles on a candlestick chart, is hard to mistake for anything other than a strong uptrend. Because candlesticks tend to have a body in most cases, the overall trend of the market is often easier to identify.
- **Trend changes are easier to spot.** Candlestick patterns can be dramatic and can help you identify trend changes before you can recognize them on bar charts. Some candlestick patterns are reliable at predicting future prices.
- **Shifts in momentum are as easy to spot.** Conditions in which a security is oversold and over-bought, along with trends and other kinds of indicators, may be easier to spot on candlestick charts than they are on bar charts due to the presence of doji candles and color. For example, an engulfing pattern, which can be either negative or positive, is easier to spot in a candlestick chart.

For Dummies: Bestselling Book Series for Beginners

About the Author

Dr. Joe Duarte is a widely read market analyst, writer, and an active trader. His daily Market IQ column is read by thousands of investors, futures and stock traders, information seekers, intelligence aficionados, and professionals around the world.

Dr. Duarte is well recognized as a geopolitical and financial market analyst combining a unique set of viewpoints into an original blend of solutions for his audience. His daily columns appear at www.joe-duarte.com and are syndicated worldwide by FinancialWire.

He is author of *Successful Energy Sector Investing, Successful Biotech Investing, Futures and Options For Dummies,* and coauthor of *After-Hours Trading Made Easy.*

He is a board certified anesthesiologist, a registered investment advisor, and President of River Willow Capital Management.

Dr. Duarte has appeared on CNBC and appears regularly on *The Financial Sense Newshour with Jim Puplava* radio show, where he comments on the energy markets and geopolitics. He has logged appearances on Biz Radio, Wall Street Radio, JagFn, WebFN, KNX radio in Los Angeles, and WOWO radio.

One of CNBC's original Market Mavens, Dr. Duarte has been writing about the financial markets since 1990. An expert in health care and biotechnology stocks, the energy sector, as well as financial market sentiment, his daily syndicated stock columns have appeared on leading financial Web sites, including Reuter's e-charts, afterhourtrades.com and MarketMavens.com.

His articles and commentary have appeared on Marketwatch.com. He has been quoted in *Barron's, U.S.A. Today, Smart Money, Medical Economics,* Rigzone.com, and in *Technical Analysis of Stocks and Commodities* magazine.

Dedication

To my mother, whose long fight with cancer is remarkable and a sign of the human spirit's ability to persevere in the toughest of circumstances.

Author's Acknowledgments

A book is always more a product of circumstances than of the author's wits and ability to research data and synthesize it. No author can create without the help of others. So here's the list of important people for this one:

My family, my office staffs from my other life, and the Wiley editorial staff, especially Stacy and Tracy who worked with me despite the inevitable circumstances that arose in the production of this book.

Grace, "the wonder agent" and purveyor of recurrent gigs.

Frank, "the master of all things Web-related," without whom there would be no Joe-Duarte.com.

To the inventor of audio books, because they keep me sane in my travels between the places that I must go to in my search for truth, justice, and bucks.

As always, coffee, tea, vitamins, sports drinks, nutrition bars, and the game of tennis also help.

Especially to those who read my books, subscribe to my Web site, and have kept this thing going for 18 years.

And also to two long-time friends, John and Greg, whose interactions with me always prove to be worthwhile and interesting, to say the least.

If I've forgotten to mention anyone, it wasn't intentional — I'm not as young as I used to be.

Publisher's Acknowledgments

We're proud of this book; please send us your comments through our Dummies online registration form located at www.dummies.com/register/.

Some of the people who helped bring this book to market include the following:

Acquisitions, Editorial, and Media Development

Project Editor: Tracy Brown Collins

Copy Editor: Christy Pingleton

Acquisitions Editor: Stacy Kennedy

Technical Editor: Brian Richman

Editorial Manager: Jennifer Ehrlich

Editorial Supervisor and Reprint Editor: Carmen Krikorian

Art Coordinator: Alicia South

Editorial Assistants: Erin Calligan Mooney, Joseph Niesen, David Lutton, and Jennette ElNaggar

Cartoons: Rich Tennant (www.the5thwave.com)

Composition Services

Project Coordinator: Katie Key

Layout and Graphics: Reuben W. Davis, Melissa K. Jester, Ronald Terry, Christine Williams

Proofreaders: Laura Albert, Melissa Bronnenberg, Valerie Haynes Perry

Indexer: Bonnie Mikkelson

Publishing and Editorial for Consumer Dummies

Diane Graves Steele, Vice President and Publisher, Consumer Dummies

Joyce Pepple, Acquisitions Director, Consumer Dummies

Kristin A. Cocks, Product Development Director, Consumer Dummies

Kathleen Nebenhaus, Vice President and Executive Publisher, Consumer Dummies, Lifestyles, Pets, Education Publishing for Technology Dummies

Gerry Fahey, Vice President of Production Services

Debbie Stailey, Director of Composition Services

Contents at a Glance

Table of Contents

Introduction

Risk and uncertainty go hand in hand with opportunities to make money. Those who can shake off the chains of preconceived notions and ideology and who discover how to make money as markets rise or fall are more successful than investors who buy and hold.

And that's what this book is about: embracing the inherent volatility of the world and the markets and using it as a wealth-building tool.

Goods, services, and basic materials probably will undergo major price swings, up and down, at one time or another during the next 20 years. The volatility of the markets is only going to increase. And the chances for sustainable trends that last for decades, the way the stock market rallied in the 1980s and 1990s, are less likely than they were a few years ago.

If global warming doesn't get you, then politicians, militants, or dictators are almost certain to try. That's why finding out how to trade futures is important for investors who not only want to diversify their own portfolios but also want to find ways to protect and grow their money when times are hard in traditional investment venues such as the stock market, a point well illustrated by the action in the financial markets in 2007 and early 2008.

The world has changed since the events of September 11, 2001. China, India, Brazil, and other economies are now competing with the United States and Europe. This competition is not likely to ebb or change for several decades, which means that market volatility is not likely to go away any time soon.

Whereas in the past investors could afford the luxury of buying and holding stocks or mutual funds for the long term, the post-September 11, 2001, world calls for a more active and even a speculative investor. The new world calls for a trader. And the futures markets, although high risk, offer some of the best opportunities to make money by trading in volatile times.

So you need to get ready to work as a stock trader, a geopolitical analyst, a money manager, and an expert in the oil and commodity markets. In my line of work, I have to keep up with news about the economy, disruptions in the supply of oil, the weekly trends of oil supply, weather patterns, and the stock market, both in a macro and micro universe. As a futures trader, you have to do the same with your contract of choice, and you have to pay attention to time factors, especially expiration dates and how much time you have left to decide whether you have to exercise your option.

Remember that successful traders

- ✔ Have a plan, follow it, and adjust it to changing conditions
- ✔ Look at trading as a business
- ✔ Are disciplined in their personal and professional lives
- ✔ Understand the risks and the game they're playing
- ✔ Know and accept that they will make mistakes
- ✔ Never forget their mistakes and benefit from them
- ✔ Never enter into a trade without knowing their exit strategy — how they'll get out of the market
- ✔ Never risk money that they aren't willing to or can't afford to lose
- ✔ Never allow a bad trade to lead to a margin call

Trading futures isn't gambling; it's speculating. It's also about being prepared, gathering information, and making judgment calls about situations that are unfolding, and it's a process of self-protection and an ongoing education.

You may think of yourself as a dummy. But after you read this book, you'll know how trading futures is done and how to stay in the game as long as you want, not necessarily by hitting home runs but rather by showing up to work every day, getting your uniform dirty, and playing good, consistent, fundamental baseball.

About This Book

Futures markets are resurging and are likely to be hot for several decades, given the political landscape. Changing world demographics and the emergence of China and India as economic powers and consumers, coupled with changing politics in the Middle East, are likely to fuel the continued prominence of these markets.

I take you inside these markets and give you tools that you can use for

- ✔ **Analyzing, trading, or just gaining a better understanding of how money works and affects your daily life.**
- ✔ **Starting fresh in your views of how the markets work.** A traditional buy and hold mind-set is a recipe for trouble in futures and options trading, while profit-taking or hedging a position before the weekend is normal operating procedure.

✔ **Discovering that time is on your side in the stock and bond markets, but it's your enemy in futures.** You have to be on top of how much time you have left before your trading position expires, becoming worthless, or you have a load of something delivered with a bill for a large sum of money.

✔ **Reading a sentence just the way it's written.** No tricks, hidden clues, political agendas, or attempts to make you look foolish. If you don't get it, I didn't do a good job of writing it.

✔ **Remembering that measuring the return *of* your money is more important than measuring the return *on* your money.**

Conventions Used in This Book

To help you make the best use of this book, I use the following conventions:

✔ *Italic* is used for emphasis and to highlight new words or terms.

✔ **Boldface text** is used to indicate key words in bulleted lists or the action parts of numbered steps.

✔ `Monofont` is used for Web addresses.

What I Assume about You

I had to start somewhere, so I assumed some things that may or may not apply to you. I'm not trying to offend you or to be condescending. So here's what I've assumed about you:

You're not a beginner. In fact, you've got some experience in investing and at least conceptually know that professionals are not the buy and hold investors that Wall Street would like to make the public believe that they are.

✔ You're looking for a better way to make money in the markets, but even though you have some experience, don't know enough to trade futures and want to find out how to do it without losing your shirt.

✔ Even though you've been a stock trader or investor, you'd like to know more about using charts, indicators, and trading psychology.

✔ You want to find out how to decrease the risk within your portfolio.

✔ You want to become a more active trader and make money more consistently by letting your profits run and cutting your losses short.

✔ You want to know how to make sense of the big picture in the markets and to try your hand at trading currencies, bonds, and commodities.

✔ You like the idea of trading on margin, and you're not afraid of leveraging additional money.

✔ You aren't afraid of being wrong five or six times in a row when trading, but you're willing to try again until you succeed.

✔ You want to investigate more about how politics, wars, weather, and external events can be used as opportunities to trade.

✔ And most important, you know that reading an introductory or intermediate work, such as this, is an excellent beginning, but that you'll have to read more, find out more, and make changes to your trading skills as time passes.

If these assumptions describe you, you've picked up the right book. Nevertheless, I also assume that you have some tools and resources at your disposal. Here's what you need to get started in futures trading:

✔ **Plenty of money and a cast-iron stomach to boot.** You need to have at least twice the amount that your broker/advisor lists as a minimum for opening an account. And you have to be ready to lose it all, fast, although if you follow the money management rules in this book, that won't necessarily happen.

✔ **Your head screwed on straight before you start.** Futures trading is really dangerous and can wither away your trading capital fast.

✔ **A quiet place to prepare, set up your trading station, and make sure that you know your market stuff really well.** Exchange hours, what brokers do and don't do, what trading terms like bid and offer mean, and how to read a brokerage statement are only some of what you need to know.

✔ **A fast computer with a fast Internet connection.**

✔ **Access to good charts.** You can gain access to charts either through the Web or a good trading software program, which gives you the ability to test your strategies before you commit to them.

✔ **Subscriptions to newsletters, books, magazines, and software.** Be ready to spend some money for these important information resources. You can also take courses, and you need to get used to paper trading (practicing without money) before jumping into the deep end.

How This Book Is Organized

I've organized *Trading Futures For Dummies* into six parts. Parts I and II introduce you to the futures markets and market analysis — technical and fundamental. Parts III through V take you into the nuts and bolts: the exchanges, the contracts, trading strategies, and indicators. Part VI is the now-famous *For Dummies* Part of Tens, in which you can discover a little about a lot of different futures information.

Part 1: Understanding the Financial Markets

Sure, this sounds like a lot to swallow, but if you don't understand how the pieces fit together, you won't get the finer points that can make you a better trader.

This part shows you three things:

- Where money comes from and why markets move the way they do
- What the function and role of futures and options markets are
- How the financial markets work together

Part 11: Analyzing the Markets

This part is where you get your basic training. It's all about fundamental and technical analyses, and it gives you details about supply and demand, how to use economic reports, and how to take advantage of seasonal and chart patterns and market sentiment.

Part 111: Financial Futures

Most stock investors think the stock market is the center of the universe. After you read this part, you'll see things differently, because I look at the role of the bond market and how it's really the tail that wags the dog.

Part 1V: Commodity Futures

Yeah, baby! We finally get to pork bellies, soybeans, and wheat. But more important, this part is about trading oil, natural gas, steel, copper, gold, you name it — all of which are affected by strange things like weather, pollution, and electricity thrown in for good measure.

Part V: The Trading Plan

This part is a big case of the nuts and bolts of trading. Relax, it isn't catching, but it is likely to get you a bit more organized. Who can't use a little discipline, eh?

This part details how you can set up, organize, execute, and operate a trading business, starting with the trading calendar and working all the way to deciding what your best markets and surefire strategies are and how to mix and match approaches while trading and hedging.

Part VI: The Part of Tens

Here I give you lists of rules and resources that can not only help you make money but also keep you from losing big chunks of it whenever the markets turn on you.

Icons Used in This Book

For Dummies books use little pictures, called icons, to flag certain chunks of text and information that are of particular interest. Here's what they actually mean to you, the reader:

Yup, this one is important. Don't forget the stuff marked with this icon.

The bull's-eye gives you info that you can put to use right away, such as when to trade or how to engage a specific strategy.

I like this one best because it reminds me of Inspector Clouseau of *The Pink Panther* fame. The "bemb," as Clouseau would say, is a sign that you need to read the information highlighted by it carefully. If you ignore this icon, you can end up in a world of hurt.

Although you can skip this important, but not necessarily essential, information without repercussion, you may not be able to impress your friends at the water cooler as much as you otherwise would.

Where to Go from Here

For Dummies books are set up so you can start reading anywhere. Don't feel as though you have to read everything from beginning to end. If you're a true beginner, or feel as if you need to brush up on the basics of the global economy before moving on to trading, I recommend that you read Parts I and II carefully before you start skipping around. Here's to profitable futures trading.

Part I
Understanding the Financial Markets

The 5th Wave   By Rich Tennant

Defining your investment risk with the:
TOAST RETRIEVING RISK TOLERANCE TEST

LOW RISK | Waits for toast to pop up even though it's burning.

MODERATE RISK | Goes after toast with wooden toast prongs.

HIGH RISK | Goes after toast with all metal butter knife.

ULTRA HIGH RISK | Goes after toast with metal butter knife wearing a wet swim suit and a stainless steel colander on head.

In this part . . .

You get a handle on where money comes from and the important details about how the futures markets work in this part of *Trading Futures For Dummies.* I start you out with the key relationship between central banks and the bond markets and take you on a tour of the futures markets, while offering a little history lesson along the way. That leads you into an overview of today's markets — how they work with and depend on one another.

Chapter 1

The Ins and Outs of Trading Futures

In This Chapter

▶ Finding out who trades futures and what makes them successful

▶ Gathering your trading tools and know-how

▶ Checking out market analysis, short trades, and money management

▶ Understanding the effects of a global economy

▶ Discovering how much fun trading can be

*I*f you're one of those people who look at their mutual fund portfolios once a year and wonder how the results came about, futures trading isn't for you — at least until you make some changes in how you view the financial markets. Much of what the average person believes to be true is not applicable to the financial markets. One example is how sometimes the stock market rallies when people lose their jobs. The reason is that sometimes job losses lead to lower interest rates from central banks. And lower interest rates tend to be a good thing for the stock market at some point in the future.

In other words, as a trader, you need a different mind-set than that of a working or professional person. To be sure, I'm not asking you to change your personal outlook on life, every minute of the day, but it will be helpful to your trading success if you change a few of your views while trading.

No, you don't have to live in a monastery and wear a virtual-reality helmet that plugs into the Internet, has satellite TV, and features real-time quotes and charts. You are, however, going to have to take the time to review your current investing philosophy and find out how futures trading can fit into your day-to-day scheme of things without ruining your family life and your nest egg.

Trading is not investing; it's speculating. *Speculating* is defined as assuming a business risk with the hope of profiting from market fluctuations. Successful speculating requires analyzing situations, predicting outcomes, and putting your money on the side of the trade that represents the way you think the market is going to go, up or down. Speculating also involves an appreciation of the fact that you can be wrong 70 percent of the time and still be a successful futures trader if you apply the correct techniques for analyzing trades, managing your money, and protecting your account.

Basically that means you have to chuck all your preconceptions about buy-and-hold investing, asset allocation, and essentially all the strategies that stock brokerages put out for public consumption. And just so you don't call your brother-in-law the broker and get the publisher and me in trouble: what I mean is that buy-and-hold doesn't work in the futures markets because futures are designed for trading.

Trading futures contracts is a risky business and requires active participation. It can be plied successfully only if you're serious, well prepared, and committed to getting it right. That means that you have to develop new routines and master new things. In essence, you must be able to cultivate your trading craft by constantly reviewing and modifying your plan and strategies.

To be a successful futures trader, you have to become connected with the world through the Internet, television, and other news sources so you can be up-to-date and intimately knowledgeable with regard to world events. And I don't mean just picking up on what you get from occasionally watching the evening or headline news shows.

Setting up for this endeavor also requires a significant amount of money. You need a computer, a trading program, and a brokerage account of some sort, not to mention how well capitalized you have to be to be able to survive.

In essence, in order to morph from couch potato to futures trader, you have to work at it, or you'll be out of the game very quickly.

Who Trades Futures?

Aside from professional speculators and hedgers, whose numbers are many, the ranks of futures traders essentially are made up of people like you and me who are interested in making money in the markets. A wide variety of people trade futures contracts at the retail level.

In his book *Starting Out in Futures Trading* (McGraw-Hill), author Mark Powers cites a study by the Chicago Mercantile Exchange (CME) that described the profile of a futures trader in the 1970s as a male between 35 and 55 years of age with middle- to upper-class income. The study indicated that

- Fifty-four percent were professionals, including doctors, lawyers, dentists, and white-collar workers, especially upper-management types.

✔ Sixty-eight percent were college graduates.

✔ Their overall tendency was toward short-term trading.

By 1999, *Futures Industry* magazine surveyed futures brokers regarding online futures trading. A summary of the results identified

✔ Some general tendencies but couldn't settle on a description for a typical online futures trader

✔ Account sizes ranging from $14,000 to $30,000 at brokerages aimed at retail investors, with average transaction sizes within that group ranging from 1.6 to 5 contracts

✔ Account sizes ranging from $40,000 to millions of dollars at brokerages with mostly institutional clienteles, with average transaction sizes within that group ranging from 17 contracts to even larger transactions

Yet, this is a fluid situation, and it's important to keep the macro demographics of society in mind. For example, as the general population ages, the potential for massive shifts in investment trends increases. Will a significant number of retirees begin to look at futures markets as a potential set of investments? Will this large group of investors start to cash in their stock portfolios? The answers to these questions will be of importance over the next 20 years, as baby boomers begin to leave full-time work and start to cash in long-term equity investments.

The bottom line seems to be that to be able to trade futures you need to have a certain amount of education and the technological and financial means to get started.

What Makes a Futures Trader Successful?

Everyone knows that it helps to know a few things about the financial markets and that you need the ability to at least consider online trading. And, of course, you need the financial resources to trade futures contracts.

But how do you become good at it? How do you manage to survive, even when you're not particularly good at it?

The answer is simple. You must have the money and the ability to develop a trading plan that enables you to keep making trades in the markets long enough to make enough money to capitalize your next big trade.

Simply put: If you don't have enough money, you won't last. And if you don't have a good trading plan, your money quickly disappears.

Ninety-five percent of all futures traders lose money consistently. You have to prepare yourself to be one of the 5 percent who beat the odds. Your success depends more than anything else on how you prepare yourself financially, intellectually, technologically, and personally through the development of a detailed and easy-to-implement trading plan.

What You Need in Order to Trade

You need money, knowledge, patience, and technology to be able to trade futures contracts.

In terms of money, many experienced traders say that you need $100,000 to get started, but the figures from the previous section show that retail investors rarely have that much money in their accounts — at least as of 1999. The truth is that there are many talented traders who have made fortunes after starting out with significantly less than $100,000. However, it would be irresponsible for me to lead you astray and give you the false impression that the odds are very much in your favor if you start trading at a very low equity level.

The reality is that different people fare differently, depending on their trading ability, regardless of their experience level. A trader with a million dollars in equity can lose large amounts just as easily as you and I can with $10,000 worth of equity in our accounts. My only point here is to make sure that you understand the risk involved and that you go into trading with realistic expectations.

If you're looking for a magic number, $25,000 might be a goodcompromise; $10,000 might get you by. And $5,000 is the absolute minimum.

If you don't have that much money and are not sure how to proceed, you need to either reconsider trading altogether, develop a stout trading plan and the discipline required to heed its tenets, or consider managed futures contracts. I discuss these topics in detail in Chapter 17. Would-be traders who have less than $30,000 should also consider the managed futures opportunities like the ones I tell you about in Chapter 17.

When it comes to technology, you need an efficient computer system that has enough memory to enable you to look at large numbers of data and run either multiple, fully loaded browsers or several monitors at the same time. You also need a high-speed Internet connection. If you get serious about trading, you may need to consider having two modes of high-speed Internet access. For a home office, a full-time trader often has high-speed Internet through the cable television service and through DSL (digital subscriber line), with one or the other serving as a backup.

Seeing the Two Sides of Trading

Trading futures contracts is truly a hybrid that lies somewhere between the types of trading that are separately based on technical analysis and fundamental analysis.

The fundamental side of trading (see Chapter 6 for all the details) involves getting to know the following:

✔ The industry in which you're making trades

✔ Contract specifications

✔ Seasonal tendencies of the markets

✔ Important reports on which you need to keep an eye

The technical side of trading (at least the part that I concentrate on) focuses on what the market is doing in response to fundamentals. When you use technical analysis, you look at jargonistic things, such as trading volume, price charts, and open interest, and how they respond to factors like the global economy, interest rates, and politics — to name just a few influences on prices. To do that, you need to have access to and be able to read charts and know how to use indicators, such as trend lines, moving averages, and oscillators. (I show you how in Chapters 7, 8, and 20.) These instruments and indicators help you to keep track of prices and guide you in choosing when and how best to place your trades — in other words, when to get in and out of the markets. Without them, your trading is likely to suffer.

To be sure, there are other approaches to technical analysis, ranging from those listed in this book to rather esoteric techniques that are not mentioned, such as using astrology or rather precise, but not so commonly seen, chart patterns. My goal here is to give you methods and examples that you can begin to see and use immediately. See Chapter 7 for more on technical analysis.

Making money is always better than being right. The key is not what you think should happen, but rather how the market responds to events and fundamental information and how you manage your trade. Success comes from letting winning positions go as long as possible and cutting losses short before they wipe you out.

Getting Used to Going Short

Going or selling short is the opposite of going long. Shorting the market, as it is often referred to, usually troubles stock investors. *Going short* means that you're trying to make money when prices fall, while going long means that you are trying to make money when prices rise. In the stock market, going short involves borrowing shares of stock from someone, usually your broker, so you can sell it at a high price, wait for prices to fall, buy it back at the lower price, return the asset to the lender, and pocket the difference between what you sold it for and what you paid for it.

In the futures market, going short means that you're trying to make money as a result of falling contract prices. No borrowing is involved.

Although this may sound confusing, trading software simplifies the concept for futures traders, by giving you a button choice for short selling. Chapters 7 and 8 offer nice examples, including illustrations of what short selling is and when it's the correct strategy to follow.

In futures trading, every transaction involves a trader who's trading short and one who's trading long.

If selling short confuses you, you definitely need to read this book carefully before you consider trading futures contracts or, for that matter, aggressively trading stocks.

You can also bet on the market falling by using options strategies, a subject that I touch on briefly in Chapter 4 and throughout the book as appropriate, but that is covered in much greater detail in *Trading Options For Dummies* by George A. Fontanills (Wiley).

Managing Your Money

To be a successful trader, you must have a successful money management system that includes a minimum of these four components:

- **Having enough money:** You need enough money to get a good start and to keep trading. Undercapitalization is the major reason for failure. See "What You Need to Trade," earlier in this chapter.

- **Setting appropriate limits:** You need to set reasonable limits on how much you'll risk, how you'll diversify your account, how much you're willing to lose, and when and how you'll take profits. Knowing your limits and sticking to them with regard to all these factors is important to successful trading. You get there by doing things like developing and regularly reviewing your trading plan, and using techniques such as placing stop-loss orders under your trades to limit losses if you're wrong. See Chapters 17, 18, 19, and 20 for trading strategies.

- **Setting realistic goals:** Know where you want to be on a monthly, quarterly, and yearly basis. This will help you evaluate the efficacy of your trading plan.

✔ **Avoiding margin calls:** Margin calls will come if your account's equity falls below critical levels. Margin levels are different for each contract that you trade. A *margin call* is what happens when you hold a position that is falling in value beyond a limit set by the exchange. For example, if you are trading widgets with a margin set at $1,000 and your widget contracts fall below $1,000, your broker calls you and asks you for more money. If you can't put more money in the account, either by wiring it or by selling what's left of your widgets, the broker sells the widgets to raise the money, and your account is inactive until you raise the amount of money needed to meet future margins.

Analyzing the Markets

One of the most important steps you can take toward being a good trader is developing a knack for analyzing the markets. That means you need to understand the technical and fundamental aspects of the market with respect to the underlying asset that you're trading.

The two basic ways for choosing what to trade are

✔ **Monitoring different markets to see which ones are moving or are likely to move.** The more markets that you understand and become familiar with, the better off you'll be. When you have an understanding of the environment and the variables that move more than one market, you can trade each of them individually, based on your knowledge and within the overall trend that they are displaying at any given time. In other words, you're not locked into just trading stocks when the market is going up, because you can also trade oil, natural gas, bonds, currencies, and grains.

The advantage to knowing more than one market is that you'll almost always have something to trade. The disadvantage is that when you're just getting started, you certainly won't be an expert in too many markets, so don't be in a hurry. Chapters 6 through 8 focus on technical and fundamental analyses of the economy, the futures markets, and basic speculating strategies.

✔ **Becoming an expert (on the technical and fundamental aspects) in at least one or two markets, and then trading them exclusively.** The advantage is that you get a good feeling for the subtleties of these markets and your chances of success are likely to increase. The disadvantage is that you may have a good deal of dead time or dull stretches if the markets you choose don't move much. Chapters 10 through 16 cover the major mainstream futures markets in detail, including trading strategies.

Noodling the Global Economy

The dominant economic variables currently emerging in the world are the advance of militant Islam, the Chinese economy, and the emerging purchasing power of the developing world, which now competes effectively for commodities with the developed world.

Every era has one major trend that separates it from the others. In the 1970s, investing was all about commodities, real estate, and oil. In the 1980s, it was about the first generation of technology companies bursting onto the scene. And in the 1990s, it was all about the Internet. These major dynamics came about because a specific set of political and economic circumstances spawned them.

The 21st century has brought inflation back, which means that the commodity markets are the place to be in the foreseeable future. Trends of this magnitude tend to remain in place for many years, but are not guaranteed to go straight up, or straight down, which gives you ample opportunity to trade on the long and the short side. But, at some point, the dominant trend will reverse, and you need to be ready for that moment. Thus, the key to better trading is to know when a major change is occurring and whether that particular trend has changed temporarily or permanently.

The China phenomenon

The first bull market of the 21st century has arguably been in industrial commodities, and much of it has been spurred by the demand for oil, steel, and other raw materials from China as it has transitioned from a centrally run economy to one that's more market oriented.

From that transition, all variables with regard to the financial markets in the early part of the century emerged, as money flows began to chase the seemingly incessant growth story in China. To be sure, this story, as all stories do, will change. And when that unwinding takes place, it will provide smart traders the opportunity to make money by betting against China. As with most bull markets or other economic phenomena, things don't happen overnight. These events take several years to set up, and they slowly emerge until they become evident to the majority. After that they eventually collapse because smart money traders who establish positions early on take their profits and unload their high-priced assets onto the unsuspecting greater fools who come late to the party and spend much more to attend.

The underlying cause of China's miracle boom of the early 21st century started in the late 1970s when President Richard Nixon made his historic visit to Communist China. The pieces already were falling into place before that historic event, but what ensued was a steady opening up of the Chinese economy to foreign capital. Slowly, often in fits and starts, infused money led to a domestic building boom and later to an export boom of Chinese goods.

The Fed's massive lowering of interest rates after the events of September 11, 2001, fueled a more rapid rate of advance in the Chinese economy. Cheap money and easy credit, meaning money borrowed at lower interest rates, moved money to China where it attracted high rates of return based on that country's economic growth rates. When China joined the World Trade Organization in the early 21st century, however, problems surfaced. A corrupt and frail banking system was exposed, and massive environmental problems and significant social inequalities, especially between farmers and city dwellers, became evident.

The Chinese economy at present seems headed for an inflationary spiral, a situation that has the potential to rattle the global economy. This kind of action will have a major impact on the futures markets, and you should be very aware of it.

China's economy is now a key to what happens in the world financial system. Therefore, you need to know that the Chinese economy

✔ Had large sums of money sunk into it by virtually every major bank, brokerage firm, mutual funds that invest in international assets, and major significant individual investor in the world. When the Chinese economy eventually hits the skids, a major trading opportunity in bonds, currencies, short-selling of commodities, and other trading vehicles will take place.

✔ Is a double-edged sword. Although the potential for growth exists, so does the potential for losing lots of money fast.

✔ Can be a major risk. Despite its size, it will remain a risk for many years because of the Chinese government's close involvement.

✔ Will cause futures markets to play a significant role in global financial developments because major players use these markets to hedge their bets or to make large trades with less risk than directly owning Chinese assets.

Europe: Hitting the skids

Unlike China, Europe is a region in decline. After decades of stable growth following World War II, Europe began to fade because large outlays of state money were needed to keep a welfare system afloat, and that led to rising budget deficits.

When the Berlin Wall fell in 1989, Germany, the engine of growth for the continent, started to feel the weight of extending its social safety net to East Germany's Russian-style economy. Outdated East German technology and a poorly trained, unmotivated workforce that was unfamiliar with capitalism became an economic albatross around the country's neck.

France suffered a similar fate as an influx of Middle Eastern and African refugees moved there, in many cases putting increased strain upon that country's social safety net.

The cumbersome socialist regulations of France and Germany, combined with high taxes and a tendency for short workweeks and long vacations, completed the circle that led to the significant decline of the European economy. Badly conceived political ploys by France at a time when the countries of Europe were banding together in the European Union (EU), and again when it expanded in 2004, put a strain on the unity of the entire continent. The war in Iraq is another divisive stake that pits the more established EU states against newer members. As the 21st century evolves, you'll probably see Germany and France moving away from each other ideologically in search of other alliances. Right now, France leans toward China, while Germany leans toward Russia. That could change at any moment.

Friction between the United States and Europe, especially France and Germany (together or separately) will appear regularly. As a futures trader, you can make money from this naturally strained relationship, especially in the bond and currency markets where geopolitical situations tend to get played out more aggressively than in stocks (although stocks are becoming increasingly volatile).

Here's the lay of the fractured land in Europe:

- ✔ Germany is the economic engine of Europe, as is France to a variable degree, depending on the political leanings of the government in power.

- ✔ Germany and France are deeply in debt because of their socialist tendencies, high tax rates, and lack of growth incentives in their economies.

- ✔ Heavily unionized industries and the expense of subsidizing East Germany after unification made Germany weaker during the latter part of the 20th century.

- ✔ France sees itself as the leader of a united Europe, but not all members of the EU agree.

- ✔ Divisions between the members of the EU offer futures traders opportunities to trade currencies and international bonds.

- ✔ The euro is a good antithesis to the dollar, because some governments and political entities have mounted a campaign to make the euro the world's reserve currency, the traditional place of the U.S. Dollar. As with any currency, when a trend is established, the euro tends to trend in one direction for weeks to months at a time.

✔ Interest rates don't change direction in Europe as often as they do in the United States. This is because the European Central Bank (ECB) uses inflation targets as a guide, while the Fed uses multiple indicators, anecdotal evidence, and indicator data when dealing with interest rates.

✔ The United Kingdom, although smaller than the European continent, still is a major player because it's an oil-producing nation, it has its own military, and it has its own currency.

North America: Ignore it at your own risk

North America is comprised of the United States, Canada, and Mexico. Together, they form NAFTA, or the North America Free Trade Agreement.

Three countries at different stages of development with vastly different ideologies share a vast land rich with natural resources, industry, cross-border commerce, and, in the United States, the world's most powerful financial institutions and most advanced military.

Those last two factors are most important to traders. Yes, it may sound crass, but that's the way traders think when they go to work. Everything is built around whatever it takes to make money. And because of its financial and military might, the United States still has the world's number-one economy.

Sure, this assessment is fluid, and the terrorist attacks of September 11, 2001, and the Iraq War have caused the United States to take a small step back in its ability to compete in the transatlantic economy. However, ignoring the United States, especially the Federal Reserve, the Pentagon, Congress, and private power brokers — Wall Street brokers, insurance companies, and hedge funds — is a recipe for disaster from a trader's perspective. So here's what you need to know about the United States, Canada, and Mexico:

✔ The U.S. dollar and the U.S. Treasury-bond market still are the most liquid markets in the world. U.S. Treasury bonds still are considered the flight-to-quality financial instruments in times of crisis.

✔ Despite the setbacks of the Iraq War, the U.S. military still is the most advanced in the world.

✔ The combination of a strong military, a still sought-after currency, and a liquid and highly respected bond market makes the United States the center of the world's financial system.

✔ Although they belong to NAFTA, Mexico and Canada are not on par with the United States; however, each plays a significant role in the region's financial stability. When the Mexican economy was in danger of defaulting during the Clinton administration, the United States wisely bailed out its trading partner.

- ✔ The United States has high budget deficits that it finances with foreign money. Much of that money comes directly from foreign central banks that buy dollars and treasury bonds.
- ✔ The United States also
  - May be in the early stages of a social security crisis
  - Depends on foreign oil for most of its energy
  - Has a political system that is steadily deteriorating into partisan bitterness

As a futures trader, especially in the bond and currency markets, you must consider these observations on a daily basis because they point to the kinds of factors that big-money traders tick off in their heads as they focus on support and resistance levels while poring over their charts. This basic set of assumptions about North America is what you need as you sit down in front of your trading screen right before the employment report hits the wires. (For more information about vital reports and their effects, see Chapter 6.)

Emerging markets: There's more to keep tabs on than you may expect

In the old days before the Internet, things were easier to keep straight. The developed world traded for and used the commodities produced by the developing world. But in the last few decades, globalization and advances in communications have enabled trading to evolve into a platform for developing and developed countries to compete for the commodities each produces.

From a futures trader's point of view, Brazil and India are the most important emerging markets outside of China. Brazil is a major producer of natural resources and a rapidly growing political power in South America, where the populist capitalism of President Lula da Silva is behind aggressive attempts to

- ✔ Curb the country's foreign debt
- ✔ Pursue foreign money from non-U.S. sources, such as China, the Middle East, and India

These kinds of emerging and ever-changing dynamics are perfect examples of what futures traders have to contend with.

India is on the verge of making the transition from a developing country to a more developed one, although not on par yet with the United Kingdom or the United States.

Although the distinctions are subtle, from a trading standpoint, you need to keep them in mind because the bottom line is that serious money not only filters into but it also emerges from places like India, Brazil, and other countries where governments and private enterprises increasingly buy raw materials from outside their borders.

India is probably the best example at this time. Although it's a ravenous user of petroleum, its economy is growing, especially its information technology (IT) sector where many U.S. companies use Indian/English speakers to provide customer support services. Other energy-guzzling, IT-related businesses in India include server farms, software development firms, and manufacturing.

Aside from being a producer of lumber and oil, Brazil has an active pharmaceutical manufacturing industry that is a big user of energy and other resources.

When considering the big picture about the emerging markets, you need to think globally. Here's why:

✔ Everyone has money now and can move it around with the push of a mouse button.

✔ Virtually all countries in the world, except for the poorest and most politically isolated ones, now are involved on both ends of the production/user equation.

✔ Demand for commodities, although it may rise and fall much as it always has, more than likely has been reset at a higher baseline, meaning that more people are going to want more things. And that translates to higher demand and a general upward pressure on prices.

✔ Resetting demand, coupled with increasing supply tightness, creates the potential for frequent squeezes in the market.

This new set of dynamics — which is very fluid, meaning that the whole picture can, and probably will, change often — will be the major influence in futures trading for the next several decades to come.

Militant Islam

The events of 9/11 and the subsequent aftermath changed the world forever, as it brought what was only known to the most niche-oriented players in the various global intelligence agencies to the forefront of the menu for dinner conversation.

Yes, there is a growing group of people in the world who are willing to commit acts of violence in order to convert the world to their ideology.

From a trading standpoint, that is a variable that cannot be ignored. And because of the geographical and political factors that are involved, the energy, metals, commodities, and currency markets are the most likely markets to provide plenty of trading opportunities with regard to this factor.

Relating Money Flows to the Financial Markets

The more money that sloshes around the world, the better the chances that futures, options, and financial markets in general will move aggressively. And that means a more profitable trading atmosphere for those with know-how.

Money is only good as long as the people who are exchanging it for goods and services have faith in the fact that it's worth something. Money is a creation of the human mind that is extremely convenient, but it isn't one of the basic tenets of the universe.

Keep that in mind, and you can steadily develop the steely-eyed gaze of a trader. If you buy into the widely held notion that the U.S. dollar or any other currency is anything more than a vehicle for storing the value of something, you'll probably have trouble making decisions about what to do with it in the futures market or life in general.

For most of the business cycle, demand is not always as important as the supply side of the equation.

The higher the money supply, the easier it is to borrow, and the higher the likelihood that commodity markets will rise. As more money chases fewer goods, the chances of inflation rise, and the central banks begin to make it more difficult to borrow money. If you keep good tabs on the rate of growth of the money supply, you'll probably be ahead of the curve on what future trends in the markets are going to be.

To make big money in all financial markets, futures included, you have to find out how to spot changes in the trend of how easy or difficult it is to borrow money. The perfect time to enter positions is as near as possible to those inflection points in the flow of money — when they appear on the charts as changes in the direction of a long-standing trend.

These moves can come before or after any changes in money supply or adjustments to borrowing power appear. However, when a market trends in one direction (up or down) for a considerable amount of time and suddenly changes direction after you notice a blip in the money supply data, you know that something important is happening, and you need to pay close attention to it.

Enjoying Your Trading Habit

I trade regularly, based on market conditions and my time commitments to other activities. What I've discovered through years of trading is that few times have I not enjoyed the process of analysis and decision making that it involves. To me, trading is just about as good as it gets. Maybe it's something that's programmed into my DNA, personality, or mojo that just keeps me coming back.

As you progress through this and other books about trading futures and options, you'll discover whether your connection to the force (your karma) is good for trading.

Just remember that when you're ready to trade, you're going to be excited. That's okay, because the thrill of the hunt is one of the reasons everyone trades. However, you need to temper that excitement and hone it to your advantage. If you can manage the exhilaration of trading and turn it into an awareness of what is happening, you're likely to be more successful.

Welcome to one of the final frontiers left on the planet earth.

If you start trading and you're not enjoying it, you need to revise your trading plan or find another way to put your investment capital to work.

Chapter 2

Where Money Comes From

Money doesn't grow on trees. But the truth isn't far from that. In fact, money is manufactured inside the world's central banks, especially the United States Federal Reserve System, essentially from thin air.

Okay, so there is some method to the madness. But the global monetary system mostly seems like madness that is far from leading to any certain outcomes, which, of course, is what makes trading a potentially profitable occupation — as long as you know what to look for. The big picture is that central banks are part think tank, part political and public relations offices, and above all, lenders of last resort.

If you know how the system works and how to use it, you can turn it to your advantage. In this chapter, I tell you how the Federal Reserve System in the United States (also referred to as the Fed — the central bank of the United States) and other central banks around the world have branch offices throughout their respective countries, where economists directly monitor economic activity. They do this by going out into the community and talking to businesses, by designing and refining models, and by compiling reports based on all the data collected.

I also let you in on what happens when the Fed and its branch chiefs meet a few times every year to look at all this economic information so they can make informed decisions about how much money to pump into the system and how easy (or hard) they're going to make it to borrow that money.

You can't get into the inner workings of the Fed without knowing about the interactions between money supply, interest rates, and inflation, so I also include these topics and tie them together with the Federal Reserve, central banks, and money and the markets in general.

When I talk about the Federal Reserve, unless I say otherwise, I also refer to other central banks, because they all work in similar fashion. When there are important differences in the way they go about their business, I let you know.

Discovering How Money Works: The Fiat System

As a result of globalization, the world's central banks are finding it difficult to determine their own country's monetary policy without keeping an eye on what goes on in other countries. They watch how the financial markets respond to the global economy.

The global monetary system is what's called a *fiat system,* in which *money* is a storage medium for purchasing power and a substitute for barter. Each dollar bill, euro, yen, gold ingot, or whatever currency you choose enables you to buy things as the need or want arises, thus making the barter system (trading one service or product for another) mostly obsolete.

Before there was money, if you owned land you produced your own necessities and traded the surplus with other people for whatever else you needed. Money changed that system by its inherent ability to store purchasing power, thus giving people the opportunity to make plans for the future and to specialize. For example, if you're a good wheat farmer, then you can specialize in wheat, buying equipment, hiring workers, and looking for neighbors' land to buy to expand your wheat farm.

Markets and central banks value the relative worth of the paper (currency) based on the perception of how a particular country is governing itself, the current state of its economy, and the effects the interplay of those two factors have on interest rates.

Money's money because we say it's money

Most of the world's money is called *fiat money,* meaning it is accepted as money because a government says that it's legal tender, and the public has confidence in the money's ability to serve as a storage medium for purchasing power. A *fiat system* is based on a government's mandate that the paper currency it prints is legal tender for making financial transactions. *Legal tender* means that the money is backed by the full faith and credit of the government that issues it. In other words, the government promises to be good for it. I know how it sounds. But that's what the world's financial system is based on.

Fiat money is the opposite of *commodity money,* which is money that's based on a valuable commodity, a method of valuation that was used in the past. At times, the commodity itself actually was used as money. For instance, the use of gold, grain, and even furs and other animal products as commodity money preceded the current fiat system.

Where money comes from

Central banks create money either by printing it or by buying bonds in the treasury market. When central banks buy bonds, they usually buy their own country's treasury bonds, and their purchases are made from banks that own bonds. The money from the central banks goes to the bank vaults, and becomes loan-making capital.

When the Fed wants to increase the money supply in the United States, it buys bonds from banks in the open market. It uses a pretty simple formula to calculate how much money it actually is creating.

Instead of using gold as the basis for the monetary system, as was the custom until 1971, the Fed requires its member banks to keep certain specific amounts of money on reserve as a means of keeping a lid on the uncontrolled expansion of fiat money — in other words, to keep the money supply from exploding. These reserve requirements are the major safeguard of the system.

When the economy slows down, the Fed attempts to jump-start it by lowering interest rates. The Fed lowers interest rates by injecting money into the system through the purchase of government bonds from the banking system. This is the nuts and bolts of what happens when they lower the Fed Funds rate. The monetary injection is sort of like a flu shot for an ailing economy. But instead of a vaccine, the Fed injects money into the system by buying bonds from the banks.

To keep the system from becoming inflationary, the Fed keeps a lid on how much banks can actually lend by using a bank reserve management system. The reserve management system, to be sure, is not an exact science, but over the long haul, it tends to work as long as the public buys the validity of the system, which, in the United States, it does.

Here's how the reserve requirements work:

- ✔ If the current formula calls for a 10 percent reserve ratio, it means that for every dollar that a bank keeps in reserve, it can lend ten dollars to its clients.

- ✔ At the same time, if the Fed buys $500 million in bonds in the open market, it creates $5 billion in new money that makes its way to the public via bank loans.

> ✓ The reverse, or opposite, is true when the Fed wants to tighten credit and slow down the economy. It sells bonds to banks, thus draining money from the system, again based on the reserve formula.

Fiat money is created (and gotten rid of) out of thin air, but the process isn't by hocus-pocus from some wizard's wand. Its power comes from its use as accurate storage for purchasing power that is based on

> ✓ The public's acceptance of the legal-tender mandate. See the earlier section, "Money's money because we say it's money."
>
> ✓ The market's expectations that a government's promise to make its currency legal tender, by law, will hold.

Introducing Central Banks (Including the Federal Reserve)

Central banks are designed to make sure that their respective domestic economies run as smoothly as possible. In most countries, central banks are expected at the very least to combat inflationary pressures.

The overarching goal of the central banks is to repeal (or keep in check) the boom-and-bust cycles in the global economy. So far this goal is only an intention, because boom and bust cycles remain in place and are now referred to as the *business cycle*.

One good impact has come from the actions of the Fed and other central banks. They've been able to lengthen the amount of time between boom and bust cycles to the extent that they've smoothed out volatile trends and created an environment in which the futures markets offer a perfect vehicle for hedging and speculation.

Prior to the advent of central banks, booms and busts in the global economy came about as often as every harvest season. Because money was hard to come by prior to the centralization of the global economies, a bad harvest, a spell of bad weather, or just a bad set of investment decisions by a local bank in a farming community could devastate the economy in an area or even a country.

The central bank of the United States (and the world): The Federal Reserve

The Federal Reserve, otherwise known as *the Fed*, is the prototype central bank because of its relative success, not because it was the first central bank. Created in 1913 to stabilize the activities of the money and credit markets, it

Inside the central banks' boom and bust cycle

Just because the world's central banks have somewhat smoothed out the boom and bust cycle, the system is still nowhere near risk free. And that means opportunity for you and me as futures traders.

Sure, innovation is a good thing, as is tweaking an old practice in order to make it available to more people for less money. But, history shows that every so-called "new" financial practice eventually leads to excess, and outright cheating. The cheating eventually leads to the collapse of the trend, and a liquidity crisis. When the eventual liquidity crisis comes along, the world's central banks are essentially forced to act in order to keep the global economy from collapsing.

The difference between what has happened in modern times and what happened in past cycles is that the actions of the Federal Reserve, despite significant criticism, have at least kept the U.S. economy from reaching a recession so deep that it could be called a Depression. In the 20-year period from 1987 to 2007, the Federal Reserve has, depending on your point of view, "corrected" or "bailed out" Wall Street and the U.S. economy, in one way or another, at least seven times by lowering interest rates and providing loans as the lender of last resort. Here's a list of those occasions:

1987 — Junk bonds and the savings and loan crisis led to the stock market crash of 1987.

1991 — The U.S. economy was in a recession that worsened due to worries about the first Gulf War.

1994 — The United States was in a run-of-the-mill economic recession.

1997 to 1998 — The Asian currency crisis, a phenomenon that started in Thailand, spread throughout Asia and eventually led to the Russian debt default and the bailout of the Long Term Capital Management hedge fund in a deal brokered by then Fed Chairman Alan Greenspan.

2000 — The dot.com boom imploded, an event that led to the start of a bear market in the U.S. Stock market, which lasted well into 2003.

2001 — The 9/11 attacks on the World Trade Center accelerated an economic contraction in the United States that was already in progress due to the dot.com implosion. When the Twin Towers fell, money started to move to foreign shores, a fact that was accelerated by the aggressive lowering of interest rates by the Federal Reserve.

2007 — The subprime mortgage crisis is the latest example of the boom-bust cycle that has not been eradicated, as central banks would have you believe. In fact, this example of the phenomenon followed the script fairly well. Too many people made bets that were too far beyond their ability to pay off. And the result was the same as always, the financial ruin of many at all levels of the food chain.

administers the Federal Reserve Act, which mandated the creation of an agency intent on "improving the supervision" of banking and "creating an elastic currency."

The current objectives of the Fed are to fight inflation and maintain full employment to keep the consumption-based U.S. and global economies moving.

Under Chairman Alan Greenspan (whose appointment as a member of the Fed Board of Governors expired on January 31, 2006), the Federal Reserve became the most important financial institution in the world. In reality, the Fed is the central bank to the world, especially having grown in prestige and deeds during Greenspan's more than 18 years as chairman.

Greenspan's successor, Ben Bernanke, was tested in his abilities to guide the U.S. economy during the summer of 2007, as the subprime mortgage crisis unfolded. Despite having a different management style than Greenspan, Bernanke had no choice but to lower interest rates, which he did in August and September of 2007 with moderate success, at least as of late September 2007.

The Fed had a tough act to follow in Greenspan. His 18-year tenure gave the markets a time-tested pattern of action from a central bank that, prior to his stewardship, had been less than stellar during several crucial periods.

How central banks function

The Fed has two official mandates: keeping inflation under control and maintaining full employment. However, it has some leeway and in many ways has outgrown its mandates, becoming lender of last resort and source- of money in times of crises. In many speeches, especially after September 11, 2001, Greenspan and other Fed governors made it clear that their perception of the Fed's duties included maintaining the stability of the financial system and containing systemic risk.

Some central banks, such as the European Central Bank (ECB), use inflationary targets to gauge their successes. Unlike the Fed (which didn't set such targets under Chairman Alan Greenspan, but may do so in the future), the ECB must keep raising interest rates until the target is achieved, even if unemployment is high in Europe, as long as inflation is above the central bank's target.

The positive side of inflation targeting is that it gives the market a sense of direction with regard to what the central bank's actions may be toward interest rates. The negative side, as is evident in Europe, is that the use of inflation targets often prevents the ECB from moving on interest rates. As a result, the European economy has lagged in its ability to grow. In other words, the dogma of adhering to the target set by the central bank has hurt the European economy. In contrast, despite frequent criticism, the U.S. economy, albeit in fits and starts, has continued to be the leading economy in the world. Much of that is because of the relatively good management of interest rates by the Fed.

The ECB's mandate opens up opportunities for trading currency, interest rates, and commodity futures, because after a central bank starts down a certain policy route, it usually stays with it for months, creating an intermediate-term trend on which to base the direction of trading.

For example, after September 11, 2001, the Fed lowered interest rates six times, — starting on September 17, 2001 — and left them at 1 percent until the summer of 2004, when it began to raise them until the summer of 2006. The Fed had already lowered interest rates six times prior to the post 9/11 reductions. In September 2007, the Federal Reserve lowered the Discount rate and the Fed Funds rate, in response to the subprime mortgage crisis.

Understanding Money Supply

Money supply is how much money is available in the economy to buy goods, services, and securities. The Federal Reserve stopped emphasizing the role of money supply on the economy in the year 2000, and stopped publishing the M3 money supply figure in March 2006, because "M3 did not appear to convey any additional information about economic activity that was not already embodied in M2. Consequently, the Board judged that the costs of collecting the data and publishing M3 outweigh the benefits," according to a summary of money supply on the New York Fed's Web site. That leaves three figures to get to know:

- **M0:** The total of all physical currency plus the currency in accounts held at the Federal Reserve that can be exchanged for physical currency.

   M1: The *M1* money supply is M0 minus those portions of M0 held as reserves or cash held in vaults plus the amounts in checking or current accounts.

- **M2:** The *M2* money supply is M1 plus money housed in other types of savings accounts, such as money market funds and certificates of deposit (CDs) of less than $100,000.

Equating money supply and inflation

It would be easy to get into the esoteric aspects of money supply, but it wouldn't do a whole lot of good. So, the key is to understand the following concept: At some point in the future, it may come to pass that global central banks will have put so much money into circulation that money supply may become as important an indicator as it was in decades past. If and when that time comes, the inflation-sensitive markets, such as gold, energy, and grains, are likely to become very active. When that happens, you need to be able to trade them effectively. See the remember icon, directly ahead, for a more specific summary.

I don't like equations (and my guess is that you don't either), but this one is important. It's called the *monetary exchange equation,* and it explains the relationship between money supply and inflation as:

Velocity × Money Supply = Gross Domestic Product (GDP) × GDP Deflator

Velocity is a measure of how fast money is changing hands, because it records how many times per year the money actually is exchanged. *GDP* is the sum of all the goods and services produced by the economy. The *GDP deflator* is a measure of inflation, or a sustained rise in prices. *Inflation* is usually defined as a monetary phenomenon in which prices rise because too much money is in circulation, and that money's chasing too few goods.

Here's what's important about the money supply as it applies to futures trading:

- Money supply is related to inflation because of the number of times it actually changes hands (see the definition of velocity in thepreceding paragraph).

- More money in the system — chasing goods and services at a faster rate — is inflationary.

- A rising money supply tends to spur the economy and eventually fuels demand for commodities.

- A rising money supply usually is spawned by lower interest rates.

- Whenever the money supply rises to a key level, which differs in every cycle, eventually inflationary pressures begin to appear, and the Fed starts reducing the money supply.

- *Deflation* is when money supply shrinks because nobody wants to buy anything. Deflation usually results from *oversupply,* or a glut of goods in the marketplace. The key psychology of deflation is that in contrast to inflation, consumers put off buying things, hoping that prices will fall farther — as opposed to times of inflation when consumers are willing to pay high prices in fear that they will rise farther.

- *Reflation* is when central banks start pumping money into the economic system, hoping that lower borrowing costs will spur demand for goods and services, create jobs, and create a stronger economy.

- The more money that's available, the more likely it is that some of it will make its way into the futures markets.

As a general rule, futures prices respond to inflation. Some tend to rise, such as gold, and others tend to fall, such as the U.S. dollar (see Chapters 11 and 14). Each individual area of the futures market, though, is more responsive to its own fundamentals and its own supply-and-demand equation at any given time. With that noted, here is a quick-and-dirty guide to general money supply/commodity tendencies:

✔ Metals, agricultural products, oil, and livestock contracts generally tend to rise along with money supply. This tendency is not a daily occurrence but rather one that you can see over an extended period of time if you compare graphs and charts of economic indicators with futures prices. The overall trend is toward higher consumer prices, which have resulted from higher commodity prices.

✔ Bonds and other interest-rate products do the opposite. Generally, bond prices fall, and interest rates or bond yields rise in response to inflation (see Chapter 10).

✔ Stock index futures are more variable in their relationship with the money supply, but eventually, they tend to rise when interest rates — either from the Fed or market rates in the bond and money markets — are falling, and they tend to fall when interest rates reach a high enough level. In other words, the relationship of money supply to the stock market and stock index futures is indirect and has more to do with how effectively the Fed and the bond market are bringing about the desired effect on the economy, whether slowing it down or speeding it up. However, during some periods, such as 1994 and most of 2005 when the Fed raised interest rates, stocks and stock index futures stayed in a trading range.

✔ Currencies tend to fall in value during times of inflation.

In a global economy, many of these dynamics occur simultaneously or in close proximity to each other, which is why an understanding of the global economy is more important when trading futures than when trading individual stocks.

Seeing how something from something is something more

The wildest thing about money is how one dollar counts as two dollars whenever it goes around the loop enough times in an interesting little concept known as the *multiplier effect.* For example, say the Fed buys $1 worth of bonds from Bank X, and Bank X lends it to Person 1. Person 1 then buys something from Person 2, who then deposits the dollar in Bank 2. Bank 2 then lends the money to Person 3, who then deposits it in Bank 1, where the $1, in terms of money supply, is now $2, because it has been counted twice.

By multiplying this little exercise by billions of transactions, you can arrive at the massive money supply numbers in the United States, where, as of late 2004, the M0 alone was $688 billion. As of March 7, 2008, M1 was $1.38

trillion, unchanged from March 2005 and M2 was $7.63 trillion, compared to $6.41 trillion in March 2005. The growth in M2 was one of the reasons that gold prices were rising during this period as inflation was heating up.

Getting a handle on money supply from a trader's point of view

Although you and I can use money supply data in many ways from an academic point of view, believe me, it won't make you the life of the dinner party. The key to making money by using money supply information is to have a good grip on whether the Fed actually is putting money into the system or taking it out. What's even more important is how fast the Fed is doing whatever it's doing at the time. In the old days, I used to keep strict money supply data and plug it into a formula that I invented. It used to work fairly well. But like other indicators that used to work, it became fairly irrelevant, and I stopped using it.

Instead, I pay more attention to what the Fed says and does, and how the market anticipates events and responds to the words and actions of the central bank(s). In other words, the market, by its actions, factors in what it thinks the money supply is doing, and what effects it will have on the economy and the way the world works. All you and I, as traders, have to do is to pay attention and follow the overall trend of the market.

For example, if the Federal Reserve starts to lower interest rates, and the market responds by rallying gold prices, lowering the dollar, and raising long-term bond yields, the market is betting on inflation becoming a factor at some point in the future.

I can follow those trends and trade those markets. That, in my view, is better than using a formula that stopped working a few years ago.

Don't get caught up in jargon or the opinions of talking heads in the media. You can do quite well for yourself, just by paying attention to what's going on in the markets.

Recognize when the Fed is being cautious in its conduction of monetary policy, say, by using ambiguous statements after its Federal Open Market Committee meetings or in its members' speeches to the public. You need to be cautious in how you trade, but you also need to be monitoring the markets for their response. You don't want to let a good set of opportunities pass you by.

A perfect example is what happened in September 2007 and into 2008. The Federal Reserve, and other global central banks, lowered interest rates and offered discount rate loans to banks and financial institutions in response to a liquidity crunch in the global credit markets, which had resulted from the subprime mortgage crisis. The response of the markets to the Fed's actions was to deliver not only a rally in stocks, at least initially, but also a rally in gold, along with a significant breakdown in the U.S. dollar and significant volatility in the U.S. Treasury bond market. That combination of events suggested that the market was concerned about inflation at some point in the future.

Putting Fiat to Work for You

The average person may find the fiat concept difficult to grasp. But as a futures trader, it is the center of your universe. If you can figure out which way interest rates are headed and where money is flowing, most of what happens in the markets in general will fall into place, and you can make better decisions about which way to trade. Keep these relationships in mind:

- ✔ Futures markets often move based on the relationship between the bond market and the Fed, which means that when either the Fed or the bond market moves interest rates in one direction, the other eventually will follow. See Chapters 6 and 10.

- ✔ Higher interest rates tend to eventually slow economic growth, while lower interest rates tend to spur economies.

Another excellent example of how the system works occurred after the events of September 11, 2001. In response to the catastrophe, the Fed lowered key official interest rates, such as the Fed funds and discount rates, but it also bought massive amounts of government treasuries, thus making much more money available to the banking system.

Currency traders, who are not well known for their patriotism, sold dollars and bought euros, yen, and other currencies, and effectively moved money out of the United States.

Much of the money that the Fed injected into the system made its way to China and ended up fueling the major economic boom in that country that marked the post September 11, 2001, economic recovery. China used the infusion of foreign money to finance a building boom that, in turn, led to increased demand for oil and raw materials, such as copper, steel, and lumber. This major change in the flow of money spread to all the major futures markets and led to a bull market in commodities because China bought increasing amounts of steel, copper, and the fuel needed to power the boom — oil.

When the Fed began to raise interest rates, it did so partially with the intention of cooling off the growth in China and diverting the flow of dollars away from Beijing and back to the U.S.

Get in the habit of watching all the markets together. When the Fed starts lowering interest rates, it is doing so because it wants the economy to grow and jobs to be created. When the Fed starts to ease rates, as a trader, you want to start looking at what happens to commodities like copper, gold, oil, and so on. The commodities markets provide you with confirmation of what the markets in general are starting to expect as the Fed makes its move.

Normally, you begin to see these markets come to life at some point before or after the Fed makes a move. For example, if you see the copper market starting to move, you want to check on what the bond and stock markets are doing, because smart money starts pricing in expectations of a change in trend by the Fed.

Bonding with the Fed: The Nuts and Bolts of Interest Rates

If you want to make money in futures, you need to become intimately familiar with what the Fed does and how it goes about it. Credit makes the world go around. Credit enables everyone to have the things they want now and to pay for them later. How much stuff you can buy depends on how easy the Fed makes it for you to borrow the money. The Fed wants to create an environment that prompts consumers to buy as much stuff as they want without letting them create inflation.

One way the Fed raises and lowers interest rates is by buying or selling U.S. Treasury bonds in the open market. In past decades, the market had to guess what the Fed was trying to do with interest rates where the bond market was concerned. In the latter years of Alan Greenspan's terms as Fed chairman, the central bank became more open in its communications with the markets, but a fair amount of *Fedspeak,* the often-difficult-to-decipher language from the central bank, still was in use. In some cases, it was even conjecture.

Greenspan's successor, Chairman Ben Bernanke, used a different formula in 2007, at least initially, in order to calm the credit markets during the subprime mortgage crisis. Instead of initially lowering the Fed Funds rate, Greenspan's favorite weapon, Bernanke lowered the Discount Rate, the rate of last resort used by banks that can't get credit anywhere else and have to borrow from the Fed. Because he didn't want to flood the whole economy with easy money, Bernanke targeted those financial institutions that were in trouble and "destigmatized" the Discount window by making it known that the Fed would not be penalizing those banks that used the credit facility. This bought Bernanke some time, which he used to gather more data, before finally lowering the Fed Funds rate a couple of weeks after lowering the Discount rate.

No matter what you think of the Fed and central banks in general, they're a fact of life, and the better you can understand them and decipher some of the things they say and do, the better you can trade and make other decisions about your money. Finding out how central banks work is easier than trying to decipher what they say and do. They buy and sell bonds and inject or extract money from the banking system they control. When the Fed buys bonds, it gives the markets and the economy money. When the Fed sells bonds, it takes money out of the markets and the economy. Pretty simple, right?

The amount of money that the Fed uses to buy bonds can signal which way the Fed's Board of Governors wants interest rates to go. This relationship is pretty simple any more, because the Fed rarely goes into the bond market — other than for routine maintenance of the money supply — without making a statement. The New York Fed conducts routine maintenance. An example is when the Fed adds more reserves than usual during holiday periods, such as Christmas, to make sure banks have enough money on hand to handle the shopping season. In the new year, the Fed drains the extra reserves from the system. The Fed usually doesn't mean this maneuver as a major economic action.

The Bernanke Fed, following the tradition started by the Greenspan Fed, will usually announce its "target rate" for the Fed Funds rate. This is the rate that banks charge each other for overnight loans, and is the primary interest rate that the Federal Reserve manipulates to set the overall trend for all other rates. When the Fed makes significant changes in monetary policy, the central bank clearly announces it has made a move, and why it has made it.

Central Banks

Central banks have convinced the world's corporations and population that money and its wonderful extension, credit, are the centerpieces of the world's economic system. And the easier it is to borrow money, the more things get done and the bigger things get built.

When central banks buy bonds from banks and dealers, they're putting money into circulation, making it easy for people and businesses to borrow. At the juncture where money becomes easier to borrow, the potential for commodity markets to become explosive reaches its zenith.

Commodity markets thrive on money, and their actions are directly related to

- ✔ Interest rates
- ✔ Underlying supply

✔ The perceptions and actions of the public, governments, and traders, as they react to

- **Supply:** How much is available and how fast it's going to be used up
- **Demand:** How long this period of rising demand is likely to last

Demand is not as important for most of the business cycle as the supply side of the equation.

The higher the money supply, the easier it is to borrow, and the higher the likelihood that commodity markets will rise. As more money chases fewer goods, the chances of inflation rise, and the central banks begin to make it more difficult to borrow money.

If you keep good tabs on the rate of growth of the money supply, you'll probably be ahead of the curve on what future trends in the markets are going to be.

To make big money in all financial markets, you have to find out how to spot changes in the trend of how easy or difficult it is to borrow money. The perfect time to enter positions is as near as possible to those inflection points in the flow of money — when they appear on the charts as changes in the direction of a long-standing trend.

These moves can come before or after any changes in money supply or adjustments to borrowing power appear. However, when a market trends in one direction (up or down) for a considerable amount of time and suddenly changes direction after you notice a blip in the money supply data, you know that something important is happening, and you need to pay close attention to it.

Chapter 3

The Futures Markets

A futures contract is a security, similar conceptually to a stock or a bond, yet significantly different. When you buy a stock, you're buying part of a company, while a bond makes you a lender to a government or a corporation. Whereas a stock gives you equity and a bond makes you a debt holder, a futures contract is a legally binding contract that sets the conditions for the delivery of commodities or financial instruments at a specific time period in the future.

Futures markets emerged and developed in fits and starts several hundred years ago as a mechanism through which merchants traded goods and services in the present based on their expectations for crops and harvest yields in the future. Today, futures markets are the hub of capitalism, because they provide the base for prices at wholesale and eventually retail markets for commodities ranging from gasoline and lumber to key items in the food chain, such as cattle, pork, corn, and soybeans.

Futures contracts are available for a variety of financial products and commodities. There are contracts for trading just about anything, starting with familiar securities such as stock index futures, interest rate products like bonds and treasury bills, to lesser known commodities like propane and ethanol. Some futures contracts are even designed to hedge against weather risk and to trade electricity. The latest introduction, as of late 2007, is that of real estate market contracts.

Now virtually all financial and commodity markets are linked, with futures and cash markets functioning as a single entity on a daily basis. Thus, as a successful trader, you need to understand the basics of all major markets — bonds, stocks, currencies, and commodities — and their relationships to each other and the economic cycle.

In this chapter, you gain an understanding of who the major players are, how the futures markets evolved to their prominent role in the global economy, and what basic rules and regulations keep the markets as fair and reasonable as possible.

Taking Big Risks and Guarding Against Them: Two Types of Traders

The futures markets serve two major constituencies: hedgers and speculators. Although these two groups have differing interests, the participation of both is necessary for the markets to function.

Hedgers, in general, are major companies that actually produce the commodities, or others (like farmers) who have an inherent interest in the market. Hedgers may employ professional traders to use futures contracts on commodities and related products to decrease the company's risk of loss. Their goal is not to profit from futures trading, but rather to cover their risk of losses and keep company operations moving forward.

Speculators, the second constituency (including you and me), trade futures contracts with the goal of making money from market trends and special situations. In other words, the speculator's job is to see where the big money is going and follow it there, regardless of whether prices are going up or down.

So although hedgers may actually take delivery of or receive products specified in a futures contract, speculators are trying to ride the price trend of those products as long as possible, while always intending to cash in before the delivery date.

Hedging bets to minimize risk

Farmers, producers, importers, and exporters are hedgers, because they trade not only in futures contracts but also in the commodity, equity, or product represented by the contract. They trade futures to secure the future price of the commodity of which they will take delivery and then sell later in the cash market.

People who buy commodities, or *holders,* are said to be long, because they're looking to buy at the lowest possible price and sell at the highest possible price. Short sellers sell commodities in the hope that prices will fall. If they're correct, they offset, or close, the position at a lower price than when they sold it. (For more on the long and short of trading, see "Talking the talk," later in this chapter.)

Futures contracts are attractive to longs and shorts, because they provide price and time certainty, and they reduce the risk associated with *volatility,* or the speed at which prices change up or down. At the same time, hedging can help lock in an acceptable *price margin,* or difference between the futures price and the cash price for the commodity, and improve the risk between the cost of the raw material and the retail cost of the final product by covering for any market-related losses. *Note:* Hedge positions don't always work, and in some cases, they make losses worse.

Exxon Mobil is a good example of a hedger in the oil markets, because the company must gauge the potential risk of weather, politics, and other external factors on future oil production. Warm winter weather, for example, reduces the demand for heating oil and therefore puts downward pressure on the price of oil. Exxon wants to protect itself from such a risk.

Another good current example of a hedger is an airline in the post-September 11, 2001, world, and its fuel costs. Aside from labor, airplane fuel is by far the most expensive component of an airline's costs. A good airline also has expertise in the oil market.

Say that Duarte Air (I know, I know, it's self-serving promotion) is projecting a need for large amounts of jet fuel for the summer season, based on the trends in travel during the past decade. As the airline's CEO, I know that demand for gasoline tends to rise in the summer; thus, prices for the jet fuel I need are also likely to rise because of refinery usage issues — refineries switch a major portion of their summer production to gasoline.

In order to hedge its costs for crude oil in the summer, Duarte Air starts buying July crude oil and gasoline futures a few months ahead of time, hoping that as the prices rise, the profits from the trades can offset the costs of the expected rise in jet fuel. Say, for instance, that Duarte Air bought July crude futures at $50 per barrel in December, and by June they were trading at $60 per barrel. As the prices continued to rise, Duarte would start unloading the contracts, pocketing the $10-per-barrel profit and using it to offset the higher costs of its fuel in the spot market (during the summer travel season).

On the other hand, if Duarte's hedging was wrong and the price of oil went down, the airline could always use options to hedge the futures contracts, or go short, by selling futures contracts high and making money by buying them back at lower prices if there was a sudden price drop.

Considering the effects of a crash

The stock market crash of 1987 had one positive result. It ushered in the era of the one market. After that fateful day, October 19, 1987, anyone who'd ever invested in any market understood that all markets are linked, regardless of the underlying securities traded on them, and that money can and does flow at the speed of light from one type of market to another. In fact, the futures markets, according to Mark Powers, in his book *Starting out in Futures Trading* (McGraw-Hill), are like "convenient laboratories" for conducting market analysis.

After the 1987 crash, the Brady Commission coined and defined the concept that all markets were linked, because the action in one or more of them had an influence on one or several others. But the commission did little to dissuade the media's and the public's perception that the futures markets were not to blame for the crash — something the Federal Reserve concluded in its post-crash study released in 1988.

Another positive of the post-crash environment was the implementation of *circuit breakers,* or intraday limits on trading that slow or stop trading in specific products when the markets for those products are moving too fast. The Board of Governors of the Federal Reserve System (the Fed), the Securities and Exchange Commission (SEC), and the various exchanges (see the section "Seeing Where the Magic Happens," later in this chapter, for a list of exchanges) also developed better techniques for monitoring position sizes and overall market liquidity after the crash.

Speculating that there's a profit to be had

Speculators, in contrast to hedgers, are betting on the price change potential for one reason only — profit. Speculators do the opposite of hedgers; they look to increase risk and increase the chances of making money.

A hedger tries to take the speculator's money and vice versa. So a normal futures transaction is likely to include a member of each of these subgroups. A speculator is likely to be buying a contract from a hedger at a low price, while the hedger is expecting the price to decline farther, which is why he's selling the contract.

Think of this dance in terms of risk. Hedgers are transferring the risk of price variability to others in exchange for the cost of the hedge. Speculators assume price variability risk, thus making the transfer possible in exchange for the potential to gain. A hedger and a speculator can both be very happy from the outcome of price variability in the same market.

This interaction between speculators and hedgers is what makes the futures markets efficient. This efficiency and the accuracy of the supply-and-demand equation (see the later "Talking the talk" section) increase as the underlying contract gets closer to expiration and more information about what the marketplace requires at the time of delivery becomes available.

Limiting Risk Exposure: Contract and Trading Rules

By design, futures contracts are meant to limit the amount of time and risk exposure experienced by speculators and hedgers, those traders who use them. As a result, futures contracts have several key characteristics that enable traders to trade them effectively. I list and briefly describe these characteristics in the sections that follow and use these explanations to expand on how the contracts work throughout the book.

Checking the expiration date

All futures contracts are time based; they *expire,* which means that at some point in the future they will no longer exist. From a trading standpoint, the expiration of a contract forces you to make one of the following decisions:

- Sell the contract and roll it over by buying the contract for the next front month (the futures contract month nearest to expiration) or another that's farther into the future.
- Offset the contract (taking your profits or losses) and just stay out of the market.
- Take delivery of the underlying commodity, equity, or product represented by the contract.

Chilling out: Daily price limits

Because of the volatility of futures contracts and the potential for catastrophic losses, limits are placed on futures contracts that freeze prices but do not freeze trading. Limits are meant to let markets cool down during periods of extremely active trading.

When the limit rules are triggered, the market can trade at the limit price but not beyond it. Some contracts have variable limits, which means that the limits are changed if the market closes at the limit. For example, if the cattle markets close at the limit for two straight days, the limit is raised on the third day.

Sizing up your account

Most brokers require individuals to deposit a certain amount of money in a brokerage account before they can start trading. A fairly constant figure in the industry is $5,000.

For most people, depositing only $5,000 with the brokerage firm probably is not enough to provide them with a good trading experience. Some experienced traders will tell you that $100,000 is a better figure to have on hand, and $10,000 to $30,000 is probably the least amount you can actually work with comfortably. These are not hard and fast rules, though. The bottom line is that to be a successful trader, you should know yourself and your risk tolerance, get a good handle on your trading plan, let your winners ride, and cut your losses short.

Staying Up to Snuff: Criteria for Futures Contracts

Futures contracts are nothing like credit-card transactions. Buying something and promising to pay for it later, the way you do when you go shopping with a credit card, doesn't make a futures contract. True futures contracts must meet the following six criteria, which have developed since the inception of the futures markets:

- **Trading must be conducted on an organized exchange.** This *exchange* is a physical place, where trading actually takes place either by open-cry trading in a trading pit, which is what you see on television when you turn on the business channels, or by electronic means, which is an increasing phenomenon, especially in Europe, where trading already is done nearly 100 percent electronically, as opposed to the U.S. where both electronic and open-cry trading take place.

- **Common rules govern all transactions.** The two most important ones are as follows:

  - Trading occurs in one designated place, the ring or pit of the exchange, by open outcry or electronically, during specific trading hours, with every participant having equal access to the bids and offers and the flow of trading.

  - No exchange member can offer to fill or match an order without first offering it to the crowd. A *member* is a firm or an individual who buys a *seat on the exchange,* or the privilege to trade directly for his own account and to be an intermediary for other traders. When a floor broker *fills an order,* he is fulfilling your request from his own inventory of futures contracts. When a floor broker *matches an order,* he is fulfilling your request by finding a buyer or seller in the trading crowd and matching the buyer with the seller.

✔ **Contract sizes, delivery dates, mode of delivery, and procedure are standardized.** That means that there is consistency as each contract of each individual commodity is equal to the other contracts in its class, and the important dates of each contract year are easy to follow.

✔ **Traders negotiate only the original transaction with each other.** Beyond the original agreement, the exchange becomes a clearinghouse, and the obligation of the parties to a futures contract transaction is with the exchange.

✔ **Futures contracts are canceled, or closed out, by offset.** When a trader sells a contract to deliver a specific amount of a marketable product for December delivery, he has an obligation to deliver that product to the exchange by December. If he buys a contract for the same amount of that product before December, then he has met his obligation; he has *offset* the original sale with an equivalent buy and is out of the market.

✔ **The exchange clearinghouse acts as a guarantor, or guardian, for each transaction.** It accomplishes this by requiring its members to have minimum amounts of working capital and enough funds to meet their outstanding debts. Exchange members who are not clearinghouse members must associate with exchange members, who are to guarantee and verify all contracts.

Seeing Where the Magic Happens

Several active futures and options exchanges are open for business in the United States. Each has its own niche, but some overlaps occur in the types of contracts that are traded. In this section, I cover the basics of three of the more frequently used Chicago exchanges, along with a handful of exchanges based in other cities.

The names of the exchanges are as follows:

✔ **Chicago Board Options Exchange (www.cboe.com):** The premier options exchange market in the world, the CBOE specializes in trading options on individual stocks, stock index futures, interest rate futures, and a broad array of specialized products such as exchange-traded mutual funds. The CBOE is not a futures exchange but is included here to be complete, because futures and options can be traded simultaneously, as part of a single strategy. I discuss this throughout the book where applicable, but go into in a bit more detail in Chapter 4.

- ✔ **Chicago Board of Trade** (www.cbot.com): Trades are made in futures contracts for the agriculturals, interest rates, Dow Indexes, and metals. Specific contracts traded on the CBOT include

  - **Agricultural futures:** Corn, the soybean complex, wheat, ethanol, oats, rough rice, and mini contracts in corn, soybeans, and wheat

  - **Interest rate–related futures:** Treasury bonds, spreads, Fed funds, municipal bonds, swaps, and German debt

  - **Dow Jones Industrial Average:** Dow Jones Industrial mini contracts

  - **Metals futures:** Gold and silver and e-mini contracts for gold and silver

- ✔ **Chicago Mercantile Exchange** (www.cme.com): The CME is the largest futures exchange in North America. CME Group merged with the CBOT, forming a formidable contender in the exchange industry. The merged entity, a publicly traded company, operates both exchanges and trades on the New York Stock Exchange under the ticker symbol CME. The two exchanges, although they are one company, have two separate trading floors, and between the two distinct areas offer the opportunity to trade a wide variety of instruments, including commodities, stock index futures, foreign currencies, interest rates, TRAKRS, and environmental futures. Among the contracts traded on the CME are

  - **Commodities:** Live cattle, milk, lean hogs, feeder cattle, butter, pork bellies, lumber, the Goldman Sachs Commodities Index (and associated futures contracts), and fertilizer

  - **Stock index futures:** S&P 500, S&P 500 Midcap, S&P Small Cap 600, NASDAQ Composite, NASDAQ 100, Russell 2000, and the corresponding e-mini contracts for all the major indexes traded

  - **Other important stock-related contracts:** Single stock futures, futures on exchange-traded funds (ETFs), and futures on Japan's Nikkei 225 index

  - **Options:** Options on the futures contracts that are listed by the CME

- ✔ **Kansas City Board of Trade** (KCBT, www.kcbt.com): The KCBT is a regional exchange that specializes in wheat futures and offers trading on stock index futures for the Value Line Index, a broad listing of 1,700 stocks.

- ✔ **Minneapolis Grain Exchange** (MGEX, www.mgex.com): MGEX is a regional exchange that trades three kinds of seasonally different wheat futures, and offers futures and options on the National Corn Index and the National Soybeans Index.

✔ **New York Board of Trade (NYBOT, www.nybot.com):** A major international exchange, the NYBOT offers a broad array of products, including

   • **Commodities:** Sugar, cocoa, cotton, frozen orange juice, ethanol and pulp, and the Reuters/Jefferies CRB Index

   • **Currencies:** U.S. dollar index and a wide variety of foreign currency pairs and cross rates

   • **Stock index futures:** Russell Equity Indexes and NYSE Composite Index

✔ **New York Mercantile Exchange (NYMEX, www.nymex.com):** The NYMEX is the hub for energy trading in

   • **Energy futures:** Light sweet crude, natural gas, unleaded gasoline, heating oil, electricity, propane, and coal

   • **Metals:** Gold, silver, platinum, copper, palladium, and aluminum

Futures contracts for the Goldman Sachs Commodity Index and options on the futures contracts that the CME lists also are traded on the CME.

E-mini contracts are smaller-value versions of the larger contracts. They trade for a fraction of the price of the full value instrument and thus are more suitable for small accounts. The attractive feature of e-mini contracts is that you can participate in the market's movements for lesser investment amounts. Be sure to check commissions and other prerequisites before you trade, though.

Exploring How Trading Actually Takes Place

Around the world, most futures exchanges have converted from open-cry to electronic trading. The United States, however, still uses the open-cry system of futures trading, where traders on a trading floor or in a trading pit shout and use hand signals to make transactions or trades with each other. Futures contracts are traded in a clear, albeit nonlinear, order.

When you call your broker, he relays a message to the trading floor, where a runner relays the message to the floor broker, who then executes the trade. The runner then relays the trade confirmation back to your broker, who tells you how it went. The order is just about the same when you trade futures online, except that you receive a trade confirmation via an e-mail or other online communiqué.

Trade reporters on the floor of the exchange watch for executed trades, record them, and then transmit these transactions to the exchange, which, in turn, transmits the price to the entire world almost simultaneously.

Shifting sands: Twenty-four-hour trading

In the United States, physical commodities, such as agriculturals and oil, are still traded primarily by an open-cry system; however, most futures markets in the world also offer electronic models of trading because they provide

- A more level playing field
- More price transparency
- Lower transaction costs

Globex, the electronic data and trading system founded in 1992, extends futures trading beyond the pits and into an electronic overnight session. Globex is active 23 hours per day, and contracts are traded on it for Eurodollars, S&P 500, NASDAQ-100, foreign exchange rates, and the CME e-mini futures. You can also trade options and spreads on Globex.

When you turn to the financial news on CNBC before the stock market opens, you see quotes for the S&P 500 futures and others taken from Globex as traders from around the world make electronic trades. Globex quotes are real, meaning that if you keep a position open overnight and you place a sell stop under it, or you place a buy order with instructions to execute in Globex, you may wake up the next morning with a new position, or out of a position altogether.

Globex trading overnight tends to be thinner than trading during regular market hours (usually from 8:30 a.m. to 4:15 p.m. eastern time), and it tends to be more volatile in some ways than trading during regular hours.

You can monitor Globex stock index futures, Eurodollars, and currency trades on a delayed basis overnight free of charge at www.cme.com/trading/dta/del/globex.html.

Here are a few good questions to ask your futures broker about trading via Globex:

- Does the brokerage firm that you're using provide access to Globex? If so, what kind of an interface, front-end system, or link to Globex does it supply? You want to know whether the system is compatible with Globex and how smoothly it works.

- Are the commissions for Globex trading different than the commissions charged for using the firm's regular trade routing?

✔ Are there any other rule or requirement changes, such as limits on the number of contracts that you can trade, margin requirements, or other particulars?

✔ You may want to put in an order by phone. Does the firm offer customer support in after-hours trading?

Talking the talk

If you're going to trade futures, you have to know trader talk. Knowing several key terms helps you get the job done and helps you understand what reporters and advisors are talking about.

Some key terms that refer to your expectations of the market include

✔ **Going long:** Being bullish, or positive on the market, and wanting to buy something. When I say I'm long oil, in the context of futures trading, it means that I own oil futures.

✔ **Being short:** Being bearish, or negative on the market in which you are trading. Your goal is to make money when the price of the futures contract that you choose to short falls in price. If you deal in the stock market, you know that you have to borrow stocks before you can sell them short. In the futures market, you don't have to borrow anything; you just post the appropriate margin and instruct your broker that you're interested in selling short.

I know this can be confusing, so it is best looked upon from the point of view of reversing, or offsetting, your position. To illustrate the point, consider an example in a vacuum. If you sell a crude oil contract short at $59 and the price drops to $54, you have a $5 profit. At that point, if you decide that you've made enough of a profit, you then offset the position by buying back the contract to cover your short sale. In other words, what you're selling short is the contract, and by offsetting the position, you are now finishing the trade.

✔ **Locals:** The people in the trading pits. They're usually among the first to react to news and other events that affect the markets.

✔ **Front month:** The futures contract month nearest to expiration. This time frame may not always feature the most widely quoted futures contract. As one contract expires, the next contract in line becomes the front month.

✔ **Orders:** Instructions that lead to the completion of a trade. They can be placed in a variety of ways, including

   • A *stop-loss order,* which means that you want to limit your losses at or above a certain price.

   A stop-loss order becomes a market order (see next entry) to buy or sell at the prevailing market price after the market touches the stop price, the price at which you've instructed the broker to sell. A buy stop is placed above the market. A sell stop is placed below the market. Stop orders can also be used to initiate a long or short position, not just close (offset) an open position.

- A *market order,* which means you'll take the prevailing price that the market has to offer. (It has nothing to do with trying to get fresh fish.)

- A *trailing stop,* is an order to sell placed a certain number of ticks below the price of your contract if you're long, and a certain number of ticks above your contract if you're short. The purpose of a trailing stop is to lock in profits. Here's how it works. Say you buy one S&P 500 futures contract at 1000 and you want to limit your loss to five points. You would place your stop at 995. If the contract moves up to 1005, you then change your trailing stop to 1000.75, to give yourself some breathing room. If the contract moves up another two points, then raise your stop to 1002.75, and so on. When the market turns and your stop is hit, you're out of the market automatically.

✔ **Hedging:** A trading technique that's used to manage risk. It may mean that you're setting up a trade that can go either way, and you want to be prepared for whichever way the market breaks. In the context of large producers of commodities, *hedging* means putting strategies in place in case the market does the opposite of what is expected, such as a major and sudden rise in oil prices caused by a hurricane.

The following terms can help you understand hedging:

- *Putting on a hedge* means that you're setting up a trading situation that enables you to cover all the bases for whichever way the market decides to go. *Hedgers* often account for 20 to 40 percent of all the open, or active, futures contracts in a particular market. They're usually companies or large entities that are protecting their investments against the risk of price fluctuation in the future by buying or shorting futures contracts.

- A *cross hedge* isn't fancy shrubbery; it's the act of using a different contract to manage the risk of another contract in which you're primarily interested. For example, an oil company may use gasoline contracts to hedge the risk of their crude oil contracts.

✔ **The pit:** This isn't Hell, although if you're on the wrong end of the trade, it can feel like it. The pit is where all futures contracts are traded during a regular-hours trading session in the futures markets.

✔ **Speculators:** Traders (usually, but not always, small- to medium-sized) who are trying to make money only from the fluctuation of prices without intending to take delivery of the contract. Hedge funds are also speculators.

- **Floor brokers:** Agents who receive a commission to buy and sell futures contracts for their clients. These clients generally are futures commission merchants. A floor broker may also trade for his own account, under certain restrictions. Floor traders rarely make agent trades. They use their exchange membership to buy and sell futures for their own accounts, taking advantage of very low commissions and immediate access to market information. Floor brokers, by exchange rules, cannot place their own orders ahead of yours. Your broker can trade for himself, but he cannot put his order in ahead of yours.

- **Bid:** The price at which you want to buy something.

- **Offer:** The price at which you are willing to sell something.

- **Taking delivery:** Taking the product on which you were speculating.

- **Supply and demand equation:** Trader talk referring to whether there are more buyers than sellers. When there are more sellers than buyers, the equation tilts toward supply, and vice versa.

- **Expiration:** This isn't a reference to death or breathing out. Expiration with regard to a contract means that the contract is no longer trading.

- **Delivery:** What futures contracts are all about — someone actually delivering or handing something to someone else in exchange for money.

Making the Most of Margins

Margins are what make futures trading so attractive, because they add leverage to futures contract trades. The downside is that if you don't understand how trading on margin works, you can take on some big losses in a hurry.

Trading on margin enables you to leverage your trading position. By that I mean that you can control a larger number of assets with a smaller amount of money. Margins in the futures market generally are low; they tend to be near the 10 percent range. Thus, you can control, or trade, $100,000 worth of commodities or financial indexes with only $10,000 or so in your account.

Trading on margin in the stock market is a different concept than trading on margin in the futures market.

In the stock market, the Federal Reserve sets the allowable margin at 50 percent. So, in order to trade stocks on margin, you must put up 50 percent of the value of the trade. Futures margins are set by the futures exchanges and are different for each different futures contract. Margins in the futures market can be raised or lowered by the exchanges, depending on current market conditions and the volatility of the underlying contract.

Generally, when you deposit a margin on a stock purchase, you buy partial equity of the stock position and owe the balance as debt. In the futures market, a margin acts as a security deposit that protects the exchange from default by the customer or the brokerage house.

When you trade futures on margin, in most cases you buy the right to participate in the price changes of the contract. Your margin is a sign of good faith, or a sign that you're willing to meet your contractual obligations with regard to the trade.

In the futures market, your daily trading activity is *marked to market,* which means that your net gain or net loss from changes in price of the outstanding futures contracts open in your account is calculated and applied to your account each day at the end of the trading day. Your gains are available for use the following day for additional trading or withdrawal from your account. Your net losses are removed from your account, reducing the amount you have to trade with or that you can withdraw from your account.

You can reduce the risk of buying futures on margin by

✔ Trading contracts that are lower in volatility.

✔ Using advanced trading techniques such as *spreads,* or positions in which you simultaneously buy and sell contracts in two different commodities or the same commodity for two different months, to reduce the risk. An example of an *intramarket spread* is buying March crude oil and selling April crude. An example of an *intermarket spread* is buying crude oil and selling gasoline.

For more detailed information about margins, turn to Chapter 4.

Chapter 4

Some Basic Concepts About Options on Futures

. . . .

In This Chapter

▶ Getting the lowdown on types of options and traders

▶ Speaking option-ese (both English and Greek)

▶ Factoring in volatility

▶ Checking out other resources

. . . .

*W*hy would a book on trading futures have a chapter on options? The answer is actually fairly simple. Options on futures are quite an important part of the market, and it's important for you to be exposed to the very basics of the options market as they relate to futures. This chapter is by no means a complete treatise, but rather a broad overview of the major aspects of options on futures. You can get a whole lot more by reading *Trading Options for Dummies* by George Fontanills (Wiley).

Still, trading options, even options on futures, doesn't have to be confusing if you take the time to discover the specific nuances of the market. In fact, when used properly, options give you an opportunity to diversify your holdings beyond traditional investments and to hedge your portfolio against risk.

To be sure, investors are increasingly interested and active in the options markets. And while many of the general concepts are the same, some important differences exist between the options of individual stocks and those of a futures contract.

In this chapter, I cover the very basics of options on futures. This, though, is a highly complex topic which requires extensive space. My goal here is to expose you only to the rudimentary concepts so that you can have a base for further reading. At the end of the chapter, I provide some important sources where you can get more details.

Getting Options on Futures Straight

A futures contract is a standardized contract that calls for the delivery of a specific commodity at some time in the future. Thus, unlike options on stocks, in which you take delivery of a lot consisting of at least 100 (and possibly more) shares of stock, an option on a futures contract gives you the opportunity to buy or sell the futures contract, not the underlying commodity. So when you exercise or assign your option on a futures contract, you receive the contract, not the cash value of the index, the soybeans, or the gold.

Options on futures

- Are always for one contract of the underlying commodity.

- Require that you understand the underlying futures contract, be it for gold, soybeans, oil, or whatever, before you begin trading.

- Trade in the same price units as the underlying futures contract, in most cases. That means that a one-point move in a stock index futures contract is a one-point move in the corresponding option. T-bond futures and options are an exception. The former trade in 32nds, while the latter trade in 64ths.

- Don't move on their own in price; rather, they move along with the underlying futures contract.

- Can have quirky expiration dates. For example, March soybean options actually expire in February. What expires in March is the March soybeans contract, which is why the options are referred to as "March options." The best thing to do is to look very carefully at a well-documented futures and options expirations calendar. You can get one from your broker, or see the December issue of *Futures* magazine for good calendars.

- Offer *round turn* commission in many cases. This means that you only pay the broker when you exit your position, instead of paying to both enter and exit, as with stock options. Check with your individual broker for his practices.

SPANning your margin

Margin in futures and options on futures is different than margin on stocks. While margin in the context of stocks is a loan from your broker so you can buy stock worth more money than you have, margin in the former two is just the amount of money that you have to have in your account to trade futures and futures on options. Also, in terms of futures and options on futures, margin is a performance bond that earns interest if it's held in the form of Treasury bills, as SPAN margin allows. (Keep reading for a definition of SPAN margin.)

Moreover, margin becomes important in options on futures if you want to implement more sophisticated strategies, such as writing spreads. *Spreads* are sophisticated techniques used by traders to make money in sideways markets. The value of the spread is derived from the difference in two or more assets. Spread trading is really beyond this chapter, but it's an important aspect of options trading that you may want to look at as you gain experience.

SPAN stands for Standard Portfolio ANalysis of risk, a practice used in the exchanges where options on futures trade (the Chicago Board of Trade and the Chicago Mercantile Exchange) in order to determine the entire risk of a portfolio, including all futures and options held within it. SPAN is based on a sophisticated algorithm and is designed to help you make the best use of your trading capital.

The algorithm is designed to calculate the worst possible one-day move in all your positions. Then it automatically shifts the excess margin from any position(s) to new positions or those that don't have enough. Here are some general details on margin for options on futures strategies:

- ✔ Initial margin is just the amount needed to open the position. Margin requirements fluctuate on a daily basis.

- ✔ A good rule of thumb for options writers is to have a 2-to-1 ratio of margin to net premium collected.

- ✔ T-bill margins are valued at less than the actual value of the T-bills. For example, a T-bill with a $25,000 value gets a margin value between $23,750 and $22,500, depending on the clearinghouse. Still, the interest earned on such a T-bill may be good enough to offset some of your transaction costs, another good thing about SPAN. For more details on SPAN and options on futures, visit www.optionsnerd.com.

Types of options

Two types of options are traded. One kind lets you speculate on prices of the underlying asset rising, and the other lets you bet on their fall. Options usually trade at a fraction of the price of the underlying asset, making them attractive to investors with small accounts.

Calls

I think of a call option as a bet that the underlying asset is going to rise in value. The more formal definition is that a *call option* gives you the right to buy a defined amount of the underlying asset at a certain price before a certain amount of time expires. You're buying that opportunity when you buy the call option. If you don't buy the asset by the time the option expires, you lose only the money that you spent on the call option. You can always sell your option prior to expiration to avoid exercising it, to avoid further loss, or to profit if it has risen in value. Call options usually rise in price when the underlying asset rises in price.

When you buy a call option, you put up the option premium for the right to exercise an option to buy the underlying asset before the call option expires. Buying the call option gives you the right to exercise it. When you exercise a call, you're buying the underlying stock or asset at the *strike price,* the predetermined price at which an option will be delivered when it is exercised.

Puts

Put options are bets that the price of the underlying asset is going to fall. Puts are excellent trading instruments when you're trying to guard against losses in stock, futures contracts, or commodities that you already own.

Buying a put option gives you the right to sell a specific quantity of the underlying asset at a predetermined price, the strike price, during a certain amount of time. When you exercise a put option, you are exercising your right to sell the underlying asset at the strike price. Like calls, if you don't exercise a put option, your risk is limited to the option premium, or the price you paid for it.

Puts are sometimes thought of as portfolio insurance because they give you the option of selling a falling stock at a predetermined strike price.

Types of option traders

Option buyers are also known as *holders,* and option sellers are known as *writers.*

Call option holders have the right to buy a stipulated quantity of the underlying asset specified in the contract. Put option holders have the right to sell a specified amount of the underlying asset in the contract. Call and put holders can exercise those rights at the strike price.

Call option writers have the potential obligation to sell. Put option buyers have the potential obligation to buy.

Breaking down the language barrier

You need to know several terms to be able to trade options. Most of this stuff is fairly simple after you get the hang of it. But if you're like me, it isn't much fun when you start. Still, if you're going to trade options, you must dig in and get a grasp on the lingo, including these terms:

- ✔ **Premium:** This is the price that you pay for the option. For options that you don't exercise, this is the maximum risk.

- ✔ **Expiration date:** This is the date on which your option expires. After this date, your option is worthless.

- ✔ **Strike price:** This is the predetermined price at which the underlying asset is bought or sold.

- ✔ **In the money:** A call option is said to be in the money whenever the strike price is less than the market price of the underlying security. A put option is in the money whenever the strike price is greater than the market price of the underlying security.

- ✔ **At the money:** Options are considered at the money when the strike price and the market price are the same.

- ✔ **Out of the money:** Calls are out of the money when the strike price is greater than the market price of the underlying security. Puts are out of the money if the strike price is less than the market price of the underlying security.

Grappling with Greek

Options require you to pick up a bit of the Greek language. You only need to know four words, but they're all important. *The Greeks,* as they are commonly called, are measurements of risk that explain several variables that influence option prices. They are delta, gamma, theta, and vega.

John Summa, who operates a Web site called OptionsNerd.com (www.options nerd.com), summarizes the four terms nicely in an article he wrote for Investopedia.com. You can find it at www.investopedia.com/articles/ optioninvestor/02/120602.asp.

But before actually getting into the Greek, you need to know the factors that influence the change in the price of an option. After that, I tell you how it all fits into the mix with the Greek terminology.

The three major price influences are

- ✔ **Amount of volatility:** An increase in volatility usually is positive for put and call options, if you're long in the option. If you're the writer of the option, an increase in volatility is negative.

✓ **Changes in the time to expiration:** The closer you get to the time of expiration, the more negative the time factor becomes for a holder of the option, and the less your potential for profit. Time value shrinks as an option approaches expiration and is zero upon expiration of the option.

✓ **Changes in the price of the underlying asset:** An increase in the price of the underlying asset usually is a positive influence on the price of a call option. A decrease in the price of the underlying instrument usually is positive for put options and vice versa.

Interest rates, a fourth influence, are less important most of the time. In general, higher interest rates make call options more expensive and put options less expensive. Now that you know the major and minor influences on price, I can describe the Greeks.

Delta

Delta measures the effect of a change in the price of the underlying asset on the option's premium. Delta is best understood as the amount of change in the price of an option for every one-point move in the underlying asset or the percentage of the change in price of the underlying asset that is reflected in the price of an option.

Delta values range from −100 to 0 for put options and from 0 to 100 for calls, or −1 to 0 and 0 to 1 if you use the more commonly used expression in decimals.

Puts have a negative delta number because of their inverse or negative relationship to the underlying asset. Put premiums, or prices, fall when the underlying asset rises in price, and they rise when the underlying asset falls.

Call options have a positive relationship to the underlying asset and thus a positive delta number. As the price of the underlying asset goes up, so do call premiums, unless other variables are changed, such as implied volatility, time to expiration, and interest rates. Call premiums generally go down as the price of the underlying asset falls, as long as no other influences are putting undue pressure on the option.

An at-the-money call has a delta value of 0.5 or 50, which tells you that the option's premium will rise or fall by half a point with a one-point move in the underlying asset. Say, for example, that an at-the-money call option for wheat has a delta of 0.5. If the wheat futures contract associated with the option goes up ten cents, the premium on the option will rise by approximately five cents ($0.5 \times 10 = 5$). The actual gain will be $250 because each cent in the premium is worth $50 in the contract.

The farther into the money the option premium advances, the closer the relationship between the price of the underlying asset and the price of the option becomes. When delta approaches 1 for calls, or –1 for puts, the price of the option and the underlying asset move the same, assuming all the other variables remain under control.

Key factors about delta to remember are that delta

- ✔ Is about 0.5 when an option is at the money and moves toward 1.0 as the option moves deeper into the money.

- ✔ Tends to increase as you get closer to the expiration date for near or at-the-money options.

- ✔ Is not a constant because the effect of *gamma* is a measure of the rate of change of delta in relation to the underlying asset.

- ✔ Is affected by changes in implied volatility. (See the section "Understanding Volatility: The Las Vega Syndrome," later in this chapter, for a full discussion of implied volatility.)

Gamma

Gamma measures the rate of change of delta in relation to the change in the price of the underlying asset. It enables you to predict how much you're going to make or lose based on the movement of the underlying position.

The best way to understand this concept is to look at an example like the one in Figure 4-1, which shows the changes in delta and gamma as the underlying asset changes in price. The example features a short position in the S&P 500 September $930 call option as it rises in price from $925 on the left to $934 on the right and is based on John Summa's explanation of the Greeks. The chart was prepared by using OptionVue 5 Options Analytical Software, which is available from www.optionvue.com.

Figure 4-1:
Summary of risk measures for the short December S&P 500 930 call option.

P/L	425	300	175	50	–75	–200	–325	–475	–600	–750
Delta	–48.36	–49.16	–49.96	–50.76	–51.55	–52.34	–53.13	–53.92	–54.70	–55.49
Gamma	–0.80	–0.80	–0.80	–0.80	–0.79	–0.79	–0.79	–0.79	–0.78	–0.78
Theta	45.01	45.11	45.20	45.28	45.35	45.40	45.44	45.47	45.48	45.48
Vega	–96.30	–96.49	–96.65	–96.78	–96.87	–96.94	–96.98	–96.99	–96.96	–96.91

The farther out of the money that a call option declines, the smaller the delta, because changes in the underlying asset cause only small changes in the option premium. The delta gets larger as the call option advances closer to the money, which is a result of an increase in the underlying asset's price. In this case, the more out-of-the-money the option is, the better it gets for the short seller of the option.

Line 1 of Figure 4-1 is a calculation of the profit or loss for the S&P 500 Index futures 930 call option — $930 is the strike price of the S&P 500 Index futures option that expires in September (as featured in Figure 4-3). The –200 line is the at-the-money strike of the 930 call option, and each column represents a one-point change in the underlying asset.

The at-the-money gamma of the underlying asset for the 930 option is –0.79, and the delta is –52.34. What this tells you is that for every one-point move in the depicted futures contract, delta will increase by exactly 0.79.

The position depicts a short call position that is losing money. The P/L line is measuring Profit/Loss. The more negative the P/L numbers become, the more in the red the position is. Note also that delta is increasingly negative as the price of the option rises.

Finally, with delta being at –52.34, the position is expected to lose 0.5234 points in price with the next one-point rise in the underlying futures contract.

If you move one column to the right in Figure 4-3, you see the delta changes to –53.13, which is an increase of 0.79 from –52.34.

Other important aspects of gamma are that it

- Is smallest for deep out-of-the-money and in-the-money options.
- Is highest when the option gets near the money.
- Is positive for long options and negative for short options.

Theta

Theta is not often used by traders, but it is important because it measures the effect of time on options. More specifically, theta measures the rate of decline of the *time premium* (the effect on the option's price of the time remaining until option expiration). Understanding premium erosion due to the passage of time is critical to being successful at trading options. Often the effects of theta will offset the effects of delta, resulting in the trader being right about the direction of the move and still losing money.

As time passes and option expiration grows near, the value of the time premium decreases, and the amount of decrease grows faster as option expiration nears.

The following minitable shows the theta values for the featured example of the short S&P 500 Index futures 930 call option.

=			
T + 0	T +6	T + 13	T+ 19
Theta	45.4	51.85	93.3

The concept of how theta affects the price of an option can best be summarized by looking in the fourth column of the table, where the figure for T + 19 measures theta six days before the option's expiration. The value 93.3 tells you that the option is losing $93.30 per day, a major increase in time-influenced loss of value compared with the figure for T + 0, where the option's loss of value attributed to time alone was only $45.40 per day.

Theta rises sharply during the last few weeks of trading and can do a considerable amount of damage to a long holder's position, which is made worse when the option's implied volatility is falling at the same time.

Understanding Volatility: The Las Vega Syndrome

Vega measures risk exposure to changes in implied volatility and tells traders how much an option's price will rise or fall as the volatility of the option varies.

Vega is expressed as a value and can be found in the fifth row of Figure 4-1, where the example cited in the figure shows that the short call option has a negative vega value — which tells you that the position will gain in price if the implied volatility falls. The value of vega tells you how much the position will gain in this case. For example, if the at-the-money value for vega is –96.94, you know that for each percentage-point drop in implied volatility, a short call position will gain $96.94.

Volatility is a measure of how fast and how much prices of the underlying asset move and is key to understanding why option prices fluctuate and act the way they do. In fact, volatility is the most important concept in options trading, but it also can be difficult to grasp unless taken in small bites. Fortunately, trading software programs provide a great deal of the information needed to keep track of volatility. Nevertheless, you need to keep in mind these two kinds of volatility:

✔ **Implied volatility (IV),** which is the estimated volatility of a security's price in real time, or as the option trades. Values for IV come from formulas that measure the options market's expectations, offering a prediction of the volatility of the underlying asset over the life of the option. It usually rises when the markets are in downtrends and falls when the markets are in uptrends. Mark Powers, in *Starting Out In Futures Trading* (McGraw-Hill), describes IV as an "up-to-date reading of how current market participants view what is likely to happen."

✔ **Historical volatility (HV),** which also is known as statistical volatility (SV), is a measurement of the movement of the price of a financial asset over time. It is calculated by figuring out the average deviation from the average price of the asset in the given time period. Standard deviation is the most common way to calculate historical volatility. HV measures how fast prices of the underlying asset have been changing. It is stated as a percentage and summarizes the recent movements in price.

HV is always changing and has to be calculated on a daily basis. Because it can be very erratic, traders smooth out the numbers by using a moving average of the daily numbers. Moving averages are explained in detail in Chapter 7, which is about technical analysis. In general, though, the bigger the HV, the more an option is worth. HV is used to calculate the probability of a price movement occurring.

Whereas HV measures the rate of movement in the price of the underlying asset, IV measures the price movement of the option itself.

Most of the time, IV is computed using a formula based on something called the Black-Scholes model, which was introduced in 1973 (see the next section). The goal of the Black-Scholes model, which is highly theoretical for actual trading, is to calculate a fair market value of an option by incorporating multiple variables such as historical volatility, time premium, and strike price. I'll let you in on a little secret here: The Black-Scholes formula alone isn't very practical as a trading tool because trading software automatically calculates the necessary measurements; however, the number it produces, IV, is central to options trading.

HV and IV are often different numbers. That may sound simple, but there's more to it than meets the eye.

In a perfect world, HV and IV should be fairly close together, given the fact that they're supposed to be measures of two financial assets that are intrinsically related to one another, the underlying asset and its option. In fact, sometimes IV and HV actually are very close together. Yet the differences in these numbers at different stages of the market cycle can provide excellent trading opportunities. This concept is called *options mispricing,* and if you can understand how to use it, options mispricing can help you make better trading decisions.

When HV and IV are far apart, the price of the option is not reflecting the actual volatility of the underlying asset. For example, if IV rises dramatically and HV is very low, the underlying stock may be a possible candidate for a takeover. Under those circumstances, the stock probably has been stuck in a trading range as the market awaits news. At the same time, option premiums may remain high because of the potential for sudden changes with regard to the deal.

The bottom line is that HV and IV are useful tools in trading options. Most software programs will graph out these two variables. When they are charted, big spreads become easy to spot, and that enables you to look for trading opportunities.

Options screening software helps you cut through the clutter. For more sophisticated analysis than the bare-bones type provided by free software, you have to spend some money.

Many good options-trading programs are available. Among the most popular programs is OptionVue 5 Options Analysis Software. This program has been around since 1982, and it has just about everything anyone could want to analyze options and find trades. Many traders use OptionsVue and consider it the benchmark program.

Most programs on the market are good enough to generate decent data. You want to find the one that's easiest for you to use and in the right price range. *Technical Analysis of Stocks & Commodities* magazine, www.traders.com, has excellent software reviews, and it conducts an annual readers' poll to determine which programs its readers think are the best. This magazine/Web site is a good place to do your homework.

Some Practical Stuff

In the preceding sections, I tell you about the nuts and bolts of options. In this section, I give you a brief summary of some, but certainly not all, situations in which you might want to use options.

There are two basic reasons to choose options as a trading vehicle. One is that you have limited amounts of money and want to trade. And the other is that you are looking to combine leverage while limiting your risk. The second choice is the most sensible of the two, as it takes a lot of talent to turn a little money into a large amount by using options, although it can be done if you're clever and talented. But if you could do that, you wouldn't likely be reading this book.

✔ The simplest options strategy is buying call options, as the upside potential is theoretically limitless, while the downside risk is your option premium. This is usually the first strategy that beginners use when they enter this sector and is best used when you are expecting the underlying asset to rally.

✔ A second use of call options is option writing. In this case, you are looking to protect a long position by selling a call option to someone and collecting the premium. This works better in markets that are falling or moving sideways. In this case you're hoping that the underlying market goes mostly nowhere and that the option expires worthless, while you pocket the premium.

✔ Put option strategies are generally useful in falling markets, but tend to be more risky than call related strategies.

✔ Other, more complex strategies, such as straddles, strangles, and spreads, involve two or more options, sometimes involve more than one asset class, such as stock index options being paired with bond options, and are beyond the scope of this chapter. See the section at the end of the chapter titled "Useful information sources."

General rules of success

Become familiar with the underlying futures contract before you trade the options, and look at the two instruments simultaneously.

The following example, adapted from an article written by John Summa (optionsnerd.com), covers the S&P 500 stock index futures and related options. (If you're going to trade soybean options, become familiar with the rules and vagaries of the soybean sector, and so on.)

Figure 4-2 summarizes the facts about the S&P 500 futures contract. Figure 4-3 shows you the settlement prices for three S&P 500 futures prices as they settled on June 12, 2002, and Figure 4-4 shows the closing prices of corresponding options on the same day.

Figure 4-2:
S&P 500
futures
contract
specifi-
cations.

Futures Contract	Contract Value	Tick Size	Delivery Months	Last Trading Day	Type of Settlement
S&P 500	$250 × price of S&P 500	.10 (a "dime")= $25	March, June, Sept., and Dec.	Thursday prior to the third Friday of the contract month	Cash

Figure 4-3:
S&P 500
futures
contract
settlement
prices June
12, 2002.

Contract	High	Low	Settlement	Point Change
June '02	1022.80	1002.50	1020.20	+6.00
Sept. '02	1023.80	1003.50	1021.20	+6.00
Dec. '02	1025.00	1007.00	1023.00	+6.00

Figure 4-3: S&P 500 futures contract settlement prices June 12, 2002.

Strike	Settlement	Point Change	$ Change	Delta
June Puts				
1000*	7.50	−2.40	−$600	−.30
975	3.40	−1.70	−$425	−.15
950	1.60	−1.20	−$300	−.07
925	.85	−.90	−$255	−.04
June Calls				
1025*	11.90	+1.70	+$425	.40
1050	3.60	+1.70	+$125	.20
1075	.95	+1.70	+$50	.06
1100	.35	+1.70	+$12.50	.02
*(*Near-the-money options)*				

Figure 4-4: S&P 500 options prices at settlement on June 12, 2002.

Here's what's important: The June S&P futures contract in Figure 4-3 settled at 1020.20 on June 12. The contract gained 6.00 points, which is equivalent to a gain of $1,500 per single contract (6 × $250 = $1,500).

Looking at the options, note in Figure 4-4 that because the price of the contract rose, the price of the call options rose, and the price of the puts fell. Note also that the delta is positive for calls and negative for puts, and that the higher the delta value, the more the price of the underlying futures affects the option's price change. The reverse applies to the put options, as the figure shows.

If you understand these rules, you can then apply them to your option strategies, which are of three basic types: buying puts or calls, selling (writing) puts or calls, or setting up more sophisticated strategies, such as spreads, strangles, and straddles.

The following tips are the best advice I can give you when it comes to options, or any kind of investment or trading in the futures markets:

- Work out the kinks of your strategies on paper before you proceed.
- Avail yourself of the best possible software and quote system possible for whatever you're trading.

If you're well prepared and you have good equipment and data, your chances of success will be much higher.

Useful information sources

Finally, here are some other places to get more details about options:

- *High-Powered Investing All-in-One For Dummies* (Wiley). Check out Book III, focusing on futures and options, by yours truly.
- *Trading Options For Dummies* by George A. Fontanills (Wiley).
- *Options as a Strategic Investment* by Lawrence G. McMillan (New York Institute of Finance)
- *Options Made Easy,* 2nd Edition, by Guy Cohen (Financial Times Trading and Investing)
- The CBOE Web site (www.cboe.com)

Chapter 5

Trading Futures Through the Side Door

With exchange-traded funds (ETFs), the world of the futures markets has opened to traders whose fears of the unknown previously limited their prospects. When you understand ETFs and how to make them work successfully, you can trade just about anything.

This chapter helps you get your feet wet in futures trading through ETFs, which means you can trade without worrying about margin and when to roll over a contract.

Using the information and techniques in this chapter, you can participate in the general trends of the futures markets, including the agricultural, energy, bond, currency, and stock index futures contracts, with less threatening instruments. In other words, ETFs are instruments that let you take advantage of the overall profit potential of the futures markets without having to open a separate account for your trades.

Here are some of the things that I like best about ETFs:

✔ I can trade the trend, up or down, without having to research individual stocks. Thus, I can participate in what's happening as I make more detailed decisions about further trades.

✔ I can trade them through my online account with a click of my mouse, just as if I am buying individual stocks.

✔ I can trade anything from stock indexes to commodities, bonds, oil, natural gas, currencies, or very specific sectors in the stock market.

✔ The basic trading techniques are also applicable to the more familiar futures markets, such as bonds, commodities, oil, and natural gas. In other words, when conditions are right to buy an oil ETF, they are also right for buying oil futures. So after you master the techniques required to trade these ETFs, you can use them as a basis to trade futures directly.

Just remember, this chapter is not meant to give you a false sense of security. ETFs that use futures and commodities as their underlying assets tend to follow the same basic trends of those markets. Thus, the same risks and potential for volatility apply.

For a comprehensive listing of ETFs, visit the American Stock Exchange's Web site, www.amex.com. A great place to find commodity ETF information is the Deutsche Bank Web site for commodity ETFs, www.dbfunds.db.com/index.aspx. Also see *Exchange-Traded Funds For Dummies* by Russell Wild (Wiley) for lots of good pearls on ETFs.

Introducing Exchange-Traded Funds

ETFs are mutual funds that trade like stocks. These clever and useful instruments

✔ **Trade during the entire trading day and during extended market hours.** This property lets you trade these vehicles when and where you want to. They're even suitable for day trading. Mutual funds, on the other hand, can usually be bought at the end of the day and can't be sold until the close of the market on the next day.

✔ **Have specific qualities.** For example, the Powershares Nasdaq 100 ETF (QQQQ) can be bought or sold for 15 minutes after the stock market closes. These ETFs resume trading after a brief period of time in the after-hours session.

✔ **Behave similarly to the index, commodity, or portfolio that they're patterned after.** For example, the U.S. Oil Fund (USO) has a similar trading pattern and follows the same general price trend as crude oil.

✔ **Offer both the opportunity to go long or go short the market, without having to sell shares of stock or of an ETF short, although you can sell**

shares of any individual ETF short. See next bullet. For example, you can go long the Nasdaq 100 index by owning the QQQQ ETF. To short the Nasdaq 100, you can just buy shares of the Ultrashort QQQ Proshares (QID) or a similar fund. See "Stocking Up on Stock Index Future ETFs," later in this chapter.

✔ **Can be individually sold short.** If you prefer to sell short directly, you can sell any ETF short as you would any stock by borrowing shares from your broker in a margin account. Although that's possible, I recommend shorting the market by buying an ETF that sells short rather than shorting an ETF that goes long.

✔ **Offer options trading similar to stocks and futures.** You can trade ETF options as you would trade stock options. In some ways, long-term options (LEAPS) are well suited for ETFs. LEAPS let you bet on the long-term price of an underlying instrument, such as a stock. See *Trading Options For Dummies* by George A. Fontanills (Wiley) for full details on LEAPS and other options.

However, not all ETFs are created equal. Reading the fine print about how an ETF goes about its business is important. The Macroshare Funds for trading crude oil are an example. These funds use derivative formulas based on the bond market to mimic the action in the oil market. See "Comfort via Commodity ETFs," later in this chapter for more details.

Margin in the stock market is different than margin in the futures markets. The margin rules for the stock market are the margin rules that govern ETFs. See Chapters 3 and 4 to review margin rules.

The management fee extracted by the ETF sponsor company affects the price of the ETF and its overall performance. In other words, your ETF isn't likely to match its underlying index or its stated performance goals perfectly. Also keep in mind that ETFs pay dividends, and this may have some tax consequences, as well as affecting the price of the fund. Read the prospectus and consult your financial advisor if necessary before you invest in any ETF.

Read the fine print on the prospectus or the online description of all ETFs. For example, Amex.com notes the following in its description of "The Short S&P 500 Proshares (SH)" investment objective: "The Fund employs leveraged investment techniques to achieve its investment objective, which may expose the Fund to potentially dramatic changes (losses) in the value of its portfolio holdings and imperfect correlation to the index underlying the Fund's benchmark." See "Stocking Up on Stock Index Future ETFs" in the next section for more details.

Stocking Up on Stock Index Future ETFs

You can trade just about every single stock index by using an exchange-traded fund. But for the sake of simplicity, I concentrate on the big ones because a big part of your success here depends on liquidity and ease of trading as well as your own recognition of what you're trading. The indexes in the following sections all have corresponding futures contracts. After you get the hang of working with these, you can expand your horizons.

Futures are meant to be traded both short and long, so I list any short-selling funds that are available for any particular futures market in this section. If no fund is listed, it's because no ETF that specialized in short selling that particular market or index was available at the time. Also, due to space limitations, I limit my discussion to the most liquid ETFs.

In the following sections, I discuss the most liquid and actively traded major stock indexes and their corresponding futures contracts.

The S&P 500 (SPX)

The S&P 500 and its ETFs are important because the action in these ETFs closely matches that of the S&P 500 index futures, at least in their general direction and the size of the moves.

- ✔ **SPDR S&P 500 (SPY):** This highly recognizable and well-advertised ETF is the most commonly traded S&P 500 ETF. Also known as the S&P 500 "Spyders," it is among the most liquid of all ETFs. SPY trades at one-tenth the value of the S&P 500 cash index. That means that if the S&P 500 is at 1,400, SPY trades at 140. SPY works well when you want to trade the overall trend of the broad stock market.

- ✔ **Ultra S&P 500 Shares (SSO):** This is a leveraged ETF which rises and falls twofold the daily performance of the S&P 500. It's an excellent fund when the market is starting to come out of a significant decline. The potential risk of losing twice the drop of the S&P 500 on any given day, though, makes it a tough one to use until a rising trend is clearly in progress.

- ✔ **Short S&P 500 ProShares (SH):** This ETF is a way to sell the S&P 500 short without selling SPY short. SH is structured to work opposite to the S&P 500, without any leverage. In other words, if the S&P 500 was to lose 1 percent at any given time, SH would rise close to 1 percent.

- ✔ **UltraShort S&P 500 ProShares (SDS):** This is my favorite way to sell the stock market short because it follows the trend of the S&P 500 quite closely, and it gives me the opportunity to leverage my gains. The investment goal of this fund is to deliver twice the opposite performance of the S&P 500 (200percent), before fees and expenses. I use it when I get sell signals for the stock market. See Chapter 12 for more detail on stocking up on indexes. See "Using ETFs in Real Trading" at the end of this chapter for a real-life trading example.

The Nasdaq 100 Index (NDX)

The Nasdaq 100 Index is a basket of large technology stocks including familiar names such as Intel and Apple. The index often moves in a big way, both up and down, offering great opportunities for active trading.

- ✔ **PowerShares Trust (QQQQ):** This highly popular and liquid ETF contains the largest 100 stocks that trade on the Nasdaq. It works well as a proxy for the Nasdaq 100 futures and the E-mini Nasdaq futures, which are both very popular contracts.

- ✔ **Ultra QQQ Proshares (QLD):** This ETF is designed to double the returns of the Nasdaq 100 Index twofold. It's a good vehicle to use when you're expecting a significant rally and want to get more bang for your buck. Just remember that what goes up twofold also falls twofold.

- ✔ **Short QQQ Proshares (PSQ):** This ETF shorts the Nasdaq 100 Index on a one-to-one basis, such that a 1 percent drop in the index leads roughly to a 1 percent rise in the price of PSQ. This fund is ideal if you want to sell NDX short but aren't willing to get too leveraged.

- ✔ **UltraShort QQQ ProShares (QID):** As with all "Ultra" funds, this one gives you a twofold return on the trend of the index that it mirrors. In this case, QID rises twice the amount of the Nasdaq 100 when the index falls. This is an excellent fund to use when large technology stocks are having difficulties and you're looking to leverage your short positions.

The Dow Jones Industrial Average

The Dow Jones Industrial Average is the most widely followed stock index in the world. Its corresponding ETFs are great trading tools, and they have an excellent correlation to the Dow Jones Industrial Average futures.

- ✔ **Diamond Shares (DIA):** This is the way to trade the general trend of the Dow Jones Industrial Average. Its value is roughly one-tenth of the Dow Jones Industrial Average.

- ✔ **DDM, DOG, and DXD:** Ultra Dow30 Proshares (DDM), Short Dow30 Proshares (DOG) and UltraShort Dow30 Proshares (DXD) round out the quartet of highly liquid Dow Jones Industrial average–based ETFs. As with other Ultra ETFs, the ones corresponding to the Dow Jones Industrial Average are leveraged. To short the Dow Jones Industrial Average on a one-to-one basis, use the Short Dow30 Proshares (DOG).

Comfort via Commodity ETFs

Commodities, at least as of February 2008, seem to be in the midst of a multi-year, and perhaps a multidecade, bull market. Indeed, even dummies (like us) can trade oil, natural gas, commodities like wheat and soybeans, and bonds with little trouble as long as we have online stock trading accounts.

Still, it's a good idea to check out Chapter 10 for information on trading bonds, see Chapter 13 to get a good idea as to what's involved in trading energy, and review Chapter 16 to get the lay of the land on agricultural commodities before you jump in with both feet. Other chapters that are likely to be helpful in trading ETFs include Chapter 7 (on technical analysis), Chapter 14 (on trading metals) and Chapter 17 (on setting up your trading plan).

Energizing your ETF Trades

The energy markets captured the spotlight for the last seven years, since oil began its climb before topping out at $110 in March 2008. Whether that's the final top or not remains to be seen, but one thing is certain: The energy markets offer great trading opportunities, and there are plenty of ETFs that you can use to participate.

- **The U.S. Oil Fund (USO):** This was the first ETF introduced to allow the actual trade of crude oil futures without owning futures contracts. It remains the most liquid, although it has some competitors. The key to success is to remember that USO follows the general price trend of crude oil, but the price is not the same as the leading crude oil futures.

  As Russell Wild points out in *Exchange-Traded Funds For Dummies* (Wiley), USO is a commodity pool. It doesn't invest in oil companies, but rather in crude oil futures. Thus, it's a risky and volatile fund, whose value is based on the value of the futures contracts owned by the management company that runs the fund.

  Wild goes to great lengths to give you the negative aspects of the ETF, and they're worth reading so you get the whole picture. But for my money, the fund, which has been around since 2006, is very liquid and serves my purposes as it follows the trend of crude oil futures closely. When oil prices are rising, I want to own shares in USO.

- **The PowerShares DB Energy Fund (DBE):** This fund lets you trade West Texas Light Sweet Crude oil, Brent Crude, RBOB gasoline, heating oil, and natural gas under one banner. The problem with the fund is that there is no guarantee that all five energy components will be in bullish or bearish trends at the same time. As a result, this ETF may lag a single commodity fund such as USO or UNG. Still, if the energy sector is firing on all cylinders, this one is a good one. Both crude grades get a 22.5 percent weighing here, as do gasoline and heating oil. The more volatile natural gas component gets a 10 percent weighing.

✔ **Macroshares Oil Down Tradeable shares (DCR):** This ETF has not been very successful given its inability to track the price of crude oil, either in price itself or in percentage terms. Much of the problem has been the illiquidity of the product. On some days, only a few hundred shares trade hands, in contrast with USO, where hundreds of thousands of shares trade daily.

The problem with Macroshares DCR is that the fund is not invested in the short sale of oil or oil futures; rather, it's invested in treasury bonds, which in turn are worked into a formula that's supposed to generally track the trend of crude oil. If this fund worked correctly, it would rise in price when crude oil prices fall. But it doesn't always work that way. In fact, on January 17, 2007, the price of crude oil fell and DCR shares fell. Aside from embarrassing the issuer of the fund at the time (Claymore Advisors), the incident raised questions about whether this fund would be viable.

Nevertheless, knowing about it is worthwhile, assuming it stays around. As of February 2008, the fund was still available. And if oil ever falls for any extended period of time, this might be a good way to try to make money from the event, after careful scrutiny of how the fund is functioning at the time.

✔ **The United States Gas Fund (UNG):** UNG actually works pretty well at moving along with the fortunes of natural gas. It correlates with the rises and falls of the price of the underlying futures. The major problem with UNG is the fact that natural gas is hugely volatile. So even in an ETF you could experience big intraday volatility. I have traded this fund many times and have had a difficult time making money, due to the nature of the underlying asset. Yet, if natural gas ever hits a bull market like crude oil has had since 2001, this would be a good way to play it.

✔ **The PowerShares DB Commodity Index Tracking Fund (DBC):** This fund tracks a diversified commodity portfolio, including crude oil, heating oil, aluminum, corn, wheat, and gold. It generally tracks the overall price of the commodities it houses, but is heavily weighted toward energy with crude oil (35 percent) and heating oil (25 percent) making up over half of the asset allocation. Aluminum accounts for 12.5 percent, while corn, wheat, and gold make up the rest of the fund. Make no mistake about it, though; despite the diversification, this is no wallflower of an ETF.

✔ **The PowerShares DB Agriculture Fund (DBA):** This is a good play on the agricultural commodities. It's designed to track, before fees and expenses, the Deutsche Bank Liquid Commodity Index — Optimum Yield Agriculture Excess Return. DBA tracks the price of corn, wheat, soybeans, and sugar with each commodity getting a 25 percent weighing in the ETF. It functions similarly to DBC, but is more volatile since it concentrates its assets on agriculture. Both DBA and DBC were doing well in early 2008, as commodities were rising in price due to higher demand for goods in China and other emerging markets. Both DBA and DBC are direct commodity pools.

The golden touch — metal ETFs

Precious metal ETFs are fairly liquid and trend with the price of the underlying commodity quite well. Several fairly liquid gold funds exist, but the most liquid and most popular is Streettracks Gold Shares (GLD). This fund offers access to gold bullion without having to trade futures or take custody of bullion bars. It also saves transaction fees.

Other gold and silver ETFs are

✔ **PowerShares DB Precious Metals (DBP)**, which houses both gold and silver futures. Gold makes up 80 percent of the portfolio, with silver carrying 20 percent of the load. This makes sense, given the volatility of the silver market.

✔ **PowerShares DB Gold Fund (DGL) and iShares DB Silver Trust (SLV)** are self-explanatory.

✔ **The PowerShares DB Base Metals Fund (DBB)** lets you trade aluminum, zinc, and copper. Each represents 33.3 percent of the portfolio. This is a good fund when the global economy is booming and demand for industrial metals is high.

Getting Current with Currency ETFs

Foreign currencies are an excellent way to profit from global market volatility, political instability, and other crises. At the same time, they're excellent trading vehicles when interest rates change.

A good general rule is that higher interest rates and a strong economy tend to favor a country's currency. And while there isn't a 100 percent correlation between any one variable and a currency's price, if you know how to trade with the trend, currencies are an excellent vehicle. For the whole story on currencies, read Chapter 11. In this section, I provide a good list of currency ETFs. All of them trade along the same trends as their underlying currencies.

In the world of currency trading, not only can you trade dollars versus other currencies, but you can also engage in what is known as cross trading, or trading of Yen versus Swiss francs, euros versus Australian dollars, and so on. In this section, though, I concentrate only on ETFs that feature the dollar versus other currencies.

There are plenty of opportunities to trade currencies via ETFs:

- You can bet on a rising U.S. dollar with the PowerShares DB U.S. Dollar Bullish Fund (UUP). This ETF has relatively low volatility and is not the best way to trade the dollar when the trend is sideways because it generally rises and falls with the U.S. Dollar Index, a slow-moving composite of the dollar against ten global currencies.

- The same can be said about the PowerShares DB U.S. Dollar Bearish Fund (UDN). This would be a good way to trade the dollar in a very long-term downtrend, but it has fairly low volatility and is not as good a vehicle for trading as are the individual currency funds that I describe in the next two bullets.

- The Currency Shares EuroTrust (FXE) has an excellent correlation to the exchange rate between the euro and the U.S. dollar.

- The Currency Shares Swiss Franc Trust (FXF), the Currency Shares Australian Dollar Trust (FXA), the Currency Shares Yen Trust (FXY), the Currency Shares Swedish Krona (FXS), the Currency Shares Canadian Dollar Trust (FXC), the Currency Shares Mexican Peso Trust (FXM), and the Currency Shares British Pound Trust (FXB) round out the ETF offerings for the currency markets.

For more information on these ETFs, visit www.currencyshares.com.

Using ETFs in Real Trading

In this final section I describe a real trade that I recommended at www.joe-duarte.com, and that I made in my own portfolio at the same time. In order to illustrate both the concept of trading futures and how to use an ETF in the process, I chose a sale in which I shorted the UltraShort S&P 500 ProShares (SDS).

The market had been acting fairly poorly since the start of January, but by January 15, (2008) things were getting pretty dicey. On December 26, 2007, on `Joe-Duarte.com` I recommended the purchase of S&P 500 SPDRs (SPY), which was triggered at 149.53. The trade moved mostly sideways, which is rare for the week between Christmas and New Year's Eve. Traditionally, the holiday week is one of the best trading weeks of the year, as portfolio managers tend to "window dress" their portfolios by adding more shares of winners and making their results look better. Figure 5-1 shows the uncharacteristically flat market during the holiday period in 2007 and the subsequent decline as well as the catalysts of the decline in early 2008.

On January 4, 2008, I recommended the purchase of SDS on a price above 60.05, as the S&P 500, which had crossed below its 200-day moving average at the end of 2007, looked to weaken once again. (See Chapter 7 for more on the 200-day moving average.) The market stayed that way until January 10, when it rallied briefly and again tried to stabilize. Figure 5-2 shows the entry and exit points for the trade.

Figure 5-1:
The S&P 500 failing to rally and finally breaking down during the traditionally bullish holiday period.

Figure 5-2:
ProShares
Ultrashort
S&P 500 ETF
entry and
exit points
during a
short-term
trade via
the short-
selling ETF.

But the stabilization process of the S&P 500 (refer to Figure 5-1) looked weak, as volume dried up on each day thereafter. Weaker volume on a rally is usually a sign of poor conviction. As I saw this phenomenon and noted that the market was still trading below its 200-day moving average, the dividing line between bullish and bearish trends, I recommended entering SDS on a price above 60.05.

The entry point on SDS was triggered on January 15, when the market started selling off during the middle of the day. This was due to several announcements made by Apple Inc.'s CEO Steve Jobs during a news conference. The news did not sit well with traders, who were already jittery about the general state of affairs.

The stock market drifted off for the rest of the day, and all hell broke loose after the bell when Intel's earnings announcement again disappointed the street. The S&P 500 started a five-session decline that finally stopped on January 23. The position was stopped out that day at 66.23, pocketing a 10.29 percent gain in an eight-day period.

Here are some other important things to note on Figures 5-1 and 5-2:

- ✔ Note the generally inverse nature of the charts. This makes perfect sense as SDS is supposed to move in the opposite direction of SPX. It's important for an ETF to do what it's designed to do. In this case, SDS acted perfectly, as it rallied when the S & P 500 fell.

- ✔ Note also that when SPX fell below its 200-day moving average, SDS moved above its 200-day line.

- ✔ Next, look at the sideways action until the January 14 break in SPX, which corresponded to the breakout in SDS.

- ✔ In other words, the key to this trade was to watch what happened in the S&P 500 and to be ready to pull the trigger on SDS.

To be sure, there is more to this trade than just watching the two instruments and the 200-day moving average. Yet, the key concept is that if you match an ETF to an index and you're careful as well as decisive, you can make a nice profit over a relatively short period of time.

Other things to note:

- ✔ It helps to be patient and to keep an eye on the overall trend of the markets. In this case, it was clearly down. It took this trade 11 days to materialize. I recommended the entry point of 60.05 on January 4, and waited until January 15 for the right circumstances to develop before the trade was actually triggered.

- ✔ Next, it always pays to watch how the market responds to news. Steve Jobs (Apple's CEO) didn't really say anything too horrible during his keynote address at MacWorld; yet, the market sold off during his speech. When good news leads to selling, the market is weak and you should be looking to either get out or sell short.

- ✔ Finally, you have to be disciplined when you sell as well as when you buy. When the market started to rally on January 23, it was time to sell, and we did.

Part II
Analyzing the Markets

The 5th Wave   By Rich Tennant

"My portfolio is gonna take a hit for this."

In this part . . .

Part II of this book is about cutting through jargon and getting comfortable with trading concepts. This section gives you the tools you need to wade through trader talk and use economic reports effectively to make money. I also tell you about the world of technical analysis, showing you the basics of reading price charts and using key technical indicators. You get effective tips on trading techniques, how to spot key market turning points by using market sentiment, and knowing when to trade against the grain.

Chapter 6

Understanding the Fundamentals of the Economy

To the beginner, the financial markets and reality seem to often be disconnected. That lack of connection, most often associated with stock trading, is not as often visible in the futures markets. This is especially so in the case of commodities, such as grains and the energy complex, because price changes in the markets often move through the system fairly rapidly and can be seen at the grocery store.

When I started trading, I was overwhelmed by the amount of data that was available, and I had a hard time correlating how that data was related to the movement of prices. To be honest, I thought that the whole thing was random.

My first reaction was to ignore the data and concentrate on the charts. And although chart-watching worked well for a while, it wasn't good enough to get me in and out of trades fast enough or to prevent getting taken out of positions only to see them turn around and go in the direction that I expected them to go in the first place. I knew I needed something else, so I began watching how the market moved in response to economic data.

To be sure, this is not the only approach to trading, as there are purists on both sides of the aisle: those who propose charting as the best method, and those who swear by the fundamentals. But rather than confuse you with a bunch of jargon and useless justifications on either side, I can tell you that you'll decide what works best for you, and that for me, the best method is to use charts as well as to keep my hands on the pulse of the economy.

It's also fair to say that my problem in my early trading career was one of a lack of experience. This could have been remedied by a much finer use of different charting methods, as well as a better use of charts with different time frames. See Chapter 7 for more on technical analysis.

Just remember that the more experience you get, the more insight you'll gain into what works best for you. Think of this book as a great place to get started.

Achieving a balance among what I want to know about the economy, what I need to know, and what I can use took time. So, after considerable trial and error, I've reached a comfortable middle ground: I am both an avid *chartist,* or someone who studies price charts and uses technical analysis of the financial markets to make trades, and also an avid follower of trends in the economy, although not in as much depth as you'd expect from a Nobel Prize–winning economist.

For me, the bottom line is this: Like many other successful traders, I understand how the markets and the monthly economic indicators can morph into a nice, reliable trading method. And so this chapter focuses on the effects of important economic indicators on the bond markets, stock indexes, and currency markets.

When I write, my goal is to make the examples not only as current as possible, but also universal, so that you can use them for an extended period of time. Most markets behave similarly, but certainly not identically, over time, so you have to be flexible in your interpretation of real-time trading. When I provide examples, my goal is to give you as classic a set of parameters as possible.

I purposely chose examples from April 2005 of how economic reports can affect the market for two major reasons. First, I wanted to show you that the concepts that I describe in the chapter are relevant to recent history, where the big event is the global economy during a controversial period in U.S. history — the post-September 11, 2001, era. And second, the period of time chosen had just about anything that a futures trader could ask for in the way of data that can move the markets, especially a significant amount of activity in the oil market, a booming housing market, and a Federal Reserve that was just hitting its stride in a major cycle of interest-rate hikes.

If you fast forward to 2007 or beyond, you will likely see different things happen, depending on the overall economy and how the market perceives the situation at the time. Yet, in the current world, the primary set of rules and circumstances that govern trading are no longer exclusive to the U.S. economy and its effect on the world. As a trader you also have to be keenly aware of the effect of China and other emerging markets on the macro-market, that linked beast that was unleashed in the stock market crash of 1987.

Understanding the U.S. Economy: A Balancing Act

Market experts and those well versed in economic theory, along with politicians and pundits, like to muddle things up when it comes to interpreting data and formulating working summaries of economic activity. That's how they keep their jobs — by confusing the public when it comes to what's really happening with the economy.

But understanding how the economy works and making it fit your trading approach doesn't have to be that complicated. Simply stated, the U. S. economy, the largest in the world, is dependent upon a series of delicately intertwined relationships, so keep these factors in mind:

- Consumers drive the U.S. economy.

- Consumers need jobs to be able to buy things and keep the economy going.

- The ebb and flow between the degree of joblessness and full employment, how easy or difficult it is to get credit, and how much the supply of goods and services is in demand drive economic activity up or down.

As a rule, steady job growth, easy-enough credit, and a balance between supply and demand are what the Board of Governors of the Federal Reserve (the Fed) like to see in the economy. When one or more of these factors is out of kilter (teeters off balance), the Fed has to act by raising or lowering interest rates to

- Tighten or loosen the consumer's ability to obtain credit

- Rein in a too-high level of joblessness

- Increase or decrease the supply side to bring it in line with demand, or vice versa

Several government agencies and private companies monitor the economy and produce monthly or quarterly reports. These reports, in turn, are released on a regularly scheduled basis throughout the year. They provide futures traders with a major portion of the road map they need to decide which way the general direction of prices in their respective markets are headed.

Trading, in turn, is highly influenced by the government and private-agency reports and how the markets respond. Businesses are just the pawns of the Fed and the markets, and their reaction to changes in trend usually takes some time to be noticed.

The overall focus of the markets is on only one thing: What the Federal Reserve is going to do to interest rates in response to the report(s) of the day (see Chapter 1). Based on how traders (buyers and sellers) perceive their markets before the Fed makes its move and their reactions after the Fed's response to economic conditions is announced, prices move in one direction or the other.

As a futures trader, you need to understand how each of these important reports can make your particular markets move and how to prepare yourself for the possibilities of making money based on the relationship between all the individual components of the market and economic equation. Given these basic truths about the U.S. economy, I discuss the most important sets of data released by key reporting agencies and how to use the information to make trades.

Getting a General Handle on the Reports

Economic reports are important tools in all markets, but they're a way of life for futures traders.

Each individual market has its own set of reports to which traders pay special attention. But some key reports are among the prime catalysts for fluctuations in the prices not only of all markets, but especially in the bond, stock, and currency markets, which form the centerpiece of the trading universe and are linked to one another. Traders wait patiently for their release and act with lightning speed as the data hit the wires.

Some reports are more important during certain market cycles than they are in others, and you have no way of predicting which of them will be the report of the month, the quarter, or the year. Nevertheless, Gross Domestic Product, the consumer and producer price indexes, the monthly employment reports, and the Fed's Beige Book, which summarizes the economic activity as surveyed by the Fed's regional banks, are usually important and highly scrutinized.

The Institute for Supply Management (ISM) report (formerly the national purchasing manager's report) also is important, and so is the Chicago purchasing manager's report, which usually is released one or two days prior to the ISM report. Many traders believe that the Chicago report is a good prelude to the national report, and the day of its release can often lead to big market moves, both up and down.

Consumer confidence numbers from the University of Michigan and the Conference Board usually are market movers, with bond, stock, and currency traders paying special attention to them. These reports are especially important when the market is particularly keen on what the Federal Reserve is expected to change the trend of interest rates as the Fed looks at consumer spending, which is related to consumer confidence as a major influence on the economy.

Sometimes weekly employment claims data can move the market if they come in far above or below expectations. Retail sales numbers, especially from major retailers, such as Wal-Mart, can move the markets, and so can the budget deficit or surplus numbers. Consumer credit data can sometimes move the market as well.

Cable news outlets, major financial Web sites, and business radio networks — CNBC and Bloomberg are two that I follow — broadcast every major report as it is released, and the wire services send out alerts regarding the reports to all major financial publishers not already covering the releases. The government agencies and companies that are responsible for the reports also post them on their respective Web sites immediately at the announced time.

Exploring how economic reports are used

From a public policy standpoint, economic reports find their way into political speeches in the House of Representatives and on the Senate floor. The president and his advisors, other politicians, bureaucrats, and spin doctors quote data from these reports widely and often, using them to suit their current purposes.

From a trader's point of view, you can best use them as

- ✔ **Sources of new information:** No one should ever have access to the data in economic reports prior to their release — other than the press, which receives it expressly under embargoed conditions with instructions not to release the data prior to the proper time, and key members of the U.S. government, such as the Fed and the president. Anyone else who has the data before the release can be prosecuted if they leak it to anyone else.

- ✔ **Risk management tools:** You can place your money at risk if you ignore any of the reports. Each has the potential for providing important information that can create key turning points in the market.

- ✔ **Harbingers of more important information:** Individual headlines about economic reports are only part of the important data. The markets explore more data beyond what's contained in the initial release. Sometimes data hidden deep within a report become more important than the initial knee-jerk reaction characterized within the headlines and cause the market to reverse its course. In other words, sometimes it's best to wait a few minutes or even longer before making trading decisions based on trading reports.

✔ **Trend-setters:** Current reports may not always be what matters. The trend of the data from reports during the last few months, quarters, or years, in addition to expectations for the future, also can be powerful information that moves the markets up or down. When looking through these reports, keep in mind what the prior reports have said, and pay attention to the revisions by the releasing agency that are included in the current report.

✔ **Planning tools:** Trading solely on economic reports can be very risky and requires experience and thorough planning on your part. Make the reports part of your strategy, not the center of your strategy. How the market responds to the reports is what really matters.

Gaming the calendar

As a trader, your world is highly dependent on the *economic calendar,* the listing of when reports will be released for the current month.

Each month a steady flow of economic data is generated and released by the U.S. government and the private sector. These reports are

✔ A major influence on how the futures and the financial markets move in general

✔ A source of the *cyclicality,* or repetitive nature, of market movements

You can get access to the calendar in many places. Most futures brokers post the calendar on their Web sites and can mail you a copy along with key information on their margin and commission rates — pretty convenient, eh? Customer service in the futures market actually is quite awesome if you can handle the greasy guys that you sometimes have to talk to.

The *Wall Street Journal,* Marketwatch.com, and other major news outlets also publish the calendar, either fully posted for the month or for that particular day or week.

The reports follow a familiar pattern, usually following each other in similar sequence from one month to the next.

Exploring Specific Economic Reports

Some reports are more important than others, but at some point, they all have the potential to influence the market. The reports that consistently carry the most weight and result in the biggest shifts in the markets tend to be the employment report, the Producer Price Index (PPI), the Consumer Price Index (CPI), and two reports on consumer confidence. Other economic data that have an important bearing on the markets include the Purchasing Manager's report from the Institute for Supply Management (ISM), Beige Book reports produced eight times a year by the Federal Reserve, housing starts compiled by the U.S. Department of Commerce, and of course, the grand-daddy of all, the Index of Leading Economic Indicators, which the Fed also produces.

In addition to these major economic releases, each individual market has its own set of key reports. For example, the cattle markets (Chapter 15) aren't likely to be moved by data in the Purchasing Manager's Report, but may be moved by grain storage prices. I highlight key reports that affect each individual market in the chapters that deal specifically with those markets.

Working the employment report

The U.S. Department of Labor's employment report is the first piece of major economic data released each month. It's released on the first Friday of every month and is formally known as the Employment Situation Report. Bond, stock index, and currency futures are keyed upon the release of the new jobs and the unemployment rate numbers at 8:30 a.m. eastern time. See the Remember icon directly ahead for more.

The release of the employment data usually is followed by frenzied trading that can last from a few minutes to an entire day, depending on what the data shows and what the market was expecting. The report is so important that it can set the trend for overall trading in the entire arena of the financial markets for several weeks after its release.

When consecutive reports show that a dominant trend is in place, the trend of the overall market tends to remain in the same direction for extended periods of time. The reversal of such a dominant trend can often be interpreted as a signal that bonds, stock indexes, and currencies are going to change course.

The employment report is most important when the economy is shifting gears, similar to the way it did after the events of September 11, 2001, and during the 2004 presidential election. During the election, the markets not only bet on the economic consequences of the report, but they also bet on how the number of new jobs would affect the outcome of the election.

Traders use the employment report as one of several important clues to predict the future of interest rates.

For trading purposes, the major components of the employment report are

- ✔ **The number of new jobs created:** This number tends to predict which way the strength of the economy is headed. Large numbers of new jobs usually mean that the economy is growing. When the number of new jobs begins to fall, it's usually a sign that the economy is slowing. More important, weakness in the employment report often leads the Federal Reserve to lower interest rates, while rising strength may lead the Fed to stop lowering rates, and even raise them if the report is seen as potentially creating inflation.

- ✔ **The unemployment rate:** The rate of unemployment is more difficult to interpret, but the trend in the rate is more important than the actual monthly number. A workforce that is considered to be fully employed usually is a sign that interest rates are going to rise, so the markets begin to factor that into the equation.

Other subsections of the employment report have their moments in the sun. For example, the *household survey,* which uses interviews from people that work at home, was heavily scrutinized during the 2004 election season. The *numbers of self-employed people* became more important as the election neared, because the market began to price in an economic recovery based on adding together the data from both the traditional establishment survey, which measures the people who work for companies, with the household survey.

Be ready to make trades based on the reaction of the markets to the report and not necessarily what the report says.

Probing the Producer Price Index (PPI)

The PPI is an important report, but it doesn't usually cause market moves as big as those effected by the CPI and the employment report.

The PPI measures prices at the producer level. In other words, it's a measurement of the cost of raw materials to companies that produce goods. The market is interested in two things contained in this report:

- ✔ **How fast these prices are rising:** If a rise in PPI is significantly large in comparison to previous months, the market checks to see where it's coming from.

    For example, the May 2005 PPI report pegged prices at the producer level as rising 0.6 percent in April, following a 0.7 percent increase in March and a 0.4 percent hike in February. At first glance, the market viewed the April increase (compared to the previous two months) as a negative number. However, market makers discovered a note deeper in the report, indicating that if you didn't measure food and energy — in this case (especially) oil prices — producer prices at the so-called core level rose only 0.3 percent.

The market looked at the core level, and bonds rallied. You and I know that food and energy are important expenses, and that if they are more expensive, we pay more. But futures traders live in a different world when they're in the trading pits and in front of their trading screens, meaning that they trade on their perceptions of the data and not what you and I find intuitive.

✔ **Whether producers are passing along any price hikes to their consumers:** If prices at the core level are tame, as they seemed to be in the April 2005 report, traders will conduct business based on the information they have in hand, at least until the CPI is released — usually one or two days after the PPI is released. In this case, based only on the PPI, inflation at the core producer level was tame, so traders wagered that producers were not passing any added costs on to the consumer.

Browsing in the Consumer Price Index (CPI)

The CPI is the main inflation report for the futures and financial markets. Unexpected rises in this indicator usually lead to falling bond prices, rising interest rates, and increased market volatility.

Consumer prices are important because consumer buying drives the U.S. economy. No consumer demand at the retail level means no demand for products along the other steps in the chain of manufacturers, wholesalers, and retailers.

Here are some key factors that govern consumer prices and the inflation that they measure:

✔ **Prices at the consumer level are not as sensitive to supply and demand as they are to the ability of retailers to pass their own costs on to consumers.** For example, clothing retailers can't always or immediately pass their wholesale costs for fabric components or labor to consumers, because they'll start buying discount clothing if premium apparel is too expensive. Much of this volatility has to do with the fact that a large amount of retail merchandise is made in Asia, where labor is cheap and competition is stiff.

✔ **Supply tends to be more important in many cases than demand.** When enough of something is available, prices tend to stay down. Scarcities, however, don't necessarily mean inflation (but they certainly can accompany it).

✔ **Inflation is not a price phenomenon but rather a monetary phenomenon.** When too much money is chasing too few goods, inflation appears.

> ✔ **Inflationary expectations and consumer prices are related.** This factor is true because inflationary expectations are built into the cost of borrowing money.

> ✔ **By the time prices begin to rise at the consumer level, the supply-and-demand equation, price discovery, and pressure on the system have been ongoing at other levels of the price chain for some time.**

Understanding the relationship between prices and interest rates is key to developing an intuitive feeling for futures trading.

The true return on an investment is the percentage of the investment that you gain after accounting for inflation. If your portfolio gains 20 percent for five years and inflation is running at 10 percent during that period, you actually gained only 10 percent per year.

The release of the CPI usually moves the markets for interest-rate, currency, and stock-index futures. As with the PPI, traders want to know what the core CPI number is — that is, prices at the consumer level without food and energy factored in. The April 2005 CPI was a classic report. The initial line from the Labor Department quoted consumer prices as rising 0.7 percent, a number that, if it stood alone, would have caused a big sell-off in the bond market. However, as the report revealed that the core number was unchanged, bonds and stock futures had a big rally, which spilled over into the stock market that day.

Managing the ISM and purchasing manager's reports

The Institute for Supply Management's (ISM's) Report on Business usually moves the markets, or is a *market mover,* however you want to say it. It measures the health of the manufacturing sector in the United States. This report is based on the input of purchasing managers surveyed across the United States and is compiled by the ISM.

The Report on Business is different from the regional purchasing manager's reports, although some regional reports, such as the Chicago-area report, often serve as good predictors of the national data. You also need to know, however, that the regional reports are not used as a basis for the national report.

The report addresses 11 categories, including the widely watched headline, the PMI index. Here is how to look at the ISM report:

✔ A number above 50 on the PMI means that the economy is growing.

✔ You want to find out whether the main index and the subsectors are above or below 50.

✔ Just as important is whether the pace of growth is slowing or picking up speed. The report, which is available at the ISM Web site at www.ism.ws, clearly states whether each individual sector is growing or not growing, and whether it is doing so because its pace is slowing or picking up speed.

✔ The data for the entire report is included with a summary of the economy's current state and pace near the headline of the report.

The April 2005 report concluded that the economy had been growing for 42 straight months and that the manufacturing sector had been growing for 23 straight months. The report concluded that although prices paid by manufacturers were on the rise and inventories were low, both the economy and the manufacturing sector were still growing, but the growth rate was slowing.

The bond market rallied. The dollar strengthened. And stocks had a moderate gain.

This particular ISM report had something for everybody, especially when you compare it to the economic trends around the world in which Europe had flat-to-lower growth rates and China had a robust but also moderating growth rate. A U.S. economy that is growing is good. But one that is growing too fast can lead to inflation, so the bond markets also liked the report. Steady growth with low production costs is good for company earnings, so the stock markets liked it. Economic growth is likely to keep interest rates steady or slightly higher, so the currency markets — which like to see steady to higher interest rates — liked the report, too.

Considering consumer confidence

The report that measures consumer confidence is a big report that comes from two sources that publish separate reports: the Conference Board, a private research group, and the University of Michigan.

The Conference Board Survey

The Conference Board, Inc., publishes a monthly report based on survey interviews of 5,000 consumers. Key components of the Conference Board Survey are

✔ The monthly index

✔ Current conditions

✔ Consumers' outlook for the next six months

In April 2005, the monthly index fell, and so did the current condition and outlook portions of the survey. The result: Bonds rallied, stocks rallied, and the dollar remained steady. The report became another piece of the economic puzzle at a key time in the U.S. economy. The way the market looked at the data, following eight straight Federal Reserve interest-rate increases, showed that the economy was starting to slow. To a layman, a slowing economy would be bad news, but to a futures trader, the data meant that the Fed was nearing the end of its rate hikes (or that interest rates were leveling off).

The University of Michigan Survey

The University of Michigan conducts its own survey of consumer confidence, and it publishes several preliminary reports and one final report per month. Key components of the University of Michigan Survey are

- The Index of Consumer Confidence
- The Index of Consumer Expectations
- The Index of Current Economic conditions

In April 2005, the University of Michigan reported that "Consumer confidence sank in April, marking the fourth consecutive monthly decline, with the Sentiment Index falling to its lowest level since September 2003." The report cited rising gas prices and a poor job outlook as reasons for the sag in consumer confidence and the increasingly negative data for consumer expectations. The impact on the markets was predictable. Bonds rallied and so eventually did stocks — after an initial dip.

Again, the key to the report was that consumer confidence was falling. When consumers are less confident, the Fed is less likely to continue to raise interest rates.

Perusing the Beige Book

The Beige Book, one of my favorite reports, is a key report from the Federal Reserve that is released eight times per year. In each tome, the Fed produces a summary of current economic activity in each of its districts, based on anecdotal information from Fed bank presidents, key businesses, economists, and market experts, among other sources.

The 12 Federal Reserve District Banks are located in Boston, New York, Philadelphia, Cleveland, Richmond, Atlanta, Chicago, St. Louis, Minneapolis, Kansas City, Dallas, and San Francisco.

The Federal Reserve produces the Summary of Commentary on Current Economic Conditions, otherwise known as the Beige Book. In it, the Fed summarizes anecdotal reports on the economy by district and sector and packages it into a comprehensive summary of the 12 district reports. Each Beige Book is prepared by a designated Federal Reserve Bank on a rotating basis.

The Beige Book is released to the members of the Federal Open Market Committee (FOMC) before each of its meetings on interest rates, so it's an important source of information for the committee members when they're deciding in what direction they'll vote to take interest rates.

On April 20, 2005, the Federal Reserve district in Dallas had its turn to publish the Beige Book and summarized its findings as follows:

> "Eleventh District economic activity expanded moderately in March and early April. The manufacturing sector continued to rebound, while activity in financial and business services continued to expand at the same pace reported in the last Beige Book (the one released March 9, 2005). Retailers said they were disappointed with recent sales growth. Residential construction continued to cool from last year's strong pace, amid signs that commercial real estate markets were slowly improving. The energy industry strengthened further, and contacts said exploration activity was expanding on the belief that energy prices would remain high. Agricultural conditions remained generally positive. While activity was strong in some industries, in many sectors contacts reported slightly less optimism about the strength of activity for the rest of the year, largely because demand has not been picking up as quickly as they had hoped."

 Traders look for any mention of labor shortages and wage pressures in the Beige Book. If any such trends are mentioned, bonds may sell off, as rising wage pressures are taken as a sign of building inflation in the pipeline. In this edition, the book noted that banking and accounting were seeing some price competition caused by a shortage of qualified workers but added that "most industries said there was little or no wage pressure."

 Here's a good habit to get into so you can capitalize on knowledge from one area of the market as you apply it to another: After checking out the initial headlines and market reactions, read through the report on the Internet. You can find links to it on the Fed's Web site, `www.federalreserve.gov`, or you can do a Google or Yahoo! search for "Beige Book."

What I look for when I scan the full text on the Web is what the Beige Book says about individual sectors of the economy. Under manufacturing in April 2005, the Beige Book said that although little pickup was reported in the growth for electronics, slightly rising demand was noted for networking switches and other related products in telecommunications.

If you see something like that, you can start looking at the action of key stocks in that sector. Interestingly, the stock of Cisco Systems, the leader in switches and related products, made a good bottom in the month of April, and on April 21, a day after the Beige Book was released, it began to rally. By May 20, the stock was up over 10 percent.

The Beige Book usually is released in the afternoon, one or two hours before the stock market closes. The overall trend of all markets can reverse late in the day when the data in the report surprise traders.

For example, the Federal Reserve's Beige Book released on October 17, 2007, summarized the U.S. economy as one that was expanding "in all Districts in September and early October." Yet, in the next sentence, the Fed noted "but the pace of growth decelerated since August."

That was enough to end a nice rally in the stock market. The Beige Book was released at 2 p.m. eastern time, and by the close the market was already not acting too well. Over the next couple of days, the market started to drift lower. And on October 19, the 20th anniversary of the Crash of 1987, the Dow Jones Industrial average dropped 366 points, as the market began to worry about the prospects for the economy.

By the same token, as expected, the bond market staged a nice rally.

Homing in on housing starts

Bond and stock traders like housing starts, because housing is a central portion of the U.S. economy, given its dependence on credit and the fact that it uses raw materials and provides employment for a significant number of people in related industries, such as banking, the mortgage sector, construction, manufacturing, and real-estate brokerage.

Big moves often occur in the bond market after the numbers for housing starts are released.

Released every month, housing starts are compiled by the U.S. Commerce Department and reported in three parts:

- ✔ Building permits
- ✔ Housing starts
- ✔ Housing completions

The markets focus on the percentage of rise or fall in the numbers from the previous month for each component.

For example, the April 2005 report showed a 5.3 percent growth in the number of building permits, an 11 percent growth in housing starts (with a 6.3 percent growth in single-family homes), and a 3.4 percent growth rate in housing completions.

By contrast, the housing start numbers in the years 2006 and 2007 were dismal, as the housing boom contracted. These reports were closely correlated to the fall in the housing sector in the United States.

A volatile series of numbers, this data can be greatly affected by weather, so it is also seasonally adjusted and includes a significant amount of revised data within each of the internal components. For example, when winter arrives, snow storms and cold weather tend to halt or slow new and ongoing construction projects, so housing permits and housing starts can start to decline. If you don't know that, you can make trading mistakes by betting that interest rates are going to fall.

The problem comes when the weather clears, the projects get underway, and the numbers swell. Markets look at the seasonally adjusted numbers, which are smoothed out by statistical formulas used by the U.S. Department of Commerce.

Even then, this set of numbers is tricky. The Commerce Department disclaimer notes that it can take up to four months of data to come up with a reliable set of indicators.

Staying Awake for the Index of Leading Economic Indicators

The Conference Board looks at ten key indicators in calculating its Index of Leading Economic Indicators. Included are the

- Index of consumer expectations
- Real money supply
- Interest-rate spread
- Stock prices
- Vendor performance
- Average weekly initial claims for unemployment insurance
- Building permits
- Average weekly manufacturing hours

✓ Manufacturers' new orders for nondefense capital goods

✓ Manufacturers' new orders for consumer goods and materials

In April 2005, the overall index dropped and so did much of the economic data for that month. At the same time, the trend of economic growth remained up, once again confirming the notion that interest rate increases ordered by the Federal Reserve were starting to slow down the economy, but they weren't dragging it into a recession.

The Index of Leading Economic Indicators is another lukewarm indicator that sometimes moves the markets and other times doesn't. It is more likely to move the markets whenever it clearly is divergent from data provided by other indicators. For example, if in April the leading indicators were showing a drastic decline, the markets would start worrying about a recession looming on the horizon. That, in turn, may be a catalyst to knock down stock and commodity prices and the value of the dollar, but on the other hand, it may bring about a huge rally in the bond markets.

Grossing out with Gross Domestic Product (GDP)

The report on Gross Domestic Product (GDP) measures the sum of all the goods and services produced in the United States. Although GDP can yield confusing and mixed results on the trading floor, it sometimes is a big market mover whenever it's far above or below what the markets are expecting it to be. At other times, GDP is not much of a mover. Multiple revisions of previous GDP data accompany the monthly release of the GDP and tend to dampen the effect of the report. Although the GDP is not a report to ignore by any means, it usually isn't as important as the PPI and CPI and the employment report.

GDP has a component called the *deflator,* which is a measure of inflation. The deflator can be the prime mover whenever it is above or below market expectations.

Getting slick with oil supply data

Oil supply data became a central report outside of the oil markets in 2004 and 2005 as the price of crude oil soared to record highs during the war in Iraq. The Energy Information Agency (EIA), a part of the U.S. Department of

Energy, and the American Petroleum Institute (API) release oil supply data for the previous week at 10:30 a.m. eastern time every Wednesday.

Traders want to know the following:

- Crude oil supply
- Gasoline supply
- Distillate supply

A *build* is when the stockpiles of crude oil in storage are increasing. Such increases are considered *bearish* or negative for the market, because large stockpiles generally mean lower prices at the pump. A *drawdown,* on the other hand, is when the supply shrinks. Traders like drawdown situations, because prices tend to rise after the news is released.

Every week, oil experts and commentators guess what the number will be. Although they almost never are right in their predictions, the fact that they're wrong sets the market up for more volatility when the number comes out and gives you a trading opportunity if you're set up to take advantage of it.

Although crude oil supply is self-explanatory as the basis for the oil markets and is important year-round, two other supply factors are affected by these seasonal tendencies:

- Distillate supply figures are more important in winter, because they essentially represent a measure of the supply of heating oil.
- Gasoline supplies are more important as the summer driving season approaches.

Other holidays sometimes can affect oil supply numbers. The market tends to factor their effect into the numbers, though, so for other holidays to have a big effect on trading, the surprises have to be very big.

The market has changed, however, because of problems with refinery capacity in the United States and the aftereffects of two major hurricanes (Katrina and Rita) in 2005 in the Gulf of Mexico region. Volatility in the markets and supply numbers will evolve over the next few years. See Chapter 13 for a full rundown of the energy markets.

CNBC covers the oil supply release number live. Sometimes, the reporter gets the gist of the data wrong, and the market can be increasingly volatile because of it. Although this scenario is not frequent, I've seen it happen, and I have seen it have an effect on trading.

Enduring sales, income, production, and balance of trade reports

The hodgepodge of data that trickle out of the woodwork throughout the month about retail sales, personal income, industrial production, and the balance of trade sometimes causes a bit of commotion in the futures markets, but these individual reports mostly cause only a few daily ripples, unless, of course, the effect of the data is dramatic.

As a futures trader, you need to know that these reports are coming, but a good portion of the time, they come and go without fanfare or trouble, unless the economy is at a critical turning point and one of these reports happens to be the missing piece to the puzzle.

Of these four reports, the one most likely to get the most press, is the balance of trade report. Because the Chinese economy is getting so much attention these days, the currency and bond markets may move dramatically whenever the balance of trade report shows a much greater than expected trade deficit or trade surplus. If several consecutive reports show that the United States is reversing its trend toward more imports than exports, you may see a major set of moves in the futures markets.

The prices for imports also are an important factor in the trade data that can be a sign of inflation and, again, can affect how the Federal Reserve moves on interest rates.

Trading the Big Reports

The greatest effect that each of the reports highlighted in this chapter can have is on the futures markets associated with bonds, stock indexes, and currencies. Thus, the best strategies for trading based on these reports are found in those markets.

Any report can make the market move up or down if the market finds something in the report to justify the move, but some general tendencies to keep in mind include the following:

- ✔ Reports that show a strengthening economy are less friendly to the bond market and tend to be friendlier toward stock-index futures and the dollar. Although this isn't a hard and fast rule, as always, trade what's happening, not what you think ought to happen (see Chapters 10, 11, and 12).

- ✔ Signs of slowing growth or a weak economy tend to be *bullish,* or positive, for bonds and less friendly toward stock indexes and the dollar.

✔ Short-term interest-rate futures, such as in Eurodollars (see Chapter 10), may move in the opposite direction of the 10-year Treasury note (T-note) or long-term (30-year) bond futures.

✔ Gold, silver, and oil markets may respond aggressively to these reports. (To find out more about the markets in these commodities, see Chapters 13 and 14.)

✔ The Federal Reserve may make comments that accelerate or reverse the reactions and responses to economic reports.

Keeping It Simple

Futures traders can set up complicated strategies in advance of the release of a big economic report, but you can make trading these reports simple by keeping your eye on the trend before the report is released.

Say the trend is up in the stock market, and you are long a position in the S&P 500 stock index futures. You also know that the market is waiting for the employment report, and that it anticipates the number of new jobs to decrease.

A small number of new jobs usually means that the market is expecting the economy to weaken, which could mean that the stock market will rise or fall, depending on which way the market handicaps the response of the Federal Reserve.

If you are cautious and have a nice profit on your S&P 500 futures, you could offset it, take your profits, and wait to see what happens with the report.

Another approach is to hedge your bets in the stock market by using the bond market. Economic weakness usually leads to higher bond prices. That means that you can establish a long position in the U.S. Ten Year note futures one or two days before the employment report in hopes that if the report comes in weak, you can profit from a rally in the bond market, and thus protect any gains that you have in your stock position.

The market will respond when the report is released. If the number is weak, watch what happens in bonds and stocks in response. You can watch it on your computer, or you can watch the response on CNBC.

If things are not going your way, you can offset either one position or both of them depending on what's happening at the time. If both the stock and bond market like the report, you can hold both positions and offset them later, either based on your price targets or if the trend turns against them.

Chapter 7

Getting Technical Without Getting Tense

I'm a visual person, and my first experience with trading came from reading a chart in 1988, right before Memorial Day weekend, when I made my first stock trade: 100 shares of Quanex Corp. (NYSE:NX), a steel pipe and tube maker. I bought the stock for around $12 and sold it at essentially the same price a few days later, at which point it hadn't done much of anything. I was most unhappy with the commissions I had to pay and the fact that the stock didn't do what I had expected it to do — rise substantially in price.

I bought the stock based on a chart that exhibited a cup-and-handle pattern, a chart pattern made famous by *Investor's Business Daily* founder William O'Neil. This pattern isn't very useful in futures trading, but it can be helpful in trading stocks. It shows up when a stock forms a rounded base and then trades sideways in a narrow range, giving the appearance or impression of a cup and a handle.

In my first trade, I identified such a pattern from an *Investor's Business Daily* chart. I was lucky. My first stock trade cost me only a hundred bucks, and I had enough money left to keep on trading. But that failure within my small account — breaking even and paying a $50 commission on the purchase and the sale — is what prompted me to find out more about charts and how they work together with the fundamentals of the markets.

What I didn't realize at the time was that Quanex had only recently come out of some major difficulties and was restructuring. A longer-term view of the chart would've revealed that trading was volatile and that the stock was, in fact, stuck in a trading range and not in a significant up, down, or breakout trend.

I also discovered that I didn't know anything about the state of the steel industry at the time, the company's management, or its plans for the future. All are important when trading futures, options, and their underlying equities.

My mistake was that the cup-and-handle pattern, although genuine, was only a snapshot of the trading action over a few months. Had I known better — as I do now — I would've looked at a multiyear chart, and put the cup-and-handle pattern from the newspaper in its proper context.

The major lesson that I brought home during that relatively traumatic experience was that a chart pattern is only a beginning — a tool that leads you toward exploring more information about why the pattern suggests that you need to buy, sell, or sell short the underlying instrument.

In this chapter, I introduce you to the basics of recognizing interesting chart patterns that can lead you either to more study of the situation or to plug in what you already know about a market that is giving you a visual signal. See Chapters 8 and 12 for speculating strategies and using technical analysis for trading stock index futures.

Picturing a Thousand Ticks: The Purpose of Technical Analysis

I like to think of stock or futures charts as summaries of the collective opinions of all the participants in a market. In essence, a *chart* is a tick-by-tick history of those opinions as they evolve over time, factoring in everything that market participants know, think they know, and expect to happen with regard to the asset for which the chart was compiled.

And although a picture is worth a thousand words to most people, to a trader, a chart is worth a chance to make some money. *Technical analysis,* or the use of price charts, moving averages, trend lines, volume relationships, and indicators for identifying trends and trading opportunities in underlying financial instruments, is *the key* to success in the futures market. The more you know about reading charts, the better your trading results are likely to be.

After you become better acquainted with the basic drivers and influences of a particular market and how that information — key market moving reports, the major players involved, and the general fundamentals of supply and demand — fits into the big picture of the marketplace in general, the next logical step is to become acquainted with how the fundamentals are combined with the data that is compiled in price charts.

By becoming proficient at reading the charts of various security prices, you gain quick access to significant amounts of information, such as prices, general trends, and info about whether a market is sold out and ready to rally or *overbought,* meaning few buyers are left and prices can fall. By combining your knowledge of the markets and trading experiences with excellent charting skills, you vastly improve your market reaction time and your ability to make informed trades.

Technical analysis takes into account so much data and methodology that I can't possibly cover everything about it in only one chapter. So here are a few recommendations of excellent books in which you can find useful information as you progress with chart reading and trading. This list by no means is comprehensive, but these references serve as great supplements to this chapter. The books are not named in any particular order, because each has something good to offer and can serve you in different ways at different times:

- *Technical Analysis For Dummies* by Barbara Rockefeller (Wiley)
- *Trading For Dummies* by Michael Griffis and Lita Epstein (Wiley)
- *Technical Analysis of the Financial Markets* by John J. Murphy (New York Institute of Finance)
- *Candlestick Charting Explained: Timeless Techniques for Trading Stocks and Futures* by Gregory L. Morris (McGraw-Hill)

By reading the information in this book and the books in the preceding list, you can build a foundation for technical analysis. However, as you gain trading experience, technical analysis will become more of an individualized endeavor for you because you'll find that you gravitate to some areas more than others.

My own experience is that the simpler the analysis, the better, so my analytical style relies on moving averages, trend lines, and a few oscillators and indicators. Your style will develop as you gain experience.

These guidelines can help organize your expectations about reading charts:

- Charting, in my opinion, isn't meant to replace fundamental analysis. In my trading, charts are meant to complement and enhance it, enabling you to make better decisions. That's not to say that there aren't those very talented people out there who make millions as pure chartists, because there are. Just keep an open mind on this.
- Understanding the fundamentals of supply and demand in your particular segment of the futures market is necessary for you to be able to trade futures based on charted technical signals. Knowing both the

fundamentals of what you are trading and combining the knowledge with technical analysis makes investing your hard-earned money easier.

✔ You have to be flexible, so becoming familiar with more than one set of indicators and being able to combine them gives you more than one perspective from which to view the markets. I use different combinations of indicators for different types of trading to find more ways of looking at the markets. Narrow-minded traders don't go too far.

✔ Mastering the basics of following moving averages, identifying trend reversals, and drawing trend lines is important so you can add new layers of analysis, such as moving average crossover systems, and other more sophisticated techniques as you gain more experience.

✔ Continuing to expand your knowledge of technical analysis is important. You can do so by reading magazines like *Technical Analysis of Stocks & Commodities* (www.traders.com), *Futures* (www.futuresmag.com), and *Active Trader* (www.activetradermag.com) magazines, which are excellent sources of interesting articles. *Investor's Business Daily* (www.investors.com), is a chart reader's paradise for stock and futures traders.

✔ Exercising care so that you avoid clutter in your charts, even as you become more sophisticated in your approach to trading futures, is important. The simpler your charts, the better the picture you get and the better your decisions will be.

First Things First: Getting a Good Charting Service

You need a reliable *charting service* — a provider of quotes, charts, and market data — either one that your broker provides or an independent one such as Barchart (www.barchart.com), and you need a reliable set of software tools to be able to trade well. Many such services, programs, and combinations of the two are available.

Some online trading houses offer a range of services on their respective Web sites. Software and charting services are available as on websites, downloads, or as individually boxed packages that are Web-ready. They range from the bare minimum with basic charts and indicators to very complex systems used by professionals. A good way to start is with a bare-bones charting system or the next step up. You can move up to progressively more elaborate systems as your trading skills become more sophisticated.

Some brokers charge you extra for using their in-house, more sophisticated charting and software services, but others let you use them as part of a package deal, especially if you're an active trader placing trades through the sponsoring trading house. Extra charges vary, but a difference of $30 to $40 per month or more between the low- and the high-end packages is not uncommon. You need to check with each individual service before deciding on a charting service.

No matter what, you're obligated to pay exchange fees to get real-time quotes from the exchanges, and those fees can add up to hundreds of dollars per month, depending on the number of exchanges from which you get quotes.

Here are the characteristics that a charting service/online brokerage must have:

- **Reliability:** The service must be up and running when you want to place trades, and the data it provides must be accurate. If your service tells you to come back later because it's unavailable anytime when the markets are open — in other words, during peak trading times — you need to quit the unreliable service, demand a refund, and find another more-reliable service. A good way to find out whether a service is reliable is to locate users' groups, either online, where you can read their bulletin boards, or in your town, where you can attend a meeting or two and listen to any complaints. You also need to sign up for a trial period so you can see how you like the system before you pay for it. Most services offer free trials.

- **Accessibility:** The service needs to be available to you virtually anywhere, either online or by the use of a convenient online interface. You need to be able to check your quotes, open positions, and make your decisions from home, work, or elsewhere — even on your laptop, PDA, or smart phone at the airport, or at your favorite hangout that has Wi-Fi.

- **Support:** Make sure the service offers both a toll-free telephone number to call for support and online support. The toll-free number may or may not be better than the online support, so you need to try both of them out to see which works better. Call the toll-free number, log in to the support chat room, or e-mail customer support before you purchase the software, just to test the availability and level of support that you'll be getting. If your software or charting service malfunctions and you have to wait 30 minutes before anyone responds to your query, think about what effect that kind of delay may have on your investments, especially if you're trying to place a trade when a big economic release is moving the markets.

- **Charting tools:** The charts provided by your charting service must be easy to read and user-friendly. You shouldn't have to punch five or ten keys or toggle your mouse for ten minutes to make your chart look right. Sure, you can expect a learning curve with most programs, but if you can't make the software do what you want (and what the provider says it will do) after a few days, it isn't the right setup for you, and you need to consider getting a new program.

✔ **Real-time quotes:** Trading futures without real-time quotes is a sure path down the road to ruin. *Real-time quotes* are up-to-the-minute market prices, as they happen. They provide you with up-to-the-minute pricing for your particular security, futures contract, or option, thus enabling you to make timely decisions. Without them, the prices you get from your charting service may be subject to a standard 20-minute delay, during which markets can move to their limits (or even reverse course), leaving you faced with a margin call or a big loss.

✔ **Live charts:** If you're going to trade, you need access to *live charts* that actually change with every *tick* (up or down movement) of the market. You can set them up to update the bars or candlesticks in your charts over a broad range of different time frames. The key: You want your chart to be updated to reflect the direction in which the market is trading.

✔ **Time-frame analysis:** Make sure your charting service enables you to produce intraday charts. You want to be able to look at different time frames simultaneously. For example, if the long-term trend in the S&P futures is headed up on a six-month chart, but you see that a top is building on your intraday chart, your strategy for your S&P 500 Index fund may not be affected. But if you have two S&P 500 long contracts open and a few call options, you may need to adjust the strategies on your futures positions. For example, you may want to consider moving a sell stop closer to the current price if you're concerned about remaining in the position. Or you may want to sell the position outright.

✔ **Multiple indicators:** Make sure the service to which you subscribe lets you plot price charts and multiple indicators at the same time. A standard page may include prices, a combination of moving averages, stochastics, and MACD and RSI oscillators. I go into more details on these indicators and how to use them in Chapter 8. Chapter 13 features a great example of how to use RSI in the energy markets. But for now, you need to concentrate on the charting information you need for technical analysis.

Also important is the amount of data that you can get on one chart and having the ability to save it as a template. Set up your charts the way you like them when the market is closed, and then save them as your favorites. Most services will let you set up different sets of charts. That way when you start trading you won't waste time setting up your indicators when you should be pulling the trigger on your trade.

Some charting services offer access on hand-held electronic devices. This feature may be attractive to you if you're on the road and have open positions. Don't trade and drive, though.

You can get a pretty good preview of a good, basic, real-time charting program online at currency and futures brokerages optionsXpress.com or FX charts.com (`http://www.fx-charts.com/pgs/toolbox_livecharts.php`)(www.Xpresstrade.com). These pages gives you free access to both basic tutorials, as well as real-time quotes in the currency markets — while providing a good overview of several levels of charting that are available. You can scroll through many free currency real-time charts on these sites, which also offers trading software. In general, these are good places to get your feet wet and to make use of some of the concepts in this chapter as they apply to the currency markets. The basic charting principles that you discover in one market are easily applicable to other markets.

Stockcharts.com (www.stockcharts.com) has an excellent free Java charting system on which you can practice drawing trend lines and analyzing charts. These are not real-time charts, but they are a good place to practice your craft after the market closes.

Deciding What Types of Charts to Use

Security analysis relies on these four basic types of charts: line charts, bar charts, candlestick charts, and point-and-figure charts. Line charts almost never are used in trading. Bar and candlestick charts commonly are used in stocks and futures trading, and point-and-figure charts have a smaller but loyal following as trading tools.

I don't use point-and-figure charts, so I won't include them in this discussion. However, for a nice short overview of point-and-figure charting, check out *Technical Analysis For Dummies* (Wiley). If you like what you read there and want even more information about it, I also recommend John Murphy's *Technical Analysis of the Financial Markets* (New York Institute of Finance).

In general, I concentrate on bar and candlestick charting, but the bulk of my explanation in this chapter is based on candlestick charts, because they're the most commonly used charts in futures trading. They offer the best information for shorter holding periods (like the ones common to day trading) or for longer trading periods where you have open positions that you may stay with for a few days.

Confused? Don't be. Both types of price charts are useful, and you'll develop your own style and preferences for the ones that work best for you. At this point, however, you merely need to be aware of what these charts are, how to recognize them, and how you can start thinking about putting them to use. Both sets of charts offer the same basic kind of information — price, volume, and general direction of the market.

Bar charts are made up of thin single bars that define the movement of a price over a period of time. You can use one for analyzing a longer period of the market. I like them for this purpose because they're a bit less cluttered.

Candlestick charts, on the other hand, are made up of thin- and thick-bodied candles, such as in Figure 7-1, which shows how they basically look like candles with wicks at both ends. Figure 7-3 shows how you can incorporate candlestick patterns with key indicators, such as moving averages and oscillators.

Stacking up bar charts

Bar charts used to be the most commonly displayed charts on most trading software programs. The bars displayed low and high prices for the specific time frame of the chart, with the body of the bar representing the range of trading action during that time frame. The time frame of a bar chart can be set according to whatever time period the user wants to use, regardless of whether it's for part of a day, a day, a week, a month, a year, or longer.

No hard-and-fast rules govern whether one type of chart is better than another. For example, bar charts and candlestick charts can be used for trading during any time span that you like, whether day trading or trading intermediate-term positions in which you stay with the underlying asset as long as the trend remains in your favor.

I prefer to use candlestick charts for intraday charts, because the color tells me what I want to know rapidly. For longer-term charts from which I just want to get the big picture about whether I want to buy or sell the underlying asset, I tend to use bar charts. The best thing to do is work with both kinds of charts when you are a beginner and develop your own tendencies.

Bar charts are useful when

- ✔ You're looking for a quick snapshot of a particular instrument, sector, or market, or when you're doing basic trend analysis.
- ✔ You're trading individual stocks or mutual funds, and you're looking at a long-term chart, such as a five-year time span.

Weighing the benefits of candlestick charts

Candlestick charts provide the same sort of information as bar charts, but they're better for making trading decisions because they take the guesswork out of the overall trend in the underlying contract by the use of color-coding. They're especially suited for the short-term trading that's common in the futures markets.

Candlestick charts can be broken down into several parts, including the following:

- ✔ **Real body:** The *real body* is the box between the opening and closing prices depicted by the candlestick. The body can be white or black. White bodies are bullish, meaning that the price depicted is rising. Black bodies are bearish, meaning that the price depicted by the candlestick is falling.

✔ **Lower and upper shadows:** The thin lines that extend above and below the real body (the candlewicks) are the *lower and upper shadows*. The shadows, or wicks, extend to the high and low prices for the time frame.

Figure 7-1 summarizes the basic anatomy of candlestick charting.

Figure 7-1:
The anatomy of a candlestick.

Although bearish candlesticks traditionally are solid black, many software programs and charting services have replaced the black color with red to correspond with the standard method of displaying falling prices on quote systems. They've also replaced normally white bullish candlesticks with green ones, again to conform to the quote systems standards. In fact, many software programs will even let you decide which color you want to use for bullish or bearish charts. In this chapter, though, green and white refer to bullish conditions, and red and black mean bearish.

When a candlestick has no body but only vertical and horizontal shadows, meaning that it is a line with no box, it forms what is known as a doji pattern. *Doji patterns* are a sign of indecision in the market. The three types of doji patterns (see Figure 7-2) are

✔ **Plain:** A *plain doji* looks like a cross and may just be a sign of a short-term pause. Other kinds of doji bars can be important signs of a trend reversal.

✔ **Dragonfly:** A *dragonfly doji* has a long lower shadow, or single-line body — the dragonfly appears to be flying upward. If you see this kind of pattern, it means that sellers were not successful in closing the contract at the lows of the day. When that happens as the price is bottoming out, it can mean that buyers are gaining an upper hand. If a dragonfly doji occurs after a big rally, it can mean that buyers are not able to take prices any higher.

✔ **Gravestone:** A *gravestone doji* looks like an upside-down dragonfly, with a longer upper shadow — the dragonfly appears to be flying downward. Gravestone dojis occur when buyers push prices higher but can't get prices to close at those higher levels. If a gravestone doji appears after a rally, it can signal that a reversal is coming.

On the other hand, a gravestone doji in a downtrend may mean that a bottom is forming.

Figure 7-2:
The three basic doji bars.

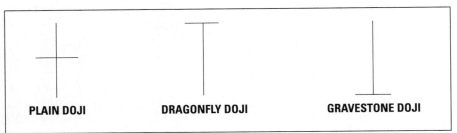

PLAIN DOJI   **DRAGONFLY DOJI**   **GRAVESTONE DOJI**

Barbara Rockefeller points out in *Technical Analysis For Dummies* (Wiley) that a doji is best interpreted in the context of the pattern that you see in the preceding candlesticks.

Candlesticks can be superior to bar charts for the following reasons:

✔ **Trends are easier to spot.** For example, a sea of rising green (or white), meaning a large grouping of bullish candles on a candlestick chart, is hard to mistake for anything other than a strong uptrend. Because candlesticks tend to have a body in most cases, the overall trend of the market often is easier to identify.

✔ **Trend changes are easier to spot.** Candlestick patterns can be dramatic and can help you identify trend changes before you can recognize them on bar charts. Some candlestick patterns are reliable at predicting future prices.

✔ **Shifts in momentum are easy to spot.** Conditions in which a security is oversold and overbought, along with trends and other kinds of indicators, may be easier to spot on candlestick charts than on bar charts because of the presence of doji candles and color. For example, an engulfing pattern (see Figures 7-3 and 7-6 and the section "Engulfing the trend," later in this chapter), which can be either negative or positive, is easier to spot in a candlestick chart.

Candlestick bars that are changing in size, especially at the end of a market run in a single direction, often signal that traders have reached a transition point in how they're looking at the market, and that an important change in the trend may have been reached. For example, a long green (white) bar after a big rally often means that buyers are out of gas, and that's when you need to start paying attention to other signs of weakness. The same can be said after a long red (black) bar that follows a major bout of selling — you can start looking for signs of strength.

Getting the Hang of Basic Charting Patterns

Charting patterns can get out of control if you're not careful, so I like to keep it simple. That means that if you understand the basic tenets of charting and the most important, easy-to-spot patterns, you can make solid trading decisions as long as you remember that charting is most useful to you when you couple it with fundamental and situational analysis of the markets.

So before you start looking for patterns, follow this three-step rule:

1. **Get the feel for whether the basic trend is up or down.**

   Just look at the chart. If the price starts low and rises, it's an uptrend. If the opposite is true, it's a downtrend.

2. **Gauge how long that trend has been in place.**

   Using longer-term charts sometimes can help you spot just how long the trend has been in place.

3. **Consider the potential for a reversal.**

   The longer the trend has been in place, the higher the chance that it can turn the other way.

After you get comfortable with this process, you can advance to looking for the charting patterns that I describe in the sections that follow.

Analyzing textbook base patterns

Bases, whether tops or bottoms, are sideways patterns on price charts; they're pauses in the uptrends or downtrends in security prices. Bases are formed as some traders take profits and other traders establish new positions in the other direction.

In futures markets, someone always buys, and someone always sells. So a *base* is what happens when the number of buyers and sellers is in fairly good balance and prices remain steady.

Bases, in general, are points in the pricing of a security at which the market takes a break before deciding what to do next. A base can come before the market turns up or down, and it can last for a long time, even years. If, after it forms a base, the market decides that more selling is called for, a new downturn, or falling prices, can start on a candlestick chart, despite the fact that the market has based after a decline. When the base forms after a rally, it can either resolve as a top, and the market can fall, or indicate only a pause in a continuing uptrend. You can't, however, predict with full certainty which way the markets will break after they pause (in either direction).

Figure 7-4 (later in this chapter) shows some key technical terms, including price tops and bottoms and basing patterns.

A base and a bottom accomplish the same thing, except that they can occur at different places. A base can be seen after the market climbs, after the market falls, or even during an uptrend or downtrend. A *bottom* usually is seen in retrospect, after the market rallies from the basing pattern. Similarly, a *top* usually is seen in retrospect, after the market declines from a basing pattern.

Although you can't predict tops and bottoms with 100 percent certainty, some reliable indicators can help you make better guesses. These indicators are

✔ Specific patterns seen in price oscillators, such as when the RSI and MACD indicators move in different directions than the price of the security (see Chapters 8 and 13).

✔ Major turns in market sentiment (see Chapter 9).

✔ Key price movements above and below important price areas, such as resistance or support points (see Figure 7-4 and the section "Using lines of resistance and support to place buy and sell orders," later in the chapter).

Downtrends

Here are some important factors to remember about a base at the bottom of a downtrend:

✔ A good trading bottom usually comes when everyone thinks that the market will never rise again.

✔ Downtrends can die in two ways: in a major selling frenzy or over a long period of time in which a base forms.

✔ At some point, all markets become oversold, and they bounce. Any such bounce can be the beginning of a new bullish uptrend in the market. After a long time of falling prices, you have to be ready to trade all turns in the market, even if you get taken out as the downtrend reasserts itself.

The most important area of a chart that is making a bottom is known as support. *Support* is a chart point, or series of points, that puts a floor under prices. That's where the buyers come in.

Uptrends

Here are some important factors to remember about a base at the top of an uptrend:

✔ Most participants at the top in the market are bullish, which is why three or four failures often occur before the market breaks toward the downside.

✔ Downturns that follow long-term rallies tend to spiral downward for a long time. That's exactly what happened with the multiyear chart of the dollar index shown in Figure 7-5, later in the chapter.

✔ Tops are more likely to lead to reflex rallies, meaning that long-term downtrends are likely to be more volatile than are uptrends. For short sellers, it's a very rough ride, no matter which market you're trading.

The most important area of a chart that is making a top is known as resistance. *Resistance* is a chart point, or series of points, that puts a ceiling above prices. That's where sellers come in.

Using lines of resistance and support to place buy and sell orders

Drawing lines of resistance and support for a particular market or security (see Figure 7-4) can help you maintain your focus when placing your buy, sell, and short-sell orders. Buy orders usually are placed above resistance lines, and sell orders and sell-short orders are placed below support levels. One thing you can count on in the futures markets is the disciplined way by which traders respond to the signals. That's what makes technical analysis ideal for futures trading.

Support and resistance lines define a *trading range*. In Figure 7-4 (later in the chapter), the trading range is called a basing pattern, because it precedes a breakout.

Support and resistance levels can be fluid, flowing up and down within the trading range. When combined with a moving average (see the next section), they provide a useful tool that indicates how market exit and entry points are progressing in relationship to the price of the security.

Moving your average

Moving averages are lines that are formed by a series of consecutive points that smooth out the general price trend. Moving averages are a form of a trend line.

In terms of a security's closing price, for example, a 50-day moving average is a line of points that represent the average of the closing prices of the security during each of the previous 50 days of trading.

Figure 7-3 shows two classic moving averages that are frequently used in technical analysis, the 50-day and 200-day moving averages. This particular figure shows a bullish long-term trend in which the bond fund is trading above the 200-day moving average and a crossover in which the price of the bond fund began trading above the 50-day moving average, a sign that prices were moving higher.

Figure 7-3: Moving averages point to a bullish trend in 20-year T-bonds, while engulfing and harami patterns point to trend changes. The MACD indicator confirms the shift.

Moving averages come in many different types, but for illustrative purposes, I use these four:

- **20 days:** The 20-day moving average traditionally is thought of as a short-term indicator.

- **50 days:** The 50-day moving average is considered a measure of the intermediate-term trend of the market.

- **100 days:** More pros are starting to use the 100-day average. The 100-day average gives the pros an edge over the public, as most people tend to follow the 20- and 50-day lines. The 100-day average gives you a chance to participate in the market's action sandwiched between the very long-term trend measured by the 200-day average and the shorter term periods measured by the 20- and 50-day lines.

- **200 days:** The 200-day moving average is considered the dividing line between long-term bull and bear markets. Use this average to make very long-term decisions about the trend of the market.

As a general rule, when a market trades above its 200-day moving average, the path of least resistance is toward higher prices; however, no hard-and-fast rules exist. Some traders prefer to use a 21-day moving averagerather than the 20-day average, while others think moving averages are useless altogether. I personally like using them to define dominant trends in the markets but not necessarily as guides to placing buy or sell stops.

Short-term charts, such as the charts used for day trading, where one price bar can equal as short a period of time as 15 minutes, have moving averages that measure minutes rather than days. The same decision rules apply, though.

The exception for me is when a market has been in a major uptrend or downtrend for an extended period, and it suddenly breaks below or above the 200-day average. This can signal that the long-term trend in that market has made a drastic change in the opposite direction.

Most trading software programs offer moving averages as part of their default charting systems. You may have to adjust these moving averages to your particular trading style or delete them if you decide that you don't like them. Also, remember that the averages I describe here are good places to start. As you gain experience, you'll find that shaving off or adding a day or two to the commonly used moving averages may give your trading a slight edge at times. The important thing is to remember the main concept first, and then you can start to add your own wrinkles.

The moving averages that you use in futures trading more than likely will be defined in terms of minutes or hours rather than days or weeks — depending, of course, on the time frame you use to make your trades. Nevertheless, knowing the longer-term trends of the markets in which you're trading is essential for knowing when to make trades with the trend rather than against it. The basic rules are the same.

You can give your position more room to maneuver by using longer-term moving averages. In the futures markets, however, that strategy is not always the best, because some markets are more volatile than others. If you're using moving-average trading methods, your best bet is to back test several different combinations of moving averages for each specific market.

Back testing is a trading method by which you review or test your proposed strategy over a period of time by using historic charts. For example, if you want to see how a market relates to its 20-day moving average, you can look at a five-year chart that includes the 20-day moving average and gauge what prices do when that market is priced above or below that average. When back testing, you're better off looking at many different indicators and combinations of them. You usually can find a combination that works best for any particular market. When you back test your strategy, you improve your chances of finding the best combination of indicators to keep you on the right side of the trend.

Breaking out

A *breakout* happens when buyers overwhelm sellers and prices begin to rise. Breakouts usually follow some kind of basing pattern or sideways movement in the market. A good rule is that the longer the base, the higher the likelihood of a good move after the underlying security breaks out of its trading range.

Figure 7-4 shows a great example of a chart breakout coming out of a head-and-shoulders pattern, a basic and easy-to-find pattern that can be found in all markets. Notice the almost perfect head-and-shoulders bottom in the crude oil contract marked *H* for the *head* and *S* for the left and right *shoulders,* as it forms the basing pattern that precedes the crude-oil price breakout in textbook fashion.

Some of the characteristics of a head-and-shoulders base are that it

- ✔ Is a common but not always reliable technical pattern. It doesn't always point to a breakout the way it does in Figure 7-4.

- ✔ Always is shaped like a head and shoulders. Arrows in Figure 7-4 illustrate how the volume drops off as the shoulders are being formed, a textbook characteristic of the head-and-shoulders bottom. Head-and-shoulder tops are the same formation turned upside down. When they happen, they can lead to a breakdown in the underlying asset.

- ✔ Indicates that any resulting breakout will take out the resistance at the neckline of the head-and-shoulders pattern.

- ✔ Results in an increase in share volume as the price breaks out above the head-and-shoulders bottom (see the five-pointed star in Figure 7-4). The volume increase is another important characteristic of a chart breakout. It indicates that many buyers are interested in the security and that prices are likely to go higher.

Figure 7-4:
Here's a
good look at
lines of
resistance
and support,
a breakout,
a base
pattern, and
a classic
head-and-
shoulders
pattern.

Using trading ranges to establish entry and exit points

Markets often trade in channels. As is what happens when a market trades up or down within defined borders. It is sort of a trading range, except usually trading ranges are defined as markets that move sideways, which are in fact horizontal channels. Don't get too bogged down in the finer points, though. Just remember that markets tend to move within upper and lower limits. Sometimes the upper and lower limits are horizontal (trading ranges) and sometimes the upper and lower limits slant (channels.) Figure 7-5 shows a rising or uptrending channel. The upper line defines the top of the channel, and the lower line defines the bottom of the channel.

Regardless of whether the trend is up or down, channel lines can point to great places to set trading entry and exit points for these reasons:

✔ The longer the channel holds in place, the more important a break above or below it becomes for a particular market or security.

✔ Channel lines can indicate a multiyear bear market if the breakout occurs below the rising channel. (That's what happened to the dollar in the late 1990s in Figure 7-5.)

✔ Channel lines can indicate that a major bottom is in place and that a bear market has come to an end if a downtrend line is broken. (That's what happened to the dollar in 1985 and 2005 in Figure 7-5.)

Figure 7-5:
Gaps,
channels,
trend lines,
triangles,
and other
basic
technical
analysis
patterns.

Resistance is the opposite of support, because it's a price point on a chart above which prices cannot move higher. It's also the place where sellers are lurking and a place where breakdowns ultimately occur. A *breakdown* is a point in the market when sellers overwhelm buyers and prices begin to fall. A breakdown usually comes after a market forms a top. Figure 7-5 shows the U.S. Dollar Index making a multiyear top. In this case, the top actually is indicated by a triple top formation, because the dollar failed to move higher in three separate attempts. (The numbers *1, 2,* and *3* correspond to the three tops, or failures, before the breakdown began in Figure 7-5.)

As with most definitive bases at the top of an uptrend, the crucial signal is the failure to make a new high for the move. Note how the number *3* top is lower than the number *2* top and then is followed by fast and furious selling.

Seeing gaps and forming triangles

Gaps and triangles are two of the more common occurrences on price charts. Each has its own meaning and importance.

Triangles, or wedge formations, can predict future price actions more reliably than gaps, but gaps can also be useful.

The three basic triangle shapes found on price charts are

  ✔ **Ascending triangles:** These triangles point upward and can be good signs of a price pattern with an upward bias (refer to Figure 7-5). In that example, the Dollar Index uses the lower rising channel line as support to build an ascending triangle. A horizontal line (above the triangle) marks the resistance point that completes the triangle.

✓ **Descending triangles:** These triangles point downward and are the opposite of ascending triangles, usually coming before downtrends.

✓ **Symmetrical triangles:** These triangles are symmetrical in that they show neither an upward nor downward trend and thus are unpredictable price formations.

Gaps, on the other hand, are unfilled points on price charts. They are more frequently visible and therefore less important in the price charts of thinly traded instruments, such as obscure futures contracts and some small stocks. However, when they occur in more common contracts and more heavily traded stocks, they can be much more important and have the following effects (Figure 7-5 shows all three such gaps):

✓ **Breakaway gap:** This gap happens when an underlying security gets out of the gate very strongly at the start of the trading day. Breakaway gaps often come after the release of economic indicators, such as the monthly employment report. They are signs of a strong market.

Breakaway gaps are more meaningful when they are bigger than the usual trading range of a security. For example, if you know that a futures contract usually trades within a range of three point ticks and it opens ten ticks higher or lower, the result is a major breakaway gap.

✓ **Runaway gap:** This gap occurs when a second gap appears on a price chart in the same direction as a breakaway gap. Runaway gaps are signs of continuing and accelerating price trends.

✓ **Exhaustion gap:** This gap is a sign that a market has run out of buyers or sellers and indicates almost a last gasp in the market before the trend is reversed. Some exhaustion gaps may have telltale candlestick patterns associated with them, such as a doji, cross, or hanging man (see the section "Hammering and hanging for traders, not carpenters" later in this chapter).

Seeing through the Haze: Common Candlestick Patterns

Even though candlestick patterns are not 100 percent reliable, they certainly are worth paying attention to. As you gain more and more experience, you'll come to know many different patterns. In this section, I concentrate on the more common and meaningful patterns that can serve as signals that a market is starting to reverse course.

Engulfing the trend

An engulfing pattern is what you see when the second (or next) day's real body, or candlestick, completely covers the prior day's candlestick. An engulfing pattern signals a potential reversal. Figure 7-6 shows a schematic of bullish and bearish engulfing patterns, and Figure 7-3 shows a real-time engulfing pattern. Note that the body of the second candle is larger than the first candle and that it predicts a change of the trend. The bullish engulfing pattern predicts a trading bottom, and the bearish engulfing pattern, a top. Action on the third day often is key to whether the pattern will hold.

Engulfing patterns are characterized by a second-day candlestick that is larger than, or engulfs, the first day's candlestick. The larger candlestick predicts a potential change in the trend of the underlying security's price. For example, a *bullish engulfing pattern* usually appears at or near a trading bottom and predicts an upturn in prices, while a *bearish engulfing pattern* appears at or near the trading top and predicts a downturn in prices.

Engulfing

Bullish   Bearish

Figure 7-6:
The engulfing
pattern.

In *Candlestick Charting Explained* (McGraw-Hill), Greg Morris, a mutual fund manager (PMFM funds), software designer, and an early proponent of candlestick charting, offers several important rules of recognition for engulfing patterns:

✔ **A definite trend must be underway.**

✔ **The second-day candlestick's body must completely engulf the prior day's candle.** In other words, the high and low prices of the second-day candlestick must be higher and lower than the respective high and low for the previous day. Morris points out the subtleties of engulfing patterns by indicating that if the tops and bottoms of both candlesticks are identical, the pattern isn't engulfing, but if one or the other is equal and the second-day candle still engulfs the previous day's candle on the other end, the pattern is valid.

✔ **The color of the first day's candle must reflect the trend.** So if prices are trending upward, and the first candle is red, the pattern doesn't hold.

✔ **The second day's candle must be the opposite color of the prevailing trend.** This rule is the corollary to the preceding rule. If the first day's candle is red or black, showing a downtrend in prices, the second day's candle must be green or white.

Figure 7-3 (earlier in the chapter) offers a great example of a real-life engulfing pattern that meets all criteria. Notice the following:

✔ The bar started out at a higher opening price, but clearly closed at a lower level, a sign of a clear reversal.

✔ The engulfing bar was huge compared to the prior day.

Hammering and hanging for traders, not carpenters

The hammer and the hanging man also are common patterns. A *hammer* is a small white candlestick with a long shadow, while a *hanging man* is a small black candlestick with a long shadow (see Figure 7-7).

Making sense of these patterns is difficult, because they can appear virtually anywhere on just about any chart. They are best used after a long series of bars of the same color and are most reliable as indicators of a possible reversal.

A white-body hammer that follows a long series of black bars in a downtrend usually means that a reversal is coming. A black hanging man pattern that appears after several white bars in an uptrend usually means that some selling and a downturn is on the way.

Figure 7-7:
Hammer
and hanging
man
patterns.

HAMMER

HANGING
MAN

Seeing the harami pattern

A *harami pattern* is an excellent example of a reversal pattern. It forms when a long candlestick of one color is followed by a smaller candlestick of another color. The color of the second candle indicates which way the market is likely to go. You can see it in a real-world example back in Figure 7-3.

The harami is an excellent pattern for indicating a trend change or pause. The stock needs to be in a strong trend, and for the harami to be a valid pattern, the second real body must form completely inside the first. The color of the second candle needs to be the opposite of the first. Confirmation of this pattern is recommended.

A harami pattern is most useful when a trend has been in place for some time, like the six-week downtrend in Figure 7-3, but you need to keep close tabs on the volume along with the candlesticks (the way I explain in the next few paragraphs).

Say, for example, that you've been selling bonds (I use the exchange traded fund TLT in this example, but it is equally applicable to bond futures) short for several days and suppose that you're starting to get comfortable with a downtrend when you spot a long red (black) candle on your chart. Your initial response, especially if you're using bar charts, is to think that the downtrend is extending and that you're going to make more money in the next few days.

Bears, bulls, and a bunch of crazy names

According to John Murphy's *Technical Analysis of the Financial Markets* (New York Institute of Finance), 68 different candlestick patterns are commonly used by futures traders. Murphy lists 8 bullish continuation patterns, 8 bearish continuation patterns, and 26 bullish and bearish reversal patterns. Some candlestick patterns are composed of two, three, four, and five candlesticks. Some of my favorite names for patterns are

✔ Abandoned baby

✔ Dark cloud cover

✔ Concealing swallow

✔ Three white soldiers

✔ Three black crows

However, on the next day, prices reverse and close higher after other short sellers have covered their short positions.

Although the bar for the second day is green (white), it's nevertheless smaller as new short sellers come into the market at the end of the day. They're thinking that the downtrending security is a good opportunity to initiate new short sales after missing out on the last move.

You gain a more accurate picture of the situation by looking at the volume on the two days, as shown by the down-pointing arrow in Figure 7-3. Average volume on the long black day followed by higher volume on the short white day suggests that the trend is about to change, and you indeed have a harami pattern.

The action on day three tells you whether the harami pattern will hold true and send prices higher.

Figure 7-3 shows real-time candlestick patterns that defined the trend in the bond market in 2005. The chart is of the Long-Term Bond Exchange-Traded fund (TLT). The TLT is closely related to the U.S. 10-year Treasury note and the U.S. Long Bond (30-year) futures contracts. The TLT can be traded both long and short, and offers a good trading vehicle for investors who want to participate in the overall trend of futures markets without actually opening an account with a futures broker. The commission and the effort spent trading the TLT is the same as with trading any stock.

Several important technical-analysis-related points to get out of the harami pattern in Figure 7-3 include

- ✔ The arrow shows the close correlation between the low-volume red or down day and the higher volume up day and clearly conforms to the rules laid out by Morris where a low-volume down day is followed by a higher volume up day.

- ✔ Day three is an up day, confirming the trend change.

- ✔ The harami was followed by more selling until the market hit a lower bottom.

- ✔ The MACD indicator also correctly correlated the bottom by crossing over a few days after the harami pattern occurred.

This is a perfect example of how you can use candlestick charts and standard indicators together to form accurate buy and sell signals.

Chapter 8

Speculating Strategies That Use Advanced Technical Analysis

In This Chapter

▶ Understanding one market's effects on other markets

▶ Using moving averages, oscillators, and trend lines to understand your market

▶ Aligning technical indicators to make a trade

*I*nexperienced investors tend to ignore the value of a good understanding of technical analysis. That ignorance, on the part of those who ignore charting, is, of course, bliss for traders like you (and me), because it gives you an advantage, albeit a small one, in light of the fact that the big guys with the big money are all chartists, and most of them are excellent at the craft. Bob Woodward, in his book about Alan Greenspan, aptly entitled *Maestro* (Simon & Schuster), describes how the former chairman of the Federal Reserve had one of the best technical charting data arrays in the world and was an avid watcher of the financial markets, using charts during his time at the Federal Reserve.

The truth is that any good speculator with an ounce of honesty will tell you that they rely as much on their charts as they do on information gathered by other means. The true money-making trader uses both fundamental and technical analyses. To be sure, analyzing the futures markets is both an art and a science and just a little bit of cooking, like when you add that extra salt and pepper to a pot of chili.

The bottom line is that your trading will be enhanced when you apply what you know about the economy and the markets to your charts. And in this chapter, I put together several topics from the fundamental and technical worlds to help you do just that.

Using Indicators to Make Good Trading Decisions

Indicators are instruments that help you confirm what you see when you look at a chart. They are an intrinsic part of trading if you use technical analysis. Graphs produced by the indicators are displayed along with the prices of the underlying asset on the same chart. The indicators are derived from formulas whose components include the prices of the underlying asset.

The more common indicators are known as moving averages, oscillators, channels (of which there are several kinds), and trend lines. These indicators are part of most price charts in the futures markets (see Figure 8-1).

Making good use of moving averages

A *moving average* is a series of points that enable you to determine which way a major trend is moving within a market and whether your trade is with or against the trend (see Chapter 7). Long-term charts use days and weeks for moving averages. Short-term, *intraday* (within the same trading day) charts use minutes to create moving averages. Generally speaking, moving averages are useful tools because

- Markets trade higher when prices are consistently above the moving average.

- When markets cross over a moving average in one direction or the other (above or below), you need to be mindful of a potential change or shift in the existing trend.

- The longer the moving average, the more important the trend and trend reversals become. For example, when the dollar crosses above its 200-day moving average, the chance that the trend has changed from a falling market to one that's about to rise is greater than when it crosses a 50-day moving average.

Trading by using only moving averages is risky business. Market prices can jump above and below them many times before actually starting a new trend or continuing an old one. Prices repeatedly jumping above or below a moving average during a short period of time are a great example of a *whipsaw*. Whipsaws can occur when you use extremely short-term moving averages or even when you use long-term moving averages (like the 200-day moving average).

Comparing multiple moving averages of varying lengths (20, 50, 100 and 200 days) with the daily price for an instrument enables traders to find important breakout and crossover points that they use to formulate their trading plans. Figure 8-1 compares these key data from June 2004 to June 2005 with that of the euro currency. Note how in October 2004 the value of the euro rallied above its 20- and 50-day moving averages and how the 20-day moving average of the euro moved above its 50-day moving average, creating a bullish crossover. A *bullish crossover* is an episode in which a shorter-length moving average crosses above a longer-term moving average, which usually is good confirmation of a rising trend and a signal to buy the underlying asset. A *bearish crossover* is the opposite, when a shorter-length moving average falls below a longer-term moving average. It usually confirms a falling trend. Figure 8–1 highlights a bearish crossover.

A good trading technique is to buy a small stake in a market when a bullish crossover occurs. That's what you see labeled as "buy point 1" in Figure 8-1. You can see that the euro moved sideways for a bit longer and then broke out; that's "buy point 2" in Figure 8-1.

The buy signal held true, and the euro's rally stayed alive until the bearish crossover occurred and the euro fell below both its 20-day and 50-day moving averages in January 2005.

Figure 8-1: Two buying points — Buy point 1, when you can establish your position, and Buy point 2, when you can add to your position.

Figure 8-1 is important because the chart points to a significant amount of information about the value of the euro, including the following:

- **Downtrends:** When the euro traded below its 20-, 50-, and 200-day moving averages, it progressed through short-, intermediate-, and long-term downtrends.

- **A negative crossover:** When both the 20- and 50-day moving averages crossed below the 200-day moving average, the resulting *negative crossover* confirmed a long-term downtrend.

- **A positive crossover:** When the 20-day moving average crossed above the 50-day moving average, the resulting positive crossover confirmed an uptrend.

- **A sustained uptrend:** The rally in the euro that followed the positive crossover points to a sustained uptrend.

Understanding and using oscillators

Oscillators are mathematical equations that are graphed onto price charts so you can more easily decide whether the price action is a correction in an ongoing trend or a change in the overall trend. Oscillators usually are graphed above or below the price charts.

Traders commonly use several oscillators. In this section, I show you two of them, the MACD and stochastic oscillators, in detail. Discovering the basics of these two oscillators will enable you to easily understand the rest of them, because they all share the same characteristics.

Biting into a Big Mac without special sauce: MACD

The *Moving Average Convergence Divergence* (MACD) is the result of a formula that's based on three moving averages derived from the price of the underlying asset. When applied to the asset prices, the MACD formula smoothes out fluctuations of that asset. For example, in Figure 8-1, the MACD is smoothing out three moving averages based on the price of the euro. The software provided by your charting service will help you to display MACD oscillators based either on your own trading criteria or the software's default criteria.

The MACD data shown in Figure 8-1 are displayed as a histogram. A MACD oscillator that's moving up usually is considered a bullish development, confirming that an uptrend has been well established when it actually crosses above the zero line.

On the left side of the MACD oscillator chart, note how the line under the MACD slopes higher, while the line under the price of the euro on the index chart above it is flat. The sloping MACD means the oscillator established a higher low, even though the price remained flat, which is called *positive divergence*.

Although prices did not rise, the positive divergence points to selling momentum that is less than it was during the previous low on the MACD oscillator, and that's a signal that prices may be getting ready to rise. In Figure 8-1, the MACD oscillator was right.

In November, however, a turnaround occurred as the MACD histogram rolled over. The price of the euro continued to rise, but the MACD provided a *non-confirmation* signal, meaning that its overall direction was now lower. Note how the line above prices is on the rise from late November through early January, but the second peak on the MACD is lower than the first. This divergence is a sign that buyers are getting tired and that prices may be getting ready to fall. And again, Figure 8-1 shows that the MACD was right.

Taking stock with stochastics

Stochastic oscillators indicate classic overbought and oversold situations in the markets. An *overbought market* occurs when prices have been in a rising trend for a long time and buyers are starting to get tired. An *oversold market* is just the opposite; sellers are getting tired as prices are trending down. Whenever either of these situations occurs, as a trader, you need to know whether your position is in danger of getting caught in a trend change.

Markets can remain in overbought or oversold conditions for short or long periods of time before the trend changes. A four-month rally in the euro during the fall of 2004 was overbought for a long time based on stochastic oscillator analysis. So if you had sold based on this indicator alone, you would've missed out on making a lot of money. In fact, looking at Figure 8-1, you can see that the stochastic indicator showed that the market was overbought when the breakout occurred at buy point 2. Without the crossover and MACD indicators for backup, you would've sold way too early.

Thus, like any indicator, stochastics need to be used in combination with other indicators. Figure 8-1 shows how you can combine MACD, stochastics, and moving-average crossovers to execute your trading plan most efficiently.

I use stochastic indicators as an early warning system. When stochastics signal overbought or oversold markets, I take it to mean that I should start paying close attention to my other indicators, such as MACD and moving averages.

Note in Figure 8-1 that before the rally, the second low on the stochastic indicator was higher than the first, just like the pair of lows on the MACD, thus providing *confirmation* of the MACD data by the stochastics, which also ultimately turned out to be correct.

The trend became clear in January when the stochastic oscillator indicated that the market was oversold. The second low was lower than the first, correctly indicating a negative situation in which the euro fell to a lower low soon after the lower low was reached on the stochastic oscillator.

By using moving averages and two simple oscillators, you could've easily traded those profitable moves in the euro on the long and the short sides.

When watching moving averages and oscillators together, use minute-based moving averages for shorter-term trading. The method is the same except that you're reading the pricing data in a different, shorter, time frame. You may want to give yourself another layer of information to confirm the shorter-term data by looking for key reversal patterns on candlestick charts.

Getting relative (Not Jiggy) with RSI

The RSI (Relative Strength Indicator) was developed by Welles Wilder and was introduced in 1978. I once got a letter from Wilder about an indicator that I developed in my early days in the business. I still have the letter and look at it once in a while. It was a nice thing for a well-known person in the business to do for someone who was just getting started. But more than stroke my ego, the letter got me interested in RSI.

RSI is a very useful tool, by itself or in combination with other oscillators. *RSI uses a mathematical formula to measure price momentum and calculate the relative strength of current prices compared to previous prices.* Like stochastic indicators, RSI's strength is that it's good at telling when the market is overbought or oversold (see the preceding section).

I like to use RSI in markets that tend to stay in a particular trend for an extended period. Energy markets are an example. See Chapter 13 for a classic example of how to use RSI. The key to RSI, like other oscillators, is to put it in the proper context of the market that you are trading. It can give early signals that take a while to come true, so you have to bide your time well. A good rule to remember is that when RSI, or any other oscillator, gives you a signal that the trend is changing, it's a good time for you to be watching the market closer and to be ready to make decisions about your positions.

Seeing how trading bands stretch

As your use of technical analysis grows more sophisticated, you'll want to know the potential price limits of certain trades. This information helps you ponder when to enter and exit trades and when markets may stall and reverse trend. A good tool for those purposes is a trading band.

Trading bands also are known as *trading envelopes,* because they surround prices, thus providing visual cues about where price support and resistance levels are at any given time. I like to think of trading bands as variable channels. Chapter 7 shows you trading channels that are defined by trend lines that you draw. Trading bands are similar to trend channels in that they provide you a visual framework of a trading range. The only difference is that trading bands are more dynamic, because they change with every tick in the price of the underlying asset.

Don't get confused here. Trading bands are, in fact, trading channels that change with every tick. In other words, trend channels, which are drawn by hand or with software, are straight lines, pointed either up or down, connecting the high and low points of the top or the bottom of the price range. When you look at trading channels, you're getting a visual representation of the trading range.

Trading bands go farther by giving you both the parameters of the trading range along with clues as to where the trading range may be heading in the future.

Introducing Bollinger bands

The most commonly used trading bands are Bollinger bands, which were introduced and made famous by John Bollinger, a pioneering technical analyst and television commentator. Bollinger bands essentially mark flexible trading channels that fluctuate by two standard deviations above and below a moving average. The bands are helpful in defining trading ranges and telling you when a change in the trend is coming. Bollinger introduced the bands with the 20-day moving average, but you can set them up for use with any moving average, and they'll work the same way.

In terms of the market, a *standard deviation* is a statistical expression of the potential variability of prices, or the potential trading range. The two-standard deviation method is a default used by most software programs because it catches most intermediate term trends. That means when you punch up Bollinger bands on your trading software, you'll see bands defining the trading range that are two standard deviations above and two standard deviations below the market price.

As you progress and become more experienced, you may want to use smaller or larger standard deviations. If you want more frequent signals, you shorten or use less standard deviation. For longer-term trading, you use larger or more standard deviation.

Don't get too hung up in the statistical language. The important concept to remember is that the market tends to follow some semblance of order, nonlinear order, which is predictably unpredictable.

The Bollinger bands are good at displaying the order for you. And here's how. Figure 8-2 shows you how to apply Bollinger bands to a trading situation that involves the price of the euro during the same period of time highlighted in Figure 8-1.

When using Bollinger bands to analyze the markets, you need to

 ✔ **Watch the general direction of the bands.** If the bands are rising, then the market is in an uptrend. If they're falling, the market is in a downtrend.

✔ **Watch the width between the upper and lower bands.** Shrinking Bollinger bands — where the distance between the upper and lower bands is narrowing — signal a decrease in volatility and indicate that a big move is on the way. I like to call this a *squeeze*. Arrows in Figure 8-2 point to a nice squeeze in the bands that preceded a false breakout and a clear downturn, or *breakdown*. Here's another good squeeze: Notice how the bands tightened around prices before the euro broke out and headed higher. Decreasing price volatility is usually a prelude to a big move. Widening bands usually are a signal that the trend has changed and that the general tendency of prices is likely to continue in the direction of the new trend.

Futures traders work in a time frame of a gnat, and a breakdown can be two hours of falling prices if you're using charts featuring five-minute bars (see Chapter 7 for more about charting).

The direction of a move signaled by a squeeze of the Bollinger Bands is not always certain, though, so you need to wait until the market moves, and catch the move as early as possible.

Bollinger bands also are excellent for staying with the trend. Watch for prices to be

✔ **Walking the bands.** Markets that move along either of the (upper or lower) bands for an extended time are interpreted as a signal that the current trend is going to continue for some time. The bracket from September to November shows a nice example of how the euro walked the band for a good while during its late 2004 rally.

I realize that reference to "some time" can be frustrating and may be confusing to readers who require certainty in their trading and more precise time frames. But when you're trading, all you can do is understand the possibilities and monitor your trades accordingly until the market tells you that the trend has changed. That's one of the reasons that you should never rely on a single indicator without using others as backups. In Figure 8-2, the "some time" turned out to be three months. By monitoring your trade closely, you could've followed this market movement for the entire period.

✔ **Breaking outside the bands.** When a market's price breaks outside the bands around a moving average, it usually means you can expect reversal in the market — a trip to the opposite band. Breakouts don't always indicate a shift in the market, but if the market goes outside the bands enough times, the price eventually makes a trip in the opposite direction.

When the market touches either of the bands, it's only a matter of time before it eventually touches the other band; however, the specific amount of time it takes for this kind of reversal to occur is not as predictable.

Figure 8-2:
The Euro
Currency
And
Bollinger
Bands.

The block arrow in February in Figure 8-2 points to a great example of how the lower band can serve as a launching pad for a bounce back up to the upper band. The euro not only touched the band, but spent several days just outside of it.

An easy way to remember how Bollinger bands work is to think of them as tight rubber bands that stretch and contract around a magnet, and the moving average as a magnet. When the rubber bands get stretched too far, the magnet pulls the market back into a more normal state, inside the bands.

Trading with Bollinger bands

Bollinger bands can be used alone, but they work much better when used in combination with oscillators and other moving averages. As with any indicator, Bollinger bands are not perfect. Sometimes, the price of the underlying asset rises above the upper band, and you think that a trip to the lower band is possible, thus prompting you to sell. Sometimes, you'll be right. At other times, however, prices fall back inside the band, stay there a couple of days, and rally right back up, continuing to walk along the upper band. That's when other indicators, such as MACD and stochastic oscillators and moving-average crossovers, come in handy as checks and balances.

You can visualize a good example of Bollinger bands being used in conjunction with other indicators by viewing Figures 8-1 and 8-2 together. The squeezing

Bollinger bands in Figure 8-2 occurred at the same time that the MACD oscillator failed to confirm the higher high in the euro currency. The combination of the two — the bands signaling that a big move was in the offing and the negative divergence in the MACD — was confirmed when the euro began a downtrend.

I use Bollinger bands on all my trades, regardless of whether I'm looking at intraday 15-minute candlestick charts or longer-term daily or weekly bar charts. And I always use a 20-period chart marked with candlesticks at 15-minute intervals for my intraday charting. Using short-term charts, I can tell what the market is doing much better than I can when using longer-term charts. You'll figure out what works best for you when you gain more trading experience. Only one rule applies when it comes to charting: Use the parameters that you're comfortable with and that make you money.

You can use Bollinger bands, oscillators, and moving averages as guidelines when placing your trades. Here's how:

- **When looking to go long (see Chapters 7 and 20),** you can set your buy points just above the lower Bollinger band so that you catch the bounce when prices bounce back into the band, and a new uptrend starts.

- **When looking to go short,** you're selling high; thus you put your sell-short entry point — as soon as it clear that the market is breaking, and it comes back inside the upper band. In this case, you're looking for prices to break and to profit from the break, which is why you're selling short.

- **When taking profits,** you can use the moving average to set your sell points to take profits based, of course, on where other indicators show the market is headed when market prices reach those points.

- **When adding to your position (buying),** you can use the moving average to establish new buy points to bolster your position. When prices fall back to the moving average and hold, you can add to positions there.

- **When the market breaks outside the upper band,** on the way up, you can sell your position there if you're long. See the "Take profits" sign in Figure 8-2. As the market moves back into the band, you can then change your tactics to short selling.

- **When the market drops below the lower band,** you can take profits on short positions and go long at the lower band.

Trading with trend lines

Trend lines are much like Bollinger bands but without so much flexibility. Trend lines directly reflect the overall trend of the market, but they're static because you draw them on your charts with the drawing tool in your software package. This tool is best used for spotting a key change in the overall direction of the underlying market.

Trend lines are just lines on charts, such as the ones shown in Figure 8-3 (numbered 1 through 4). The correct way to draw a trend line is to connect at least two points in the price chart without crossing through any other price areas. If you can draw the trend through more than two points, it can become more accurate; however, trend lines are another tool that needs to be used with other indicators.

You can use trend lines for both short- and long-term trading, and in both cases they tell you the same thing, the overall trend of the market. The important trend-line concept to remember is that rising prices remain in a rising trend as long as they're above the trend line. Likewise, falling prices remain in a downtrend as long as they're below the falling trend line. Breaks above or below the trend lines signal that the trend has changed. Correctly drawn trend lines (see preceding paragraph) help you stay on the right side of the market as follows:

- ✔ **In uptrends,** trend lines connect the lowest low to the next low that precedes a new high without passing through any other points. Two uptrend lines, number 2 and number 3, are shown in Figure 8-3, a long-term chart covering five years of trading in the U.S. Dollar Index. The price break above trend line 1 shows you when to buy right after a downtrend line is broken. Trend line 3 shows you how to add to your position as the price holds above the trend line.

- ✔ **In downtrends,** trend lines connect the highest high to the next high that precedes a new low without passing through any other points. Two downtrend lines in Figure 8-3 include an intermediate-term trend line, on the far left that lasts for months, (trend line 1), and a long-term trend line, trend line 4 (far right) that lasts for years. Trend line 1 shows you how to remain in a short position as long as the price remains below the falling trend. Trend line 4 shows you that you need to be buying the dollar when the price of the dollar breaks above the multiyear trend. Needless to say, as long as prices stayed below trend line 4, the primary trading direction was to be short the dollar.

Short-term trend-line trading

When trading futures, at times you can easily get caught up in the jargon. Short-term trading should never be confused with short selling. Short selling means you're betting that prices will fall. Short-term trading means you're not interested in holding a position for longer than a few hours or days at most.

To trade the long side (or buy by using trend lines), you can

- ✔ Buy a portion of your position when a downtrend that you've been following, or shorting, is broken (see Figure 8-3).

- ✔ Draw your trend line as the market is developing an uptrend and then buy when the market touches the uptrending line for the third time without breaking below it.

- ✔ Supplement trend lines with oscillators and moving averages to make sure that the odds of a winning trade are increased. You should never rely on only one indicator to make your trades.

I find it easier to trade after a trend line is initially broken. Sometimes I use *successful tests,* or price moves back to the trend line without breaking the line, to add to my position (see next section). This strategy works well in the oil markets and with the dollar.

Long-term trend-line trading

Say you've been short selling a downtrend in the value of the U.S. dollar for several weeks, but you're not sure how much longer the position will do well. Aside from using moving averages, Bollinger bands, and a few oscillators, a good trend line can be the best indicator for the job. Figure 8-3, a five-year chart of the value of the U.S. dollar, provides a great example of how drawing trend lines on long-term charts can help you spot a meaningful change in a long-term trend.

Figure 8-3:
Using trend lines to stay on the right side of the market.

A meaningful break in a long-standing trend often means that the trend is changing directions. You can see in Figure 8-3 that at least a meaningful inter-mediate-term advance in the dollar began in 2005 and lasted for several months following a break in a long-term downtrend.

If you're drawing trend lines, then it's a good bet that big-money players are drawing them, too. As Barbara Rockefeller points out in *Technical Analysis For Dummies* (Wiley), big traders sometimes sell their positions long enough to find out what happens when market prices touch the trend line. In essence, that means trend lines can encounter points of high volatility, and you can get shaken out of a position more than once if you're not careful, especially when you base your trades only on trend lines. Instead of relying on only one indicator, don't hesitate to use trend lines in conjunction with other indica-tors, just to make sure that the odds of success are as much on your side as possible.

Lining Up the Dots: Trading with the Technicals

Technical analysis is like solving puzzles — kind of like connecting the dots. You start with a price chart, and you start adding lines, bands, oscillators, and indicators.

As you go along, things can grow cluttered, and you can lose your way. The good thing is that trading software has "Clear" buttons, which means you can wipe out all the lines and squiggles on your charts and start over anytime things get out of control. Save your work first, though, in case you need to refer back to it.

In the next section, I deal with chart clutter by focusing on staying with the trend.

Identifying trends

Trading is not only about swimming with the tide; it's also about knowing when the tide is going to turn against you. Good traders figure out which way the trend is moving before they risk their money. It really is as simple as that. However, you also need to remember that several time frames are involved in price activity, and that knowing which ways the short-, intermediate-, and long-term trends are headed in your markets is equally important.

Finding the trends is easy; you simply look at price charts for multiple time frames every day. Daily, weekly, and monthly charts, spanning months, weeks, and even years, are the best way to go. Checking them all before you look at your intraday price charts will enable you to be on the right side of the market for the time frame in which you plan your trades.

If, for example, you're day trading in wheat, you at least want to know where the market has been during the last few weeks or months, because intraday prices of wheat are likely to be guided by that overall trend.

You can also use long-term price charts as the basis for spotting key long-term support and resistance points and for identifying those same points on your shorter-term charts.

Thereafter, you can use the trend lines in conjunction with moving averages and oscillators to help identify the dominant trend before you trade.

 Think of short-term charts like the zoom lens on your camera. They help you zoom in for a closer look at the long-term action.

 Before making a trade, make sure that you know the dominant trends. Keep a trading log so you can write them down on a daily basis before hitting the daily action.

Getting to know setups

As a trader, you're a hunter, and good hunters appreciate high levels of activity and the quiet periods in between. Remember, only three things can happen in a market. Prices can rise, fall, or move sideways for an extended period of time.

As a trader/hunter, your job is to look through all your charts for *setups,* or chart formations that signal when a change is about to occur in the market you're studying and want to trade in. As you look for trading opportunities, watch for the following:

- ✔ **Constricting Bollinger bands,** which point to the potential for a big move getting closer
- ✔ **Sideways price movements following advances and declines,** which indicate volatility is easing as traders try to decide what to do next
- ✔ **Breakouts** that occur when prices break above or cross over key support or resistance levels, trend lines, oscillators, moving averages, or other market indicators

After you find them, setups call for careful observation in which you apply the principles of the indicators explained earlier in this chapter.

A good rule to follow is to place your entry and exit points right above or below the setup in the direction of the dominant trend.

Buying the breakout

Breakouts are exciting. Prices suddenly burst out of a basing pattern. Volume can swell, and suddenly your trading screens are flashing my favorite trading color, green, as buyers come into the market.

A breakout is a signal for you to go to work. Because it can come at virtually any time, you need to be prepared to react.

Figure 8-1 (earlier in this chapter) shows you a classic example of a nice setup, a breakout, and the right outcome. The euro formed a 4½-month base and then delivered a nice breakout in mid-October, after testing resistance levels in July, August, and twice in September. Important features to notice about this classic basing pattern are that the euro found support twice during the basing period, and its value did not retreat to the bottom of the trading range after September.

These two factors together indicated that buyers slowly were starting to take the upper hand. In addition, higher lows indicated by the MACD oscillator and positive basing action (see Chapter 7) predicted the breakout.

The ideal entry point for buying the breakout (labeled in the figure) is after the price clears all the previous resistance and begins moving higher — in a hurry.

Don't be too concrete here. Setups are setups. They look the same on long-term charts as they do on short-term charts. For example, if you're using a chart to cover one day's trading, say around 6 hours, your bars or candlesticks may be anywhere from 5 to 15 minutes, meaning that by the end of a few hours, your chart will be full. You can use the same indicators on these charts. Bollinger bands shrink just the same. Prices will rise and fall above nine-minute moving averages. And MACD and stochastic oscillators will be just as applicable. The key is that the principles stay the same, no matter the time frame.

Swinging for dollars

Swing trading enables you to take advantage of markets that are stuck in trading ranges, whether they are moving sideways, rising, or falling within trading channels. The euro in Figure 8-1 was in a narrow trading range before it broke out in October, and offered opportunities for short-term swing trading before its breakout.

To be able to make profitable trades in markets that are within trading ranges, swing traders rely on trend lines, Fibonacci levels, and moving averages to identify the levels of support and resistance that they use to establish price points at which they buy, sell, and sell short their investments. When prices reach support and resistance levels, swing traders take action, in general buying on weakness at the bottom of the trading range and selling on weakness at the top of the trading range. In other words, swing traders set targets for their trades and anticipate trend changes when the market reaches those targets based on their analysis of their respective markets.

You can combine support and resistance lines with Bollinger bands and stochastic oscillators to become an effective swing trader. The euro provided plenty of opportunities for swing trades in the 4½ months before its October breakout — shown in Figures 8-1 and 8-2. Note how the support and resistance lines, the market action close to the Bollinger bands, and overbought and oversold readings on the stochastic oscillator all worked together as the euro reached the tops and bottoms of its multimonth trading range.

Swing trading, however, is risky business, the same as any other form of trading. In the Figure 8-1 example, you could've lost significant amounts of money if you happened to use the 200-day moving average to set up a swing trade in late April and May. The key: The MACD oscillator failed to confirm the attempted bottom above the moving average.

The bible of swing trading is Alan Farley's *The Master Swing Trader* (McGraw-Hill). Farley explains how to utilize a system based on what he calls *pattern cycles* — shifting market stages that repeat in an orderly, predictable process through all price charts and time frames.

Selling and shorting the breakout in a downtrend

Regardless of whether you're a momentum trader buying on breakouts or a swing trader setting up and knocking down targets, changing trends are the trader's bread and butter. And one of the hardest things for a trader to do is get up the guts to sell an instrument short. Fortunately, the complexities of the market, the popular psychology that shorting is immoral, and the high risk of losing large sums of money serve as three major deterrents against the practice.

And yet, if you keep close tabs on trend lines, oscillators, and moving averages to spot changes in a market's price trends, and watch Bollinger bands and Fibonacci retracement levels to predict when important shifts in the markets are likely, you can manage your risk and make some money selling short. You also need to use protective stops, just in case you're wrong.

Selling short is a different animal. It's essentially the practice of turning the world upside down and making money from someone else's miscues, whether political, corporate, or otherwise.

The two basic strategies for short selling are swing trading (see the preceding section) and selling into the breakdown of prices.

When you're *selling into the breakdown,* you have to wait for bad things to happen. A good rule of thumb is to consider that a market is worthy of short-selling consideration when it has been going up for an extended period of time. It can be weeks, months, or years.

When selling short, or shorting, you can do the following:

- ✔ Anticipate the breakdown by looking at the Bollinger bands and

    - Watching for the bands to constrict and the market to stop walking the band. If trend lines are broken toward the downside, you can short an instrument. Be sure to place a stop just above the trend line.

    - Watching for the market action near the moving average inside the bands, which can signal support.

- ✔ Monitor your short sales positions carefully at all times but especially in markets that respond to news and at times of high political tension. Bonds and currencies are especially susceptible to news and political tensions.

- ✔ Give your short sales positions room to move. Setting your exit stops too tightly can get you whipsawed. Different markets have different inherent ranges. Before you sell an instrument short, you need to become aware of its normal price movements and adjust your position accordingly.

You can count several trading periods and get an idea of the average number of days that a particular market moves along rising or falling Bollinger bands. This time frame won't be exact, but you want to have a good idea nevertheless. Shares of Starbucks, for example, usually hug the lower Bollinger band anywhere from four to ten days before they bounce up. Although knowing that time frame doesn't guarantee that the bounce will last, you still can be on the lookout for increased activity that can affect your trades during that period of time in the market you're trading and in other markets. *Technical Analysis For Dummies* offers a fairly detailed introduction to these topics.

Setting your entry and exit points

Where you set entry and exit points — whether mentally or automatically on your trading platform — can make a big difference in your trading performance. Although no hard-and-fast rules determine where to set these points, some fairly reliable guidelines are available. Here's a quick lineup:

- **Tailoring the strategy to the market:** Get to know how fast your market moves and how volatile trading can be before you ever start trading. It's a good idea to do this through *paper trading,* a way to practice trading without assuming the financial risk. Most online futures brokers will have practice trading available on their Web sites. Use this technique to become familiar with each market you trade.

- **Knowing your risk tolerance:** If you know wheat moves too fast for your liking, try the U.S. Dollar Index, which moves more slowly.

- **Giving a fast-moving market more room to maneuver than a slower one:** As a general rule, you need to give fast-moving markets a bit more room to maneuver. (**Note:** This bears repeating.) I usually give myself a few ticks above or below the support or resistance area that I'm using as my line in the sand so I avoid getting whipsawed.

- **Setting sell stops:** Where you set your sell stops depends not only on your experience, but also on the market's volatility and your risk tolerance.

- **Using trailing stops:** You can reset these manually; use prices or percentages as a guide. Again, much depends on the inherent volatility and general tendencies of each individual market, which is why you need to exercise care and be aware of how all contracts that you trade fluctuate before committing any money to a trade.

- **Hurrying gets you nowhere:** Never be in a hurry when trading. Some traders like to give markets an extra day before selling or buying. For example, if you spot a trend change on the S&P 500 futures chart on Tuesday, you may want to wait until Wednesday before you make your decision.

- **Using technical analysis to establish market entry and exit points:** Fibonacci levels, moving averages, trend lines, and support and resistance points provide you with plenty of references for where to place entry and exit points. The figures in this chapter offer a good foundation for beginning strategies.

- **Expanding your strategies:** As you gain more trading experience, you can find out more about the Fibonacci theory, Eliott waves, and Gann strategies by reading more about them and other approaches to trading. *Technical Analysis For Dummies* offers a fairly detailed introduction to those topics.

Chapter 9

Trading with Feeling Now!

● ●

In This Chapter

▶ Thinking in a contrary fashion

▶ Reacting to changes in volume

▶ Knowing how to benefit from open interest info

▶ Using put/call ratios

▶ Watching for signs of soft sentiment

● ●

As a contrarian thinker, my first real-life experience with contrarian market analysis was in 1990. Sure, I'd read the books and articles that tell stories about how stocks need to be sold when the shoeshine boy starts recommending stocks to you as he polishes your shoes at the airport. But, for me, 1990 was the literal proof in the pudding.

At some point in August 1990, stocks were failing in the U.S. markets, and the price of crude oil was testing the $40-per-barrel resistance level. At the time, $40-per-barrel oil was an extremely high price, even though it's cheap compared to the $105 prices to which it eventually soared in February 2008.

Both times the rise in the price of oil to what was then a record high was caused by a war in Iraq, at least initially. The situation in 2008 was slightly different, although there were still U.S. troops in Iraq.

As I discuss in detail in Chapter 13, we live in a world full of conflict, and it's important to keep in mind that wars and other world events affect how the psyches of investors work. As an investor, it's important to be aware of how news items impact the market.

During the latter stages of the oil rally in 1990, a picture of an Arab man holding a gun was on the cover of *BusinessWeek* magazine with the headline of headlines above it: "Hostage to Oil." That caught my eye. And sure as shootin' that cover story appeared only a few weeks before the price of oil topped out and actually collapsed when the United States invaded Iraq a few months later.

My contrarian stance was reinforced once again by the markets in 1991. That's when the first U.S. invasion of Iraq touched off a decade-long bull market in the U.S. stock market.

In this chapter, I take you through the major aspects of contrarian thinking and explain how to know when to use it and how to make it part of your trading arsenal.

The Essence of Contrarian Thinking

Contrarians trade against the grain at key turning points when shifts in market sentiment become noticeable. The most important aspect of contrarian thinking, though, is to be able to spot those important turning points that can lead to profitable trades. For example, a contrarian may

- Start looking for reasons to sell when everyone else is bullish
- Think a good time to buy is when pessimism about the markets is so thick that you can cut it with a knife

More can be made of contrarian trading than just using the prevailing sentiment in the market, because sentiment trading is inexact and can lead to losses whenever you pull the trigger too early during the cycle.

The bullish extremes reached during the buildup of the Internet bubble were unprecedented. Although traders who sold early were vindicated, they nevertheless lost a great deal of money by getting out too early. Another extreme is when the bear market in stocks ended in 2002. Traders who got into stocks during the seven-month period from June 2002 to March 2003 were *whipsawed,* or shaken out of positions with losses and tortured by the extremes in volatility that can happen as the final bottom of the mega bear market finally formed.

Throughout the three-year period during which the bear market in stocks unfolded, plenty of opportunities opened up to trade on the long side, meaning to buy stocks based on sentiment. But most of them proved false until the final bottom was reached.

Simply put, sentiment analysis is an inexact science and is only part of what you need to know to be a better trader. It is also a part that works better when combined with technical analysis.

This chapter helps you combine sentiment and technical analyses within your trading arsenal to lead you to better decision making.

Bull Market Dynamics

To understand sentiment and when it is most useful as a guide to trading, brushing up on the dynamics of a bull market is helpful. Because most people can identify with a bull market in stocks best, I use it as an example. Yet, the basic principles apply to just about any bull market in any commodity or financial asset.

The first stage of any bull market is when the market is sold out, and you see short covering, or the offsetting of short positions, which is based on the realization by the pessimists that the bulls are starting to charge. Still, because it's early in the new bull market, the bears tend to hang on, usually buying put options — options that are betting on lower prices — even as they short cover. This in turn creates a nice climate of pessimism, which is reflected in an indicator known as the put/call ratio (I discuss this later in the section "Putting Put/Call Ratios to Good Use").

This rise in pessimism, even though the bottom has been put in place, is known collectively as the "wall of worry." The wall of worry can last a few days or a few weeks. What's important is that at some point, if indeed the rally is strong enough to have launched a new bull run, the bears finally throw in the towel and the put/call ratios, which have risen mostly due to put option buying, start to trail off. It is at that time, when the wall of worry melts away, that the market becomes vulnerable.

Sentiment is most useful as an indicator at market bottoms because the crazy times at market tops can last for very long periods of time and you can miss big moves if you sell too early. See chapter 8 for how to spot market tops by using Bollinger bands.

Survey Says: Trust Your Feelings

Two popular sentiment surveys affect the futures markets: Market Vane and Consensus, Inc.

Consensus, Inc., www.consensus-inc.com, is based in Kansas City and it publishes *Consensus* weekly as a newspaper that you get in the mail or as an Internet publication. *Consensus* offers sentiment data on the following:

- **Precious metals:** Silver, gold, copper, and platinum
- **Financial instruments:** Eurodollars, U.S. dollars, Treasury bills (T-bills), and Treasury bonds (T-bonds)
- **Currencies:** The U.S. dollar, Euro FX, British pound, Deutschemark, Swiss franc, Canadian dollar, and the Japanese yen

- ✔ **Soybean complex:** Soybeans, soybean oil, and soybean meal
- ✔ **Meats:** Pork bellies, hogs, cattle, and feeder cattle
- ✔ **Grains:** Wheat and corn
- ✔ **Stock indexes:** The S&P 500 and NASDAQ 100 stock indexes
- ✔ **Foods:** Citrus fruits, sugar, cocoa, and coffee
- ✔ **Fibers:** Cotton and lumber
- ✔ **Energy complex:** Crude oil, natural gas, gasoline, and heating oil

Market Vane, www.marketvane.net, offers a similar set of measures under the name *Bullish Consensus.* Of the two sentiment surveys, Market Vane's is better known, and according to its Web site, *Bullish Consensus* has been published on a weekly basis since 1964 and on a daily basis since 1988.

Snapshots of both surveys for stocks, bonds, eurodollars, and euro currency are available weekly in *Barron's* magazine, under the Market Laboratory section or at Barron's Online, www.barrons.com.

What you find when reading *Barron's* or another of these publications are percentages of market sentiment, such as oil being 75 percent bulls, or bullish, which simply means that 75 percent of the opinions surveyed by the editors of *Bullish Consensus* or *Consensus* are bullish on oil. Usually such sentiment is interpreted as a sign of caution, but not necessarily as a sign of an impending top.

After you find out the market sentiment, technical analysis kicks in. A high bullish reading in terms of sentiment should alert you to start looking for technical signs that a top is in place, checking whether key support levels or trend lines have been breached, or checking whether the market is struggling to make new highs. See Chapters 7 and 8 for more details on technical analysis.

Sentiment surveys are popular tools used mostly by professional traders to gauge when a particular market is at an extreme point with either too much bullishness or too much bearishness. Their major weakness is that they're now so popular that their ability to truly mark major turning points is not as good as it was even in the late 1980s or early 1990s. Still, when used within the context of good technical and fundamental analysis, sentiment surveys can be useful.

Other particulars that describe the sentiment surveys are that they are

- ✔ Based on advisor polls that are conducted either by reading the latest publications sent to the survey editors or by telephone polling of a group of advisors.
- ✔ Indirect measures of public opinion about the individual markets.

✔ Interpreted as a measure of public opinion because they're based on advisory opinions usually subscribed to by the public. However, market professionals traditionally considered the public to be wrong, especially at market turning points.

Sentiment survey readings must be at extreme levels to be useful. In other words, sentiments below 35 to 40 percent for any given category usually are considered bullish, because few advisors are left to recommend selling.

You can use sentiment surveys as trend-following systems. A market that hits a new high as sentiment is rising along with it — without hitting any cautionary points on the charts — can be taken as a sign that more upside potential exists. Even so, when using sentiment to help guide your decision making, always

✔ Check your charts and other indicators to confirm what the surveys are saying.

✔ Avoid trading on sentiment data alone, because doing so is too risky.

✔ Check sentiment tendencies against technical and fundamental analyses, even though it may make you a little late in executing your entry or exit trades. Making sure is better than missing a significant part of an advance if you're long or a decline if you're short.

Even though the sentiment surveys are not giving you textbook numbers, they nevertheless can be useful. Figure 9-1 highlights a set of key market turning points in the 2004–2005 time period.

Figure 9-1: Key tops and bottoms in the S&P 500 from July 2004 to June 2005 were correctly called by sentiment surveys.

Figure 9-1 shows a good set of tops and bottoms in the stock market in 2004 and 2005. These were nearly textbook examples of how sentiment can be useful.

But, it's not always that clear. Consider this example. The stock market began a rally in August of 2007, although Consensus had a 63 percent bullish percentage and Market Vane had a 56 percent bullish percentage near the time when the market bottomed. Usually, long-lasting bull markets are spawned by much lower readings in the sentiment surveys. These are usually near or below 40 percent bullish percentages, and are known as *sentiment washouts,* meaning that there aren't enough bears around to keep prices down. Markets always follow the path of least resistance, and thus you get a rally.

The rally moved strongly into October, but by October 12, the bullish numbers were at 75 percent and 69 percent respectively. The following week saw the market start to stumble; on October 19, on the 20th anniversary of the Crash of 1987, the Dow Jones Industrial average fell over 300 points.

In fact, the market sentiment numbers in October were correct as that proved to be the top for that rally. For a stock investor with a 12- to 18-month time horizon, the 300-point down day may be seen as a long-term buying opportunity. Yet, as a futures trader, your time frame will more likely be two hours to two weeks. Had you owned stock index futures during this period, you might have taken a big loss if you hadn't been watching a wide array of indicators, including the sentiment surveys.

Keep tabs on Consensus and Market Vane. Watch how low the numbers get with market bottoms. Look for the washout as a sign that the rallies have a chance of lasting longer than a few weeks. And always look to your charts, volume (see the next section), and your other indicators and oscillators as backup.

Considering Volume (And How the Market Feels About It)

Trading volume is a direct, real-time sentiment indicator. As a general rule, high trading volume is a sign that the current trend is likely to continue. But consider that advice as only a guideline. Good volume analysis takes other market indicators into account. Figure 9-2, which shows the S&P 500 e-mini futures contract for September 2005, portrays an interesting relationship between volume, sentiment, and other indicators.

In April, the market made a textbook bottom. Notice how the volume bars at the bottom of the chart rose as the market was reaching a selling climax, as signified by the three large candlesticks, or trading bars. This combination of signals — large price moves and large volumes when the market is falling — is often the prelude to a classic market bottom, because traders are panicking and selling at any price just to get out of their positions.

Figure 9-2:
Volume and the e-mini S&P 500 September 2005 futures.

Notice how the volume trailed off as the market consolidated, or started moving sideways, making a complex bottom that took almost two weeks to form. *Consolidation* is what happens when buyers and sellers are in balance. When markets consolidate, they're catching their breath and getting set up for their next move. Consolidation phases are unpredictable and can last for short periods of time, such as hours or days, or longer periods, even months to years.

A third important volume signal occurred in late May and early June as the market rallied. Notice how volume faded as the market continued to rise. Eventually, the market fell and moved significantly lower as it broke below key trend-line support.

Finally, note in Figure 9-2 that open interest (see the section "Out in the Open with Open Interest," later in this chapter) fell during the last stage of the rally in late June, which usually is a sign that more weakness is likely. This is because fewer contracts remain open, suggesting that traders are getting exhausted and are less willing to hold on to open positions.

Using volume indicators in the futures markets has limitations. The example in Figure 9-2 needs to be viewed within the context of these limitations:

- ✔ The release of volume figures in the futures market is delayed by one day.

- ✔ Higher volume levels steadily migrate toward the closest *delivery month,* or the month in which the contract is settled and delivery of the underlying asset takes place. That migration is important for traders, because the chance of getting a better price for your trade is higher when volume is better. In June, for example, the trading volume is higher in the S&P 500 futures for the September contract than for other months, because September is the next delivery month. Volume for the delivery-month contract increases for a while as traders move their positions to the *front month,* or the commonly quoted (price) contract at the time. Say, for example, that the volume data for June 24, 2005, shows 36,717 contracts traded in the September 2005 contract, 170 in the December 2005 contract, and 21 in the March 2006 contract. None of the other listed contracts had any volume on that day.

- ✔ *Limit days* (especially limit up days), or days in which a particular contract makes a big move in a short period of time, can have very high volume, thus skewing your analysis. A *limit up day,* when the market rises to the limit in a short period of time, usually is a signal of strength in the market. Limit up or limit down days tend to happen in response to a single or related series of events, external or internal, such as a very surprising report. When markets crash, you can see limit down moves that then trigger *trading collars* (periods when the market trades but prices don't change) or complete stoppages of trading.

  The opposite is true when you have a big move on low volume, such as the first of the last two bars pictured in Figure 9-2. On the day of the first break of the rising trend line, volume was lower than in the prior few days. On the second day of selling, volume rose, suggesting that more trouble was coming.

When analyzing volume, be sure that you

- ✔ Put the current volume trends in the proper context with relationship to the market in which you're trading, instead of thinking about hard-and-fast rules. It's important to note that trends tend to either start or end with a volume spike climax (typically twice the 20- or 50-day moving average of daily volume).

- ✔ Remember the differences in the way that volume is reported and interpreted in the futures market compared with the stock market.

- ✔ Check other indicators to confirm what volume is telling you.

> ✔ Ask yourself whether the market is vulnerable to a trend change.
>
> ✔ Consider key support and resistance levels.
>
> ✔ Protect your portfolio by being prepared to make necessary changes.

Out in the Open with Open Interest

Open interest is the number of active contracts for any given security during any trading period. It is the most useful tool for analyzing potential trend reversals in futures markets.

A more formal definition is this: Open interest is the total number of contracts entered into during a specified period of time that have not been liquidated either by offsetting transactions or by actual delivery. Open interest applies to futures and options but not to stocks.

Open interest

✔ Measures the total number of short and long positions (shorts and longs)

✔ Varies based on the number of new traders entering the market and the number of traders leaving the market

✔ Rises by one whenever one new buyer and one new seller enter the market, thus marking the creation of one new contract

✔ Falls by one when a long trader closes out a position with a trader who already has an open short position

In the futures markets, the number of longs always equals the number of shorts. So when a new buyer buys from an old buyer who is cashing in, no change occurs in open interest.

The exchanges publish open-interest figures daily, but the numbers are delayed by one day. Therefore, the volume and open-interest figures on today's quotes are only estimates.

Charting open interest on a daily basis in conjunction with a price chart helps you keep track of the trends in open interest and how they relate to market prices. Barchart.com (www.barchart.com) offers excellent free futures charts that give you a good look at open interest.

Open interest is one of the most useful tools you can have when trading futures. Even though the figures are released with a one-day delay, they still are useful when you evaluate the longer trend of the market.

Rising markets

In a rising trend, open interest is fairly straightforward:

- ✔ **Bullish open interest:** When open interest rises along with prices, it signals that an uptrend is in place and can be sustained. This bullish sign also means that new money is moving into the market.

  Extremely high open interest in a bull market usually is a danger signal.

- ✔ **Bearish open interest:** Rising prices combined with falling open interest signal a short-covering rally in which short sellers are reversing their positions so that their buying actually is pushing prices higher. In this case, higher prices are not likely to last, because no new buyers are entering the market.

- ✔ **Bearish leveling or decline:** A leveling off or decrease in open interest in a rising market often is an early warning sign that a top may be nearing.

Sideways markets

In a sideways market, open interest gets trickier, so you need to watch for the following:

- ✔ Rising open interest during periods when the market is moving sideways (or in a narrow trading range; see Chapter 8) because they usually lead to an intense move after prices break out of the trading range — up or down.

  When dealing with sideways markets, be sure to confirm open-interest signals by checking them against other market indicators.

- ✔ Down-trending price breakouts (breakdowns). Some futures traders use breakouts on the downside to set up short positions, just like commercial and professional traders, thus leaving the public wide open for a major sell-off.

- ✔ Falling open interest in a trader's market. When it happens, traders with weak positions are throwing in the towel, and the pros are covering their short positions and setting up for a market rally.

Falling markets

In falling markets, open-interest signals also are a bit more complicated to decipher:

✔ **Bearish open interest:** Falling prices combined with a rise in open interest indicate that a downtrend is in place and that it's being fueled by new money coming in from short sellers.

✔ **Bullish open interest:** Falling prices combined with falling open interest is a sign that traders who had not sold their positions as the market broke — hoping the market would bounce back — are giving up. In this case, you need to start anticipating, or even expecting, a trend reversal toward higher prices after this give-up phase ends.

✔ **Neutral:** If prices rise or fall, but open interest remains flat, it means that a trend reversal is possible. You can think of these periods as preludes to an eventual change in the existing trend. Neutral open-interest situations are good times to be especially alert.

✔ **Trending down:** A market trend that has shifted downward at the same time open interest is reaching high levels can be a sign that more selling is coming. Traders who bought into the market right before it topped out are now liquidating losing positions to cut their losses.

Flat open interest when prices are rising or falling means that a trend reversal is possible.

Putting Put/Call Ratios to Good Use

The *put/call ratio* is the most commonly used sentiment indicator for trading stocks, but it can also be useful in trading stock index futures, because with it you can pinpoint major inflection points in trader sentiment. Put/call ratios, when at extremes, can be signs of excessive fear (a high level of put buying relative to call buying) and excessive greed (a high level of call buying relative to put buying). However, these indicators are not as useful as they once were because of more sophisticated hedging strategies that are now often used in the markets.

As a futures trader, put/call ratios can help you make several important decisions about

✔ Tightening your stops on open positions

✔ Setting new entry points if you've been out of the market

✔ Setting up hedges

✔ Taking profits

Put/call ratios are best used in conjunction with technical analysis, so you need to look at your charts and take inventory of your own positions during the time frame in which you're trading futures contracts. In other words, a good time to check the put/call ratio is when you have a long position in

S&P 500 Index futures and the stock market has been rising for several weeks, but it's running up against a tough long-term resistance level that it's failed to penetrate a few times during the last few weeks. From your read of the put/call ratio, you can consider which of the four strategies in the previous list you need to use. You can turn this scenario around for a falling market in which you have either a short position or hold put options.

The Chicago Board Options Exchange (CBOE) updates the ratio throughout the day at its Web site, `www.cboe.com/data/IntraDayVol.aspx`, and provides final figures for the day after the market closes.

The sections that follow describe two important ratios with which you need to become familiar when trading stock index futures.

Total put/call ratio

The total put/call ratio is the original indicator introduced by Martin Zweig, a prominent money manager and author who was one of the few traders who sidestepped the market crash of October 1987 and made money by buying put options. The put/call ratio is calculated by using the following equation:

total put options purchased ÷ total call options purchased

The total ratio includes options on stocks, indexes, and long-term options bought by traders on the CBOE. Although you can make sense of this ratio in multiple ways, I've found it useful when the ratio rises above 1.0 and when it falls below 0.5. When the ratio rises above 1.0, it usually means too much fear is in the air and that the market is trying to make a bottom. Readings below 0.5, however, usually mean that too much bullishness is in the air and that the market may fall.

Index put/call ratio

The index put/call ratio is a good measure of what futures and options players, institutions, and hedge-fund managers are up to. When this indicator is above 2.0, it traditionally is a bullish sign, but when it falls below 0.9, it becomes bearish and traditionally signals that some kind of correction is coming. Because these numbers are not as reliable in the traditional sense as they used to be, please consider them only as reference points, and never base any trades on them alone. Don't forget that put/call ratios need to be correlated with chart patterns.

In June 2005, the CBOE index put/call ratio was high during the period from June 17–23, which included an options expiration week. During those five trading sessions, three readings of the index put/option ratio were above 2.00; the highest reading of 2.75 occurred on June 21. If you had taken these numbers at face value, you probably would have gone aggressively long, expecting a likely rise in stock index futures. Unfortunately, you would have been wrong!

On June 23 and 24, the Dow Jones Industrial Average lost more than 290 points, and the rest of the market got clobbered, too. Hindsight obviously tells you that in this case, the rising put/call ratio was a signal that somebody, or a group of people somewhere, was aware of information that something interesting might happen that could shake the markets.

Common knowledge tells you that many people with lots of money have access to information to which you and I would never be privy and that we'd never be able to gather. The job of the trader is to look for signs that something may be brewing.

And there it was — on Thursday, June 23, China's third largest oil company, CNOOC, bid $18 billion to purchase American oil company Unocal. The political firestorm kicked off by this event certainly gave players a reason to sell stocks.

Put/call ratios, like all sentiment indicators, are best used as alert mechanisms for potential trend changes, not so much as the primary indicators on which you base key decisions. Traditionally, high ratios tend to signal that a great deal of pessimism exists in the markets and that the markets should move higher. However, the truth is that in current markets, where hedge funds and large institutions always are running complex derivative strategies, high put/call ratios can be misleading.

Don't ignore abnormal put/call ratio readings. Doing so can cost you significant amounts of money in a hurry. As a result, take the following actions apart from your daily routine:

- ✔ **Check the put/call ratios after the market closes.** The CBOE usually updates the numbers by 5 p.m. central time.

- ✔ **Favor thoughts of dramatic market reactions over thoughts of where the market is headed when you see abnormally high or low put/call ratios.** Be ready to handle dramatic changes.

- ✔ **Immediately look for weak spots in your portfolio whenever abnormal activity occurs in the options market.** Abnormal activity should trigger ideas about hedging.

When you see abnormal put/call ratio numbers, consider the following:

- ✔ Tightening stops on your open stock index futures positions.

- ✔ Look for ways to hedge your portfolio. Some hedges include option strategies, while others include buying or selling short positions in other markets, such as bonds, energy, or metals.

- ✔ Reversing positions. If you have a short position in the market, make sure that you're ready to reverse and go long or vice versa if you have a long position.

Understanding the Relationship Between Open Interest and Volume

Table 9-1 summarizes the relationship between volume and open interest. Figure 9-2 (earlier in this chapter) shows a great example of how to combine open interest and volume to predict a trend change.

Volume and open interest go hand in hand in futures trading. Generally, volume and open interest need to be heading in the same direction as the market. When the market starts rising, for example, you want to see volume and open interest expanding. A rising market with shrinking volume and falling open interest usually is one that is heading for a correction.

Table 9-1	The Relationship Between Volume and Open Interest		
Price	*Volume*	*Open Interest*	*Market*
Rising	Up	Up	Strong
Rising	Down	Down	Weak
Declining	Up	Up	Weak
Declining	Down	Down	Strong

Note in Figure 9-2 how the market started to rally in early June. Both volume and open interest (the line coursing above the volume bars) moved up. This chart confirmed the rising trend in the E-mini S&P futures.

After June 13, however, the market started going sideways. Volume began to fade, and open interest began to flatten out. Three days before the June 24 break, open interest fell precipitously, signaling that the rally was running out of gas. Fading volume provided a great example of how smart money was taking profits and being replaced by new, weaker buyers. Likewise, falling open interest not only confirmed an impending downturn, but it also revealed that traders with weak short positions were bailing out. The market thus was losing buyers and sellers and its liquidity, which, in turn, made it vulnerable to external events, such as the CNOOC/Unocal news.

When you plugged in rising put/call ratios with falling open interest in stock futures, the result was a sign that the smart money sensed a rising risk in the market. It was preparing itself by buying portfolio insurance in the form of put options, which rise in price during falling markets. *Smart money* refers to large institutions, hedge funds, or individuals. They have better access to information than the market at times, and they tend to act ahead of the crowd. Sometimes they're correct, and other times they're wrong. In this example, they were correct.

Using Soft Sentiment Signs

Soft sentiment signs usually are out of the mainstream and are subtle, non-quantitative factors that most people tend to ignore. They can be anything from the shoeshine boy giving stock tips or a wild magazine cover (classic signs of a top) to people jumping out of windows during a market crash (a classic sign of the other extreme). These signs can be anywhere from dramatic to humorous, and they can be quite useful. By no means should you make them a mainstay of your trading strategy. But they can at times be helpful.

Scanning magazine covers and Web site headlines

Based on my 1990 experience with *BusinessWeek* and the top in oil prices, every time crude oil rallies, I start looking for crazy headlines, especially on the Drudge Report. The Drudge Report (www.drudgereport.com) is a Web site that can be, in my opinion, somewhat sensational, but still the old-school indicators found there can be useful.

Look for clearly sensational headlines, such as those depicting the potential end of an era, and so on. Some of the ones that appeared on Drudge in March 2008, as oil made all time highs were:"'Bush: US Must "Get Off Oil"' from Reuters and "Swarm of Bay Area gas price records" from the *San Francisco Chronicle.*

When crude oil reached a then all-time high on June 17, 2005, I scanned the covers of *Time, Newsweek,* and *BusinessWeek. Time's* cover featured the late Mao TseTung, *BusinessWeek* had senior citizens, and *Newsweek* had dinosaurs. None of them even mentioned oil — a good soft sentiment sign that the oil market still had some room to rise.

Monitoring congressional investigations and activist protests

Another soft sign that a top may be near is what politicians and activists say or do in relation to how the markets move. So, as oil made a new high in 2005, I scanned the news for signs of senators and other members of Congress or of activists who were calling for investigations or alleging that the oil companies were price gouging.

It took a while, but by the end of June, with Congress in full swing, the attempted takeover of Unocal mobilized both sides of the aisle. Letters to President Bush were written. Hearings were held at which Fed Chairman Alan Greenspan and Treasury Secretary John Snow argued about China's newly found role as a world power and what the circumstances would likely be. The markets worried about protectionism, as well they should — the last depression in the United States came as a result of Congress and President Herbert Hoover concocting the Smoot-Hawley tariff.

As a contrarian, you must understand that the public going wild over an issue can be a sign that a major turning point is on the way in the market. Politicians and activists are no different these days, except that their lives usually are not touched by reality the same way yours and mine are. They start talking about something that you and I have experienced for months only after they've read a new poll or received lots of letters and phone calls from their constituents about the subject.

Political activity and outrage are no accident. They usually mean that the public is interested in the current set of developments. The thing is, when politicians and activists finally pick up the chant, they do so because they see some kind of advantage for their cause or their chances of being reelected. And that's usually a sign that things are at a fever pitch, and the trend can change, possibly in a hurry.

Don't hurry. Just because your initial scan of the news fails to reveal key findings doesn't mean that those events are not on the way. People in Washington sometimes take days to catch on to what's going on elsewhere. Keep looking, especially when the market is moving in the same direction.

Developing Your Own Sentiment Indicators

A hot market eventually changes trends. It gets cold. No one knows when that's going to happen. By using sentiment indicators and confirming one with another, you can get early warnings of pending changes.When any market makes a new high, I usually go to the Drudge Report and look for the headline. If it's sensational enough, I start being careful about that particular area of the market. Here are my favorite personal indicators:

- ✔ If I start bragging to my wife about how much money I'm making in the markets, I look for reasons to sell.
- ✔ When my mother tells me that I need to start watching the NASDAQ the way she did in the summer of 1999, I start to shake in my boots.

When everybody starts giving me tips, I run for the door. You can develop your own private set of indicators by monitoring your own excitement level. If you start feeling invincible, as if you're the best trader in the world, being a little more careful is a good idea. Make a mental checklist. I always check my gut when I trade. If I'm all tied up in knots, I'm less concerned than if I'm happy as a lark, because if I'm worried, I'm awake. Mind you, don't make yourself sick over it. If you can't stand what you're doing, then it isn't for you. The key is to search for some kind of balance within yourself by keeping your eyes open, doing your homework, and comparing what's going on in the charts with what you're reading and hearing from others.

Part III
Financial Futures

"Oh Martin, you scared me half to death! Next time let me know when you're picking a new stock."

In this part . . .

This part is where you get into the big money, starting with interest-rate futures, going international with the currency markets, and taking stock of stock index futures. These three markets are the focal point of all trading, and they often set the tone for the trading day in all markets because they form a hub for the global financial system. What's good about these markets is that they're great places for you to get started in futures trading, so I provide you with tips for doing just that.

Chapter 10

Wagging the Dog: Interest Rate Futures

....

In This Chapter

▶ Centering on bonds

▶ Comparing the full spectrum of interest rates

▶ Managing price risks by trading interest-rate futures

▶ Trading short-term interest in Eurodollars and T-bills

▶ Trading longer-term interest-rate futures

....

*T*he bond market rules the world. Everything that anyone does in the financial markets anymore is built upon interest-rate analysis. When interest rates are on the rise, at some point, doing business becomes difficult, and when interest rates fall, eventually economic growth is energized.

That relationship between rising and falling interest rates makes the markets in interest-rate futures, Eurodollars, and Treasuries (bills, notes, and bonds) important for all consumers, speculators, economists, bureaucrats, and politicians.

This chapter provides you with a detailed and useful introduction to a snapshot of how you can structure your analysis and trading in these major instruments, but it isn't meant to be an all-inclusive treatise on interest rates and trading techniques.

Globalization is here to stay. At the center of the globalization phenomenon is the entity known as the bond market. As a futures trader, you are likely to deal mostly, but not exclusively, with the U.S. Treasury bond futures. However, over the next 10 or 20 years, or perhaps sooner, the European bond market, and more than likely bond markets in Dubai and China, will play significant roles in the global economy. (See "Globalizing the markets," later in this chapter.)

Bonding with the Universe

At the center of the world's financial universe is the bond market. And at the center of the bond market is its relationship with the United States Federal Reserve (the Fed) and the way the Fed conducts interest-rate policies.

By law, the Fed's two main functions are

- ✔ Creating and maintaining conditions that keep inflation in check
- ✔ Maintaining full employment

Full employment is viewed by some as being potentially inflationary because it creates a scenario of too much money chasing too few goods and services — a primal definition of *inflation* that's not far from also defining capitalism.

Inflation decreases the return on bondholders' investments, acting the way sunlight does to a vampire. When you buy a bond, you get a fixed return, as long as you hold that bond until it matures or, in the case of some corporate or municipal bonds, until it's called in. If you're getting a 5 percent return on your bond investment and inflation is growing at a 6 percent clip, you're already 1 percent in the hole, which is why bond traders hate inflation.

The connection between the bond market, the Federal Reserve, and the rest of the financial markets is fundamental to understanding how to trade futures and how to invest in general. In the next section, I discuss the most important aspects of how it all works together.

Looking at the Fed and bond-market roles

The Fed cannot directly control the long-term bond rates that determine how easy (or difficult) it is to borrow money to buy a new home or to finance long-term business projects. What the Fed can and does do is adjust short-term interest rates, such as the interest rate on *Fed funds,* the overnight lending rate used by banks to square their books, and the *discount rate,* or the rate at which the Fed loans money to banks to which no one else will lend money.

As the Fed senses that inflationary pressures are rising through analyzing key economic reports, such as consumer prices, producer prices, the employment report, and its own Beige Book (see Chapter 6), it starts to raise interest rates. The Fed usually raises the Fed funds target rate, which focuses on overnight deposits between banks. Occasionally, when the Fed wants to make a point that it's in a hurry to make rates rise, it also raises the *discount rate,* the rate that the Fed charges banks to borrow at its discount window, which usually is a loan of last resort for banks and a signal to the Fed that the individual bank is in trouble. When the Fed raises the Fed funds and/or the discount rates, banks usually raise the *prime rate,* the rate that targets their best customers. At the same time, credit-card companies raise their rates.

As the bond market senses inflationary pressures are rising, bond traders sell bonds and market interest rates rise. Rising market interest rates usually trigger rate increases for mortgages and car loans, which usually are tied to a bond market benchmark rate. For example, most 30-year mortgages are tied to the interest rate for the U.S. one-year Treasury note. I know that sounds confusing, but that's the way these things are structured.

When it comes down to recognizing when inflation is lurking, sometimes the bond market takes action ahead of the Fed, but other times the Fed is ahead of the market. Sometimes the bond market senses inflation before the Fed does. When that happens, bond prices fall, market rates rise (such as the yield on the U.S. ten-year T-note), and the Fed raises rates if its indicators agree with the bond market's analysis. Whenever the Fed disagrees with the markets, it signals those disagreements usually through speeches from Fed governors or even the chairman of the Fed. Interest rates are a two-way street: The bond market sometimes disagrees with the Fed, and the Fed sometimes disagrees with the market.

Disagreements between the Fed and the bond market usually occur at the beginning or at the end of a trend in interest rates. Say, for example, that the Fed continually raises interest rates for an extended period of time. At some point, long-term rates, which are controlled by the bond market, begin to drop, even though short-term rates are on the rise. Falling long-term bond rates usually are a sign from the bond market to the Fed that the Fed needs to consider pausing its interest-rate increases. The opposite also is true: When the Fed goes too far in lowering short-term rates, bond yields begin to creep up and signal the need for the Fed to consider a pause in its lowering of the rates.

The Federal Reserve lowers interest rates in response to signs of a slowing economy. Two dramatic examples came in the period after the 9/11 attacks on the World Trade Center, when the central bank lowered interest rates dramatically. The first one came immediately after the attacks when the Federal Reserve lowered interest rates aggressively starting on September 17, 2001, with the Fed Funds rate reaching an all time low at 1 percent.

Another example, one in which the Fed acted with some nuance, came in 2007. The nuance came in the Fed's clear delineation between its use of the discount rate and the Fed Funds rate, something that the central bank had not done in recent times to any extent.

In this case, the Fed used the discount rate, which is meant to target the banking sector rather than the consumer sector. In August 2007, the Fed lowered the discount rate alone, as it was trying to encourage banks to borrow from the discount window during the subprime mortgage crisis.

The Fed then lowered the Fed Funds rate and the discount rate a second time on September 18 and continued to lower them into 2008 as the U.S. economy continued to show signs of slowing. In January and February 2008, the U.S. employment report actually showed job losses, usually a sign of major trouble in the economy. See chapter 6 for more on the importance of the employment report in the U.S.

The Fed aimed its August discount rate cut by saying that the purpose of the change in the rate was to "promote the restoration of orderly conditions in financial markets, to which end the Federal Reserve Board approved temporary changes to its primary credit discount window facility."

In the statement announcing the Fed Funds rate and the second discount rate cut, the Fed noted, "Today's action is intended to help forestall some of the adverse effects on the broader economy that might otherwise arise from the disruptions in financial markets and to promote moderate growth over time."

The bond market responded to the Fed's initial discount rate move with a nice rally. But the second move, because it came with a Fed Funds rate cut, led to a decline in the bond market, raising interest rates. By October, though, the bond market had started to rally again, as signs of a weakening economy, and thus the potential for a decline in inflation, began to surface.

Hedging in general terms

In general, *hedging* is taking a position in the market that's in the opposite direction of a trading position you've already established; it's a form of insurance against a reversal of trends. You need to know what the opposition is doing anyway so that you're better able to make your market move. In the world of short-term interest rates, aside from speculators, the big money comes from money-market funds and corporations.

Generally, money-market fund managers and corporate traders go long or short in the direction that's opposite their borrowing or lending. Borrowers generally want to hedge against rising interest rates, so they tend to short the market. That way, if interest rates rise, they either reduce their future interest-rate costs or actually profit from the situation.

Money-market funds and corporations borrow and lend millions of dollars on a daily basis, so the short-term interest-rate market, especially in Eurodollars and related contracts, is the way they hedge their exposure. Here's how hedging works for the various participants:

- ✔ **Lenders:** Banks and other lending institutions want to hedge against falling interest rates, so they tend to be long on the market. They know that they'll be lending money to someone in the future, and if interest rates continue to fall, their profits will be reduced accordingly. By using futures strategies, they lessen the impact of having to charge less interest and thus help curtail potential future losses.

Institutions decrease their risk when they sense that rates are going to fall by establishing long positions in bonds, T-bills, or Eurodollar futures contracts in order to protect their future earnings. The money that they make when they sell their contracts goes to the bank's bottom line, balancing revenue lost from lending to customers at lower interest rates. This strategy is by no means perfect, but if the institution does it correctly, it at least cushions the blow.

✔ **Corporate treasurers:** These big-money institutions use sophisticated formulas based on the need to protect their cash flow and future expenses. They also hedge against the risk of adverse international and geopolitical events and against nonpayment by high-risk customers by using the short- and long-term interest-rate futures markets.

For example, say you're the chief financial officer at an international paper products company that has multiple risks, such as the price of lumber and pulp to make paper and related products and a large customer base in Latin America, meaning that political instability is a major factor you must consider when running your business. By using lumber futures and currency hedges and by varying your strategies based on market conditions and analysis, you can decrease the risk of material shortages and political instability to your company's earnings.

✔ **Speculators:** Traders just like you and me always want to trade with the trend, which is why technical analysis (see Chapter 7) is so helpful in futures trading. By the time a tick is printed on a chart, it's as good of a snapshot as there is for all hedging and speculating that has taken place up to that instant in time.

Speculators generally trade on the long side when a particular market is rising and then go short when the market is falling. Speculative hedging techniques often involve setting up option strategies that are the opposite of established trading positions, such as buying stock index put options on the S&P 500 to hedge a long S&P position.

The same is true when you have a short position. In that case, speculators may buy call options on the S&P 500 or other stock index futures such as the E-mini.

In a flat market, a speculator can write S&P 500 calls to hedge the same long position. And you can use intermarket trades. I discuss the basics of the options markets in Chapter 4. For example, if you have a long dollar position and you're not sure that the market is topping out, but you're not quite ready to sell your position, you can consider buying a gold call option because gold tends to rise when the dollar falls. (For more about speculating strategies, see Chapter 8.)

Globalizing the markets

Globalization, or essentially the spread of capitalism around the world, has increased the number of short-term interest-rate contracts that trade at the Chicago Mercantile Exchange (CME) and around the world. Although details of market globalization are not the focus of this chapter, you nevertheless need to know that these contracts exist and that the volume of trades at times is just as heavy in Eurodollars as it is in T-bills.

In fact, just about every country in the world with a convertible currency has some kind of bond or bond futures contract that trades on an exchange somewhere around the world. The following are not complete lists, but they offer snapshots of some of the more liquid contracts.

Short-term global plays include the following:

- ✔ **Fed funds futures:** Fed funds futures trade on the CME and are an almost pure bet on what the Federal Reserve is expected to do with future interest rates. Fed funds measure interest rates that private banks charge each other for overnight loans of excess reserves. These inter-bank loans usually are intended to square or balance the books of the banks involved. The rates often are quoted in the media. Each Fed funds contract lets you control $5 million and is cash settled. The tick size as described by the Chicago Board of Trade (CBOT) is "$20.835 per ½ of one basis point (½ of $\frac{1}{100}$ of 1 percent of $5 million on a 30-day basis rounded up to the nearest cent)." Margins are variable, depending on the tier in which you trade, and they range from $304 to $1350 and $225 to $1000 respectively, for initial and maintenance margins. A tier is just a time frame. The longer the time frame before expiration, the higher the margin. For full information, you can visit the CBOT's margin page at www.cbot.com/cbot/pub/page/0,3181,2142,00.html#1b. Fed funds contracts are quoted in terms of the rate that the market is speculating on by the time the contract expires, and they're based on the formula found at the CBOT: "100 minus the average daily Fed funds overnight rate for the delivery month (for example, a 7.25 percent rate equals 92.75)."

- ✔ **LIBOR futures:** These futures are one-month, interest-rate contracts based on the London Interbank-Offered Rate (LIBOR), the interest rate charged between commercial banks. LIBOR futures have 12 monthly listings. Each contract is worth $3 million. The role of LIBOR futures is to offer professionals a way to hedge their interest portfolio in a similar fashion to that offered by Eurodollars. The minimum increment of price movement is "0.0025 (¼ tick = $6.25) for all contracts. The major difference: Margin requirements are less for LIBOR, at $743 for initial and $550 for margin maintenance, compared with margins of $-1013 and $750 for respective Eurodollar contracts. A good way for a new trader to decide between the highly liquid and popular Eurodollar and LIBOR contracts — which offer essentially the same type of trading opportunities — is to paper trade both contracts after doing some homework on how each contract trades.

The LIBOR contract was very important for traders and hedgers in 2007, as the initial liquidity problems from the subprime mortgage crisis occurred in Europe. Because of the LIBOR contract, both sides — hedgers and speculators — were able to profit or to some degree protect their own side of the ledger.

It's easy to be put off by the large amounts of money that are held in futures contracts, such as the $3 million in a LIBOR contract. No matter what contract you trade, though, you need to think in terms of short holding periods, especially if the position is moving against you. Consider how much you may actually have to pay up (if you're long) if you don't sell before the contract rolls over (the amount specified by the contract — $3 million). Small traders usually trade Eurodollars, while pros with large sums and more experience tend to trade LIBOR. See the section "Playing the Short End of the Curve: Eurodollars & T-Bills," later in this chapter.

✓ **Euroyen contracts:** These contracts represent Japanese yen deposits held outside of Japan. Open positions in these contracts can be held at CME or at the SIMEX exchange in Singapore. Euroyen contracts are listed quarterly, trade monthly, and offer expiration dates as far out as three years. That long-term time frame can be useful to professional hedgers with specific expectations about the future.

✓ **CETES futures:** These 28-day and 91-day futures contracts are based on Mexican Treasury bills. These instruments are denominated and paid in Mexican pesos, and they reflect the corresponding benchmark rates of interest rates in Mexico.

Longer-term global plays include Eurobond futures. The Eurobond market is composed of bonds issued by the Federal Republic of Germany and the Swiss Confederation that usually are the second most traded bond futures contracts in volume after the U.S. Treasury bonds. On some days, however, they can trade larger volumes than U.S. Treasuries.

Eurobonds come in four different categories: Euro Schatz, Euro Bobl, Euro Bund, and Euro Buxl. The duration on each respective category is 1.75 years, 4.5 to 5.5 years, 8.5 to 10.5 years, and 24 to 35 years. The contract size is for 100,000 euros or 100,000 Swiss francs, depending on the issuer. Eurobonds can be traded in the United States. The basic strategies are similar to U.S. bonds because they trade on economic fundamentals and inflationary expectations, and they respond to European economic reports similar to the way U.S. bonds respond to U.S. reports.

Some particulars about Eurobond futures:

- ✔ Foreigners hold half of all Euro Bunds.

- ✔ Euro Bunds are the most active Eurobond contract traded at the totally electronic Eurex Exchange in Frankfurt.

- ✔ Both Euro-Schatz and Euro-Bobl contracts rank in the top ten of all futures contracts in global trading volume.

Yielding to the Curve

The *yield curve* is a representation on a graph that compares the entire spectrum of interest rates available to investors. Figures 10-1 and 10-2, respectively, are excellent illustrations of the U.S. Treasury yield curve and rate structure at a time when inflationary expectations are under control and the economy is growing steadily. The curve and the table are from July 1, 2005, just 2 days after the Federal Reserve raised interest rates for the ninth consecutive time in a 12-month period.

Figure 10-2 depicts a standard, table-style snapshot of all market maturities for the U.S. Treasury. You can view a good yield curve daily in *Investor's Business Daily,* either in its digital newspaper or the newsstand version.

As you review Figures 10-1 and 10-2, notice the following:

- ✔ **The longer the maturity, the higher the yield:** That relationship is normal for interest-paying securities, because you're lending your money to someone for an extended period of time, and you want them to pay you a premium for the extra risk.

- ✔ **The yield on all securities rose:** Starting with the 3-month Treasury bill (T-bill) and ending with the 30-year bond, all yields rose, compared with the previous week and month, after the Fed raised interest rates. That's because the Federal Open Market Committee (FOMC), in remarks made after announcing the most recent rate increase in the Fed funds rate, told the market that inflation was controlled, but economic growth still warranted a "measured" pace of continuing interest-rate increases. To a bond trader, that meant that the Fed would continue raising interest rates until it otherwise saw fit, and it meant that the economic perceptions of the bond market and the Fed were in agreement.

Had the bond market disagreed with the Fed, yields for longer-term maturities would have fallen, because the bond market would be signaling to the Fed that the economy was starting to slow and that it (the Fed) needed to consider taking a pause or even ending its rate hikes.

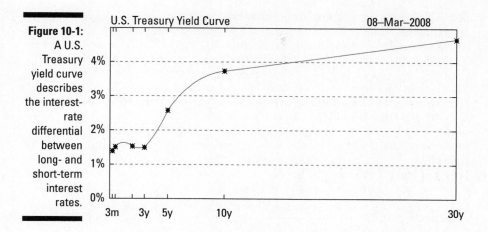

Figure 10-1:
A U.S.
Treasury
yield curve
describes
the interest-
rate
differential
between
long- and
short-term
interest
rates.

Figure 10-2:
A U.S.
Treasury
summary
shows all
the common
maturity
listings and
the price
changes.

US Treasury Bonds

Maturity	Yield	Yesterday	Last Week	Last Month
3 Month	1.35	1.27	1.71	2.00
6 Month	1.48	1.52	1.71	2.02
2 Year	1.50	1.50	1.62	1.95
3 Year	1.46	1.46	1.60	1.93
5 Year	2.42	2.46	2.47	2.66
10 Year	3.52	3.58	3.51	3.60
30 Year	4.54	4.56	4.40	4.36

Deciding Your Time Frame

From a trader's standpoint, you want to consider trading the short term, the intermediate term, or the long term.

Each position has its own time, place, and reasoning, ranging from how much money you have to trade to your individual risk tolerance, and whether your analysis leads you to think that the particular area of the curve can move during any particular period of time.

A quick-and-dirty rule of thumb is that the longer the maturity, the greater the potential reaction to good or bad news on inflation. In other words, the farther out you go on the curve, the greater the chance for volatility.

Eurodollars are the best instrument for trading the short term, because they are liquid investments, meaning that they're easy to buy and sell because the market has a large number of participants. The opposite of a liquid market is a thin market, in which the number of participants tends to be smaller, the spread between bid and offer prices tends to be farther apart, and the potential for volatility is larger. Grain markets can be thin markets (see Chapter 16). For long- and intermediate-term trading, you can use the 10-year T-note and 30-year T-bond futures.

Eurodollars are well suited for small traders, because margin requirements tend to be smaller, and the movements can be less volatile; however, don't consider those attractive factors a guarantee of success by any means. Any futures contract can be a quick road to ruin if you become careless.

Ten-year T-note and T-bond futures can be quite volatile, because large traders and institutions usually use them for direct trading and for complicated hedging strategies.

You can use options and exchange-traded mutual funds (ETFs) for trading all of these interest-rate products by applying the basic options and ETF rules and strategies described in Chapters 4 and 5.

Shaping the curve

Several informative shapes can be seen on the yield curve. Three important ones are

- ✔ **Normal curves:** The *normal curve* rises to the right, and short-term interest rates are lower than long-term interest rates. Pretty simple, eh? Economists usually look at this kind of movement as a sign of normal economic activity, where growth is ongoing and investors are being rewarded for taking more risks by being given extra yield in longer-term maturities.

- ✔ **Flat curves:** A *flat curve* is when short-term yields are equal or close to long-term yields. This type of graph can be a sign that the economy is slowing down, or that the Federal Reserve has been raising short-term rates.

- ✔ **Inverted curves:** An *inverted curve* shows long-term rates falling below short-term rates, which can happen when the market is betting on a slowing of the economy or during a financial crisis when traders are flocking to the safety of long-term U.S. Treasury bonds.

Checking out the yield curve

By keeping track of the yield curve, you're achieving several goals that Mark Powers describes in *Starting Out In Futures Trading* (Probus Publishing). By checking out the yield curve, you can

✔ Focus on the cash markets. Doing so enables you to put activity in the futures markets in perspective and provides clues to the relationships among prices in the futures markets.

✔ Watch for prices rising or falling below the yield curve, indications that can be good opportunities to buy or sell a security.

✔ Know that prices above the yield curve point to a relatively underpriced market.

✔ Know that prices below the curve point to a relatively overpriced market.

Getting the Ground Rules of Interest-Rate Trading

Interest-rate futures serve one major function. They enable large institutions to neutralize or manage their price risks.

As an investor or speculator who trades interest-rate futures, you look at the markets differently than banks and other commercial borrowers. The interest-rate market is a way for them to hedge their risk, but for you, it's a way to make money based on the system's inefficiencies, which often are created by the current relationships among large hedgers, the Fed, and other major players, such as foreign governments.

A perfect example of an inefficient market is when a large corporation wants to sell a big bundle of bonds but can't seem to find buyers. When this happens, the corporation is forced to offer a higher yield for its paper. This situation can spread into the treasury markets, as the lack of interest for the corporate offering raises the yields on the corporate bond package. At some point the yield may become attractive enough to attract buyers. Yet, in some instances treasury prices may fall and yields rise as some players sell treasury bonds to raise money to buy the corporate bonds because they offer a higher interest rate.

That kind of situation arises occasionally and can create volatility in both the corporate and treasury bond markets. Sometimes, these short-term gyrations can offer entry points into the treasury futures bond market on the long or the short side, depending, of course, on the prevailing market and the price trends at the time.

Generally, you want to watch for the following:

- ✔ Opportunities to trade the long-term issues when interest rates are falling
- ✔ Opportunities to sell bonds short when the prevailing tone is toward higher interest rates

Nevertheless, regardless of rules or general tendencies of markets, focusing on what's happening at the moment and trading what you see are important guidelines to follow.

When trading international interest-rate contracts, you must consider the effects of currency conversion. If you just made a 10 percent profit trading Eurobunds but the euro fell 10 percent, your purchasing power has not grown.

When getting ready to trade, make sure that you do the following:

- ✔ Calculate your margin requirements. Doing so enables you to know how much of a cushion for potential losses you have available before you get a margin call and are required to put up more money to keep a position open. Never put yourself in a position to receive a margin call.
- ✔ Price in how much of your account's equity you plan to risk before you make your trade.
- ✔ Canvass your charts so that you know support and resistance levels on each of the markets that you plan to trade, and then you can set your entry points above or below those levels, depending, of course, on which way the market breaks.
- ✔ Be ready for trend reversals. Although you need to trade with the trend, you also must be ready for reversals, especially when the market appears to be comfortable with its current trend.
- ✔ Understand what the economic calendar has in store on any given day. Knowing the potential for economic indicators of the day to move the market in either direction prepares you for the major volatility that can occur on the day they're released.
- ✔ Pick your entry and exit points, including your worst-loss scenario — the possibility of taking a margin call.
- ✔ Decide what your options are if your trade goes well and you have a significant profit to deal with.

Playing the Short End of the Curve: Eurodollars & T-Bills

When you trade the short end of the curve, you're using Eurodollars, T-bills, LIBOR, or short-term Eurobond futures as your trading vehicle.

Treasury bills and Eurodollars are not the same thing, although they are expressions of short-term interest rates and trade in the same direction. You can lose money trading T-bill futures, just as you can when you trade Eurodollar futures.

Eurodollar basics

A *Eurodollar* is a dollar-denominated deposit held in a non-U.S. bank. A Eurodollar contract gives you control of $1 million Eurodollars and is a reflection of the LIBOR rate for a three-month, $1-million offshore deposit. Eurodollars are popular trading instruments that have been around since 1981. Following are some facts about Eurodollars that you need to know:

- A *tick* is the unit of movement for all futures contracts, but in the case of Eurodollars, a point = one tick = 0.1 = $25. If you own a Eurodollar contract, and it falls or rises four ticks, or 0.4, you either lose or gain $100, respectively. Eurodollars can trade in ¼ or ½ points, which are worth $6.25 and $12.50, respectively.

- Eurodollar prices are a central rate in global business and are quoted in terms of an index. For example, if the price on the futures contract is $9,200, the yield is 8 percent.

- Eurodollars trade on the CME with contract listings in March, June, September, and December. Different Eurodollar futures contracts suit different time frames. Some enable you to trade more than two years from the current date. This kind of long-term betting on short-term interest rates is rare, but sometimes large corporations use it. For full details, it's always good to check with your broker about which contracts are available, or go to the CME Web site.

- Trading hours for Eurodollars are from 7:20 a.m. to 2:00 p.m. central time on the trading floor, but they can be traded almost 24/7 on *Globex,* the electronic trading home of a large variety of futures contracts. For Eurodollars, Globex is shut down only between 4 and 5 p.m. nightly.

- The *initial maintenance margins* for trading Eurodollars in March 2008 would be $1,013 and $750, respectively.

Trading Eurodollars

Eurodollars are the most popular futures trading contract in the world, because they offer reasonably low margins and the potential for fairly good return in a short period of time.

You want to trade Eurodollars when events are occurring that are likely to influence interest rates. If you grasp the concept of trading Eurodollars, you're also set to trade other types of interest-rate futures, as long as you understand that each individual contract is going to have its own special quirks and idiosyncrasies. The CME has an excellent education section on its Web site at www.cme.com/edu/.

If you trade interest-rate futures, here are some basic factors to keep in mind:

✔ Check the overall trend of the market.

✔ Consider whether the market is oversold or overbought.

✔ Decide how much you're willing to risk before you enter the trade.

✔ Look at the overall background for the trade you're going to execute before doing so.

Picking your spot to trade

A good opportunity for trading Eurodollars futures was the week ending July 1, 2005, when the economic calendar was heavy in terms of the number of releases and their importance regarding what the Fed was likely to do next with interest rates. Included on the calendar, the Fed had a two-day meeting scheduled at which it was widely expected to raise interest rates.

Aside from the Fed's announcement on interest rates the afternoon of June 30, the economic calendar featured two particularly tradable reports on July 1: the University of Michigan Consumer Sentiment Index and the Institute for Supply Management (ISM — purchasing manager's) report. Each is a key barometer of activity for a major cog in the economic food chain.

The Fed raised interest rates on June 30 and told the markets that they could expect them to be raising rates again in the future. Economic reports all showed signs of a strengthening economy. And the markets were poised for such a set of developments.

Figure 10-3 shows three months' worth of trading in the July 2005 Eurodollar contract. Note that the price break below the moving average on the far right, correctly predicted a fall in prices. Also note the overall downtrend in the Eurodollar during the three-month period, which is a sign of rising interest rates. The implied (interest) rate for this contract at the close on July 1 was 3.6175 percent, up from 3.40 in May. You can calculate the implied rate by subtracting the contract price from 100, as described in the earlier "Globalizing the markets" section.

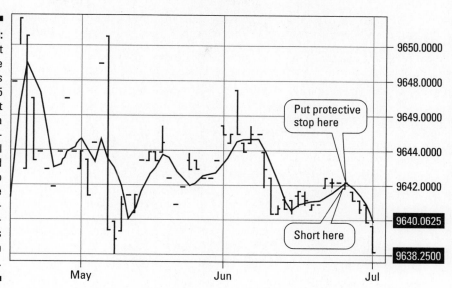

Figure 10-3: A chart of the Eurodollar's July 2005 contract illustrates a good opportunity to sell short and how to calculate implied contract interest rates based on prices.

You want to trade with the trend, so the path of least resistance in this trade was to go short. (See Chapters 7, 8, and 19 for more information about going short.)

Eurodollars trade almost around the clock, so great gains from a good intraday session can be wiped out or significantly reduced if a major event happens overnight. All futures that trade on Globex or other electronic round-the-clock systems are affected in the same way.

Managing your trade

Assume for a moment that you shorted one contract when the price slipped below the four-day moving average on June 27 so that your order was filled at the close of the regular session at 9642. To protect yourself and cover your short position, you put a buy stop five ticks above the moving average, at 9647, thus limiting your loss to $125 above the crossover price. Thereafter, you adjust the stop on a daily basis to protect your gains based on your risk tolerance. In this example, I use broad numbers, but you need to set your stop in a way that you don't risk a margin call if the trade goes against you. In other words, in this trade, your losses need to be limited to no more than $245 (roughly a ten-tick loss), because a $245 loss will get you a margin call if all you have to start with is the minimum margin of $945 (your account equity would have dropped to $700).

Setting your stop a good distance from the margin call is a good idea, though, to allow some leeway in case the market moves fast against you. The more room between your stop and the margin call, the better off you are. The more you trade, the more you'll develop a sense of what your risk tolerance is.

A stop is not a guarantee that you'll get out of a position at the point specified by your stop-loss order. Sometimes you get the closest price to the stop, depending on market conditions. See Chapter 3 for a review of different types of orders.

The trade that I describe in this section is a high-risk and purely hypothetical trade that's intended only to illustrate how to manage your margin and how the Eurodollar market works. You should never trade any futures contract unless you have enough equity in your account to do so, which in this case you don't.

As a general rule, you should never risk any more than 5 percent of your equity on any one trade with a small account. The bare minimum requirement for trading futures as an individual small speculator is widely accepted to be no less than $20,000, although $5,000–10,000 may be good enough if you're very good at managing your risk and develop a keen sense of timing and discipline. See Chapters 17, 18, and 19 to review trading plans and strategies.

By the close of trading July 1, after a five-day holding period, the gain on the hypothetical trade was $93.75. A good move then would have been to move your stop down to 9642 so that a gain would not turn into a loss if the market turned against you. You should also continue to change your stop as the market continues to gain roughly in equal increments to the gains that you're getting from the trade.

During this trade, your margin never fell to $700, because you set your stop to get you out before you got a margin call.

A ten-point move in the July Eurodollar contract (Figure 10-3) is worth $250 per contract, $25 per point.

If you happened to be short, or betting on falling Eurodollar prices, like in the example, a fall of this size would make you a good profit, as long as you continued to trade with the overall trend and continued to adjust your stop. If you were long, or betting on higher prices, you'd lose. In a small account, even a $250 loss could be significant, but if you used good risk-management techniques, such as a trailing stop like the one described in the example that accompanies Figure 10-3, you wouldn't let the Eurodollar contract move against you that far. See Chapter 17 for more about trading plans.

At this point, the example trade has earned a nice profit of 3.75 ticks, or $93.75 per contract over five days. Your account started at $945 and rose to $1,038.75. So right before a three-day July 4th holiday weekend, when the Group of Eight was meeting in London with large numbers of demonstrators present and a nine-country rock concert was planned to raise awareness for the famine in Africa, you could have

✔ Closed the position and taken your profits, less commissions.

✔ Tightened your short covering stop by setting it at 9641.05, just above the closing price (9640.0625); refer to Figure 10-3.

✔ Sold a portion of your position if you had more than one contract, taking a part of your profits and adjusting the remaining position by tightening your stop.

✔ Considered establishing option strategies. In this case, because you're short, a call option would be the correct move. A put option would be the correct choice if you were long, because a put option generally rises in price when the market falls. (See Chapter 4 for the basics of options trading.)

By now, you're probably wondering what to do if you're the subject of a margin call. For starters, you need to follow a good rule of thumb used by professionals: *Never risk more than 50 percent of your total account equity when trading.* For example, if you had followed that rule, you never would have bought the one Eurodollar contract in the example above, because you had only $945 in your account. Assuming that you had more money, and you made a good trade, in the future, you'd still buy one Eurodollar contract and keep 50 percent of your equity in your account.

If you do get a margin call, you can

✔ Liquidate your position to meet the call and then take a break for a few days until you get your wits back together.

✔ Sell some of your position to meet the call.

✔ Deposit new money into your account to meet the call.

Plan your trades so that you never get a margin call. That's the best way. Do it by carefully following the rules outlined in this section, having enough money in your account, never risking more than 10 percent of your equity on any one position (5 percent if your account's small), and calculating your maximum risk while keeping it below the amount that results in a margin call.

Trading Treasury-bill futures

A 13-week T-bill contract is considered a risk-free obligation of the U.S. government. In the cash market, T-bills are sold in $10,000 increments, such that if you paid $9,600 for a T-bill in the cash market, an annualized interest rate yield of 4 percent is implied. At the end of the 3 months (13 weeks), you'd get $10,000 in return.

Risk free means that if you buy the T-bills, you're assured of getting paid by the U.S. government. Trading T-bill futures, on the other hand, is not risk free. Instead, T-bill futures trades essentially are governed by the same sort of risk rules that govern Eurodollar trades. T-bill futures

- ✔ Are 3-month (13-week) contracts based on $10,000 U.S. Treasury bills.
- ✔ Have a face value at maturity of $1,000,000.
- ✔ Move in ½-point increments (½ point = 0.005 = $12.50) with trading months of March, June, September, and December.

Trading Bonds and Treasury Notes

The 10-year U.S. Treasury note has been the accepted benchmark for long-term interest rates since the United States stopped issuing the long bond (30-year U.S. Treasury bond) in October 2001. Thirty-year bond futures and 30-year T-bonds (issued before 2001) still are actively traded, and the U.S. Treasury issued new 30 year T-bonds in February 2006.

Ten-year T-note yields are the key for setting long-term mortgage rates. By watching this interest rate, you can pinpoint the best entry times for remortgaging, relocating, or buying rental property, and you can keep tabs on whether your broker is quoting you a good rate.

What you're getting into

Bond and note futures are big-time trading vehicles that move fast. Each tick or price quote, especially when you hold more than one contract and the market is moving fast, can be worth several hundred dollars. Some other facts about 10- and 30-year interest-rate futures that you need to know include that they are

- ✔ Traded under the symbols *TY* for pit trading and *ZN* for electronic trading in the 10-year contract.
- ✔ Valued at $100,000 per contract, the same as for a 30-year bond contract (which is traded under the symbol *US* for pit trading and *ZB* for electronic trading).
- ✔ Longer-term debt futures that have higher margin requirements than Eurodollars. As of February 2008, the initial margin for 10-year and 30-year note and bond contracts, respectively, were $-1620 and $2295. Maintenance margins, respectively, were $1200 and $1700 per contract.

✔ Quoted in terms of 32nds and that one point is $1,000 and one tick must be at least

- ½ of ⅓₂ or $15.625, for a ten-year issue

- ⅓₂, or $31.25, for a 30-year issue

When a price quote is "84-16," it means the price of the contract is 84 and ¹⁵⁄₃₂ for both, and the value is $84,500.

✔ Bonds are traded on the CBOT from 7:20 a.m. to 2:00 p.m. central time Monday through Friday. Electronic trades can be made from 7 a.m. to 4 p.m. central time Sunday through Friday.

Trading in expiring contracts closes at noon central time (Chicago time) on the *last trading day,* which is the seventh business day before the last business day of the delivery month.

U.S. note and bond futures have no price limits.

What you get if you take delivery

If you take delivery, your contract is wired to you on the last business day of the delivery month via the Federal Reserve book-entry wire-transfer system. What you get delivered is a series of U.S. Treasury bonds that either cannot be retired for at least 15 years from the first day of the delivery month or that are not callable with a maturity of at least 15 years from the first day of the delivery month. The *invoice price,* or the amount that you have to tender, equals the futures settlement price multiplied by a conversion factor with accrued interest added. The *conversion factor* used is the price of the delivered bond ($1 par value) to yield 6 percent.

Bonds that are not callable remain in circulation until full maturity, which means that the holder receives all the interest payments until the bond expires, when the principal is returned. Callable bonds put the holder at risk of receiving less interest because of an earlier retirement of the bond than the holder had planned.

For T-notes, you'd receive a package of U.S. Treasury notes that mature from 6½ to 10 years from the first day of the delivery month. The price is calculated by using a formula that you can find on the CBOE Web site. As a small speculator, your chances of getting a delivery are nil.

Figures 10-4 and 10-5 show the ten-year U.S. T-note futures for December 2005. Figure 10-4 shows a good example of a moving-average trading system during the same time period featured in the Eurodollar sections earlier.

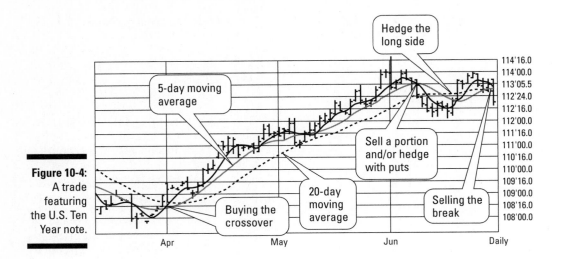

Figure 10-4:
A trade featuring the U.S. Ten Year note.

During the time frame shown in Figure 10-4, even as Eurodollars and short-term instruments fell in price, longer-term instruments rallied because the market continued to believe that higher short-term interest rates eventually would slow down the economy. Elsewhere in the mix were pressures from hedge funds, foreign governments, and big traders setting up huge derivative trades in the options market. The overall effect, however, was to keep long-term interest rates going down and bond prices rising on the long end of the curve.

In June, after the ninth interest rate increase by the Fed, the market decided that the economy was likely to keep strengthening and that the Fed would keep raising rates. According to bond trader rules, rate increases in a strong economy spell a strong sign of inflation and a reason to sell bonds. Other factors that are evident in Figures 10-4 and 10-5 include the following:

- ✔ T-note futures rose during the period of interest rate increases until the month of June, when the contract began to struggle. In the cash bond market, long-term rates had been falling until the same time period when they became volatile.

- ✔ The trend was above the trio of moving averages — the 5-day, the 20-day, and the 10-day — much of the time.

- ✔ An excellent entry point is found in April in Figure 10-4 where the 5-day moving average crosses over the 10-day and the 20-day moving averages. Buying a portion of your position at the first crossover is a common practice when using the moving average crossover as a trading method. You then buy the second portion of the position at the second crossover. You could have bought as the 5-day average crossed over the 10-day average, and again when the 10-day average crossed over the 20-day average.

✔ The uptrend stayed intact until June, so reversing the crossover is just as easy as the chart points out. You can also hedge your position if you're unsure whether the crossover is temporary or you're seeing a significant top by buying a put option.

✔ The break below all three moving averages was clear in late June, giving you an opportunity to sell short.

✔ You need to use trailing stops when trading all futures contracts so that even when you aren't sure whether a top was reached, you nevertheless are stopped out when the price falls below the three moving averages.

Figure 10-5 highlights the use of good trend-line analysis. Take note of the following:

✔ **A double top in bond prices and a key break below the rising trend line.** Note that when the Fed raised interest rates June 30, bond prices failed to close above the previous day's intraday high price, a signal that the market was exhausted. Sure enough, it closed significantly lower the next day.

✔ **The price on July 1.** Closing within the gap is a good example of how gaps become magnets for price reversals at some point in the future.

✔ **The 116 support level.** Your next indicator to watch is when the market tests the 116 key-support area. If you shorted the break in prices below 118, you'd be looking to cover at least some of your short position by buying the contract back and specifying that you are doing so with intent to cover the short position or buying some call options to hedge your position near that area.

Figure 10-5:
U.S. Key technical aspects of the U.S. Ten Year note in response to an interest-rate increase by the Federal Reserve.

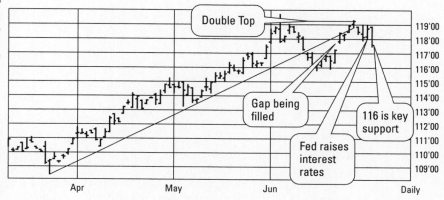

Chapter 11

Rocking and Rolling: Speculating with Currencies

*I*n a global economy, investors have come to realize that stocks and bonds are not the only games in town. Currencies are among the fastest growing segments of the capital markets.

Aside from the currency futures, foreign currencies trade in a busy spot market. In fact, explaining how much of the action in currencies takes place in the spot market takes up a good portion of this chapter.

The major goals of this chapter are to introduce you to the currency market, provide a broad overview of the important role it plays in forging relationships between other markets, and give you a good sound base from which to expand your foreign exchange (or as it's known in the business, forex) activities.

My first experience in the currency markets was with trading the U.S. dollar index. I broke all the rules and lost some money, but I discovered some valuable lessons that have enabled me to make some profitable trades since then.

These days, because of time commitments and a general distaste for volatility, I still trade currencies, but I do so by using mutual funds and exchange-traded funds (ETFs). On my Web site, www.joe-duarte.com, I provide recommendations on both for my subscribers. This is a nice development in the evolution of trading that enables me to participate in a market that I truly love while not having to suffer the hair-raising action that can go along with directly trading currencies and currency futures. That doesn't mean you should fool yourself into thinking that by using ETFs and mutual funds you can stop being careful and vigilant. These trading vehicles can be just as treacherous as the real currencies if you're not on the ball.

If participating in the currency markets indirectly sounds like your cup of tea, be sure to check out the currency mutual-fund timing system that I explain on my Web site, or check out Chapter 5, where I discuss trading futures and currencies by using ETFs. In this chapter, I deal mostly with the straight skinny on trading currencies.

Understanding Foreign Exchange Rates

Internal and external factors influence foreign exchange rates. *Internal factors* can be determined by something as simple as whether a country has specific controls or limits on its currency. The most current example of a controlled currency is the Chinese yuan, which the Chinese government maintains in a narrow trading band. This has changed some since the Chinese government began loosening the trading band on the yuan in July of 2005 by removing the currency's peg (link) the U.S. dollar.

Other global currencies, especially the ones coming from emerging markets and less developed countries, also are controlled by their respective governments. *External factors* deal mostly with trade issues (disputes) or the market's perception of the political and economic situation in a given country. Of course, wars and natural disasters also qualify as potential market-moving events.

The most important influences on currency values are

- ✔ **Interest rates:** As a rule, higher interest rates lead to higher currency prices.

- ✔ **Inflation rates:** Higher inflation tends to lead to a weaker currency. This general rule doesn't apply when the rate of inflation is leading a country's central bank to raise interest rates. In that case, despite higher inflation, the markets are likely to bid up that country's currency as they expect interest rates there to continue to rise.

- ✔ **Current account status:** Countries that tend to export more than they import tend to have stronger currencies than countries that import more than they export. This relationship is soft, however, because some countries, such as Japan, purposely keep their respective currencies weak by selling them in the open market just to keep their exports high. These countries don't export their currencies; instead, their central banks sell them into the open market by making trades just like any other trading desk. The net effect is to increase the amount of a country's currency that is floating in the markets, thus decreasing its value to indirectly affect the balance of trade.

✔ **Budget status:** Countries with budget surpluses, again, as a general rule, tend to have stronger currencies than countries with budget deficits. This rule also is soft, because it doesn't hold up all the time. For example, the United States has chronic budget and current-account deficits, but the U.S. dollar experiences long rallies in which its strength is quite impressive.

✔ **Political stability:** Along with interest rates and economic fundamentals, politics are more than likely the most consistent determinants of the exchange rates that are quoted on a regular basis. Despite a fairly strong economy, an otherwise strong dollar during the Clinton administration suffered during the Monica Lewinsky scandal.

✔ **Foreign policy:** The U.S. dollar's status as the world's reserve currency was damaged by the war in Iraq. In fact, the dollar was already weakening before the war started as traders feared Bush administration policies, such as lower taxes and the potential for increased government. The 9/11 attacks, with their negative effects on the U.S. economy and the spiraling costs of the war indeed led to a series of U.S. budget deficits, and the dollar continued to weaken into 2008.

Exploring Basic Spot-Market Trading

The *spot market* is where most of the currency trading is done. It's operated nearly exclusively by large banks and corporations. Here's the lowdown on the basics of the spot market:

✔ Trades on the spot market are made continuously Monday through Friday, starting in New Zealand and following the sun to Sydney, Tokyo, Hong Kong, Singapore, Bahrain, Frankfurt, Geneva, Zurich, Paris, London, New York, Chicago, and Los Angeles before starting again.

✔ When big banks and institutions trade currencies on the spot market, they are usually exchanging your currency with another individual party. Both parties usually know and recognize each other.

✔ One third of foreign exchange transactions in the world are done on an over-the-counter basis in the spot forex market, with no exchange being involved. Over-the-counter trades are made directly between two individuals or institutions, usually by phone.

✔ The *interbank market,* where most of the transactions in the spot market take place between banks and corporations, is a network of banks that serve as intermediaries or market makers or wholesalers. Participants buy and sell currencies in the interbank markets, where trades are settled within two days. The two-day settlement is fair to both parties, allowing plenty of time for money to change hands, considering the amount of time it sometimes takes to gather large sums together in one place.

✔ The *retail market* is where the rest of the currency transactions take place. Individual traders conduct these trades over the phone and via the Internet by using brokers as intermediaries. Settlement on the retail market is defined as the transaction day plus one day.

Dabbling in da forex lingo

Like anything else in life, foreign exchange (forex) has its own language, and your currency trading skills grow faster when you get the terms right early on; that is, before risking your money-making trades in this volatile but mostly sensible market.

Foreign exchange transactions are exchanges between two *pairings* of currencies, with each currency having its own International Standardization Organization (ISO) code. The ISO code identifies the country and its currency, using three letters. The pairing uses the ISO codes for each participating currency. For example, USD/GBP pairs the U.S. dollar and the British pound. In this case, the dollar is the *base currency,* and the pound is the *secondary currency.* Displayed the other way, GBP/USD, the pound is the base currency, and the dollar is secondary.

My favorite thing about currencies is the *pip,* the smallest move any currency can make. It means the same thing as a *tick* for other futures and asset classes. Incidentally, whether Gladys Knight trades currencies anywhere, with or without The Pips, remains unknown.

The four major currency pairings are

✔ EUR/USD = euro/U.S. dollar

✔ GBP/USD = British pound sterling/U.S. dollar (also known as *cable* from the days when a Trans-Atlantic cable was used to coordinate and communicate exchange rates between the dollar and the pound)

✔ USD/JPY = U.S. dollar/Japanese yen

✔ USD/CHF = U.S. dollar/Swiss franc

When you read an exchange rate that's quoted on a screen, you're reading how much of one currency can be exchanged for another. If you see GBP/USD = 1.7550, that means you can exchange one British pound for 1.7550 dollars. The base currency is the pound; it's the one that you're either buying or selling.

When you trade currencies, you are, in effect, buying one currency and simultaneously selling another, or vice versa.

When you view a trading screen, you see a frame with two prices. One side is marked "sell" and gives you the selling price, and the other side is marked "buy" and gives you the buying price. If you want to sell, you click on the sell side. If you want to buy, you click on the buy side. To reverse or close out your trade, you do the opposite of your current position.

Currency on the spot market is bought and sold in groups made up of 100,000 units of the base currency. On the spot market, buyer and seller are required to deposit a margin, which usually is 1 to 5 percent of the entire value of the trade. In other words, if you buy 100,000 GBP/USD at 1.7550, you put down the appropriate margin in dollars, while the seller of sterling, who is buying your dollars, reciprocates by putting down an appropriate margin in sterling.

Location, location, location

Some special currency trading issues are dependent upon where your dealer is located. If you're trading in the spot market and your dealer is in the United States, you deposit your margin in dollars. If, however, you're trading through a foreign dealer or using a currency other than the one required by the broker, you have to convert your capital and margin requirements to the currency of the foreign dealer. Each situation is different, but you need to check out all the variables before making any trades.

Here's how it works: If you're trading the USD/JPY (U.S. dollar/Japanese yen) pair, the value of your trade will be calculated in yen, JPY. If your broker uses the dollar as his home currency, then your profits and losses in this trade are converted back to dollars at the relevant USD/JPY offer rate.

Although trading currencies may seem confusing, you can work it out by carefully studying exchange rates and doing some practice trades. Most online currency dealers will enable you to open a practice account so that many of the nuances of trading currencies become self-evident with practice.

Don't get cross over crossrates

Crossrates are the exchange rates between non-U.S. dollar currency pairings. Andy Shearman of Trader House Network, www.traderhouseglobal.net, offers a nice example of how *crosses* work, as well as other tutorials that you may find helpful. An adaptation of his example follows to show the cross between the pound sterling and the Swiss franc. Say your trading screen shows the following crossrates:

- EUR/USD = 1.0060/65
- GBP/USD = 1.5847/52
- USD/JPY = 120.25/30
- USD/CHF = 1.4554/59

These four pairings are key crossrates. For example, the GBP/USD pairing is the bid (1.5847) and ask (1.5852) price for the British pound sterling and the U.S. dollar exchange rate at the moment. The difference between them, 0.0005, is the *spread,* which amounts to the commission that the dealer collects.

So to calculate the GBP/CHF (British pound for Swiss franc) crossrate, do the following:

1. **Find the GBP/USD exchange rate.**

   Bid: 1.5847 Offer (ask): 1.5852

2. **Find the USD/CHF exchange rate.**

   Bid: 1.4554 Offer: 1.4559

3. **Multiply the bid amount for the GBP/USD exchange rate by the bid amount for the USD/CHF exchange rate, and then do the same with the offer amounts.**

   $1.5847 \times 1.4554 = 2.3063$ and $1.5852 \times 1.4559 = 2.3079$

4. **Jot down the answers.**

   GBP/CHF = 2.3063/2.3079

The calculations work for all currencies if you follow these steps. Foreign exchange quotation services and trading software also give you the amounts, perhaps a little quicker.

Electronic spot trading

Aside from traditional phone-based trading, you can trade currencies in the spot market electronically, but you need to be prepared to sit in front of your screen and manage your trade actively. Otherwise, you risk losing large sums rapidly.

You also need to know that you'll pay more for trading currencies in the spot market than the pros do. That's because you're a little guy, and they're not. That's the way of the world, and you need to know that before you get into trading anything.

Something else to keep in mind is that some foreign-currency Web sites and brokers will tell you that trading on their site is commission free. That isn't true. They do collect a fee that amounts to the spread between the bid and ask prices on the currency quotes. If you keep that in mind, you'll save yourself a lot of grief, and you can get on with trading.

Getting your charts together before you trade

In order to trade forex, you need a good command of technical analysis. You can apply the principles of technical analysis that I discuss in Chapter 7, because the same general principles and indicators apply to foreign exchange rates.

Some particulars about forex that you need to keep in mind are that currencies tend to trend for a long time, usually months to even years. However, within the major long-term trends (see Figure 11-1), counter-trend moves usually occur, and a large degree of intraday volatility is common. Some other factors common to long-term currency trends like the one shown in Figure 11-1 include

- **Long-term bull (and bear) markets can last for years.** The bull market for the euro shown in Figure 11-1 lasted at least eight years. Yet, there are pauses and changes in the trend that often fool you into thinking that the long term trend has ended. Figure 11-2 enlarges and displays two periods in the multiyear bull market that are classic examples of how long term bull markets can behave and how indicators can help you make better trades.

- **Trend lines are especially useful.** In Figure 11-1, you can see the very big picture of the euro's bull market. The three trend lines demarcate the three stages of the bull market until 2008. The first trend line (up trending) shows the first multiyear run up in the euro, from 2001, after 9/11, until 2005. The break below the uptrend line was a signal that the market had entered a correction. The second trend line (down trending) covers the period of the correction that started with the double top in 2004 and lasted until 2006, when the downtrend line was broken and the next leg in the bull market started.

- **Trend indicators work well in the currency markets.** Note the *intermediate-term tops* (Figure 11-2) marked by the Relative Strength Indicator (RSI stands for *loss of momentum*) and its nice correlation with the MACD oscillator (MACD means *change of trend*). See Chapter 7 for more about oscillators.

Likewise, note how the double-top failure marked on the chart corresponds with the failure in the RSI and the break below the zero line on the MACD. A momentum failure, coupled with major breaks in the trend indicators and a break below a four-year rising trend line, was a clear sell signal that a change in the up-trend was coming.

Figure 11-1: The multi-year bull market in the Euro.

Figure 11-2: Intermediate-term tops marked by RSI.

Using long-term charts to track currencies is a great way to trade forex instruments. The long-term charts are your guides to the prevailing trend. However, within a long-term trend, you can find significant counter-trend ebb and flow, during which you can trade against the long-term trend by

✔ Going long, or buying when the long-term chart is pointing up

✔ Looking for opportunities to go short when the long-term trend is down

✔ Using shorter-term charts to guide your shorter-term trades, both long and short

Counter-trend moves are an ever-present part of the market that require adjustment. As such, you always need to keep the long-term trend in mind so you don't grow too comfortable trading in the wrong direction, or *counter* to the long-term *trend* line.

When a currency breaks below a long-rising trend line, you must consider that the long-term trend has changed direction. The trend may not change every time this situation occurs. In fact, some markets return to the original trend soon after a break. A counter-trend rally is another possible trading scenario. In a counter-trend rally, the market remains in a long-term up- or downtrend, but trades in the opposite direction for a short to intermediate period of time that can last for days, weeks, or even months before returning to the long-term trend.

You can see a counter-trend rally in Figure 11-3, which shows a one-year chart of the euro that focuses on the period of trading labeled double top, pictured in Figure 11-1.

Figure 11-3: This chart shows a perfect example of how a counter-trend rally materializes.

The vertical line in the middle of the chart connects these three key points:

- ✔ The reversal of the euro
- ✔ A bottom in the RSI indicator
- ✔ A bottom in the MACD indicator

Long-term charts are best used for keeping an eye on the big picture. When you see something that looks small on a long-term chart, use a short-term chart to magnify the time frame. Figure 11-2 magnifies the double-top and momentum failure in Figure 11-1, and Figure 11-3 highlights the counter-trend rally that occurred as the double top was forming. When you look at the shorter-term chart, the momentum failure looks much clearer, and your decision making therefore is enhanced.

Take your long-term charts seriously, but remain flexible. If you've been trading in a certain direction for weeks or months, you're bound to get a fairly good reversal. Any reversal can be big enough to change the long-term trend, so you can play every reversal as one that may be the big one. Figures 11-1 through 11-3 show how the currency markets can have fairly long-term moves in either direction, up or down, even though the dominant trend remains constant.

Keep your time frames in perspective. Intraday charts are useful for short-term trading. What looks like a major trend reversal on a three-day chart using 15-minute candlesticks may not amount to much in the big picture. But it's enough of a shift for you to use your short-term strategy.

Understanding the nuances of each individual currency is also important. For example, as well described in *Currency Trading For Dummies* by Mark Galant (Wiley), the trading patterns in the British pound and the Swiss franc are different than those of the euro and the U.S. dollar. So as you get more advanced in your trading, you can begin to factor in the specifics of each individual currency and how they can affect your trading.

Setting up your trading rig

Currency trading is heavy metal. So like heavy-metal bands, you need some serious hardware and software to keep your shirt on and your trousers dry.

Top on that list of needs is an electronic brokerage service that enables you to do *straight through processing* (STP), where you trade directly with the dealer through your computer by using integrated quotations and transactional and administrative functionality. You can gain access to STP through your online broker, and you can gain access to a decent system through many online brokerage-services providers. You can find other online brokerages that offer STP by using your favorite online search engine.

You need to evaluate different brokers before deciding on one. A good electronic brokerage service gives you access to live, streaming data and enables you to make direct trades through your broker's Web site.

Most online brokers offer plenty of free goodies that you can look at to get a feel for how the forex markets work. They also offer free real-time quotes and a good basic charting service that you can use. Here are a couple of good ones:

✔ Electronic Brokering Services (EBS) at `www.icap.com`

✔ Nostradamus at `www.nostradamus.co.uk`

I also maintain a good Web page with currency information on my Web site's directory: `www.joe-duarte.com/free/directory/software-forex.asp`.

Here are some other essentials for forex trading:

✔ A reliable margin account broker. For details on margin and how to choose a broker, see Chapters 3, 4, and 17.

✔ A fast and reliable Internet connection. You need a good, reliable, broadband connection with your computer terminal dedicated to trading — not instant messaging for your teenager or educational stuff for your homeschooler.

✔ A big-time computer system on which you can run several big programs at the same time without crashing. You need as much memory and storage as you can muster. A gigabyte of RAM (random access memory) is a good start, but if you're going to run multiple monitors, you may need more, plus the setup for it. You need a good printer for printing your statements and a good backup system. If you plan to take a break and keep a position open, a good Wi-Fi setup for a laptop is a good idea. You also need all the security — antivirus, firewall, and spyware protection — that you can muster to keep your personal data from being stolen.

✔ Good trading software on which you can open and manage positions and conduct big-time technical analysis.

✔ Separate computer monitors so you can

- Handle market data

- Submit dealing instructions

- Look at charts and indicators all at once to keep tabs on all your open positions

- Adjust your stops and place other orders

- Keep an eye on how much money you have in your margin account

Two screens is a good number to get you started, but some traders may need more, especially when they trade more than one market at a time.

Using the right orders for your forex trading goals

You can use market orders when trading forex futures and other instruments, but because the forex markets move so fast, you need to set some automatic exit and entry points to manage your risk as part of your armaments.

A *stop loss* is the same kind of order in all markets: It gets you out either at your specified price or the closest possible price depending on market conditions. Same thing's true of a *limit order,* which you use to set your entry point at a predetermined price.

Some other useful orders for the forex market include

- **Take profit orders (TPO):** A TPO enables you to get out of your position at a price that you target before you enter the trade. This kind of order specifies that a position needs to be closed out when the current exchange rate crosses a given or set threshold. You can set up a TPO above a long position and below a short position.

- **One cancels the other (OCO) orders:** An OCO is an order that has two parts; actually, it's made up of two separate orders bundled into one package. An OCO is made up of a stop-loss order and a limit order at opposite ends of a spread. When one order is triggered, no matter which direction the market is trending, the other is terminated. In effect, you enter an entry point and protect your position by limiting your losses immediately. Here's how the OCO works:

  - **Going long:** If you're going long in the market, you set the stop loss below the market spread and the limit-sell order above the market spread. If the base currency rate breaches the limit-order threshold, then your position automatically is sold at or near the price at which you set the limit, and you no longer need the stop loss, which then is canceled. Alternatively, if the rate falls to the stop-loss trigger price, the position is closed out at or near the trigger price and you no longer have any need for the limit order.

    Going short: If you're shorting the market, you set the stop loss above the market spread and the limit order below — just the opposite of the long position. If the exchange rate rises to the stop-loss trigger price, the position is closed out, thus canceling the limit order. If the exchange rate falls to the limit-order trigger price, the limit order is activated, you buy back the position at the predetermined limit-order price, and the stop-loss order is canceled.

Sampling the goods

Here's a simple example of a trade in the spot market:

- Say you buy a 100,000 lot of GBP/USD at the offer price of $1.7550.

  The trade is valued at a total of $175,500.

- You need to put your broker's margin of 2 percent, or $3,510, in your margin account. You get that amount by multiplying $0.02 \times \$175,500$.

- You profit when your trade goes well and the GPB/USD exchange rate rises to $1.760.

  Your profit is $500, or $100,000 \times (1.760 - 1.7550)$, or a 14 percent yield.

The U.S. Dollar Index

The Federal Reserve Board introduced the U.S. dollar index in March 2003. The index was the result of the Smithsonian Agreement, which repealed the Bretton Woods Agreement. What does that mean? The Bretton Woods agreement fixed global currency rates 25 years earlier. The Smithsonian agreement, which was viewed as a victory for proponents of free markets, enabled global currencies to float based on market forces.

The U.S. dollar index is used by traders to get the big picture of the overall trend of the dollar and is widely quoted in the press and on quote services. It is similar to the Fed's dollar index, which is a trade-weighted index, meaning that the Fed gives value to each individual currency in the index based on how much it trades within the United States. However, the value of each index is different, and they shouldn't be confused with one another.

The U.S. dollar index has traded as high as the 160s and as low as the 70s, with the Trader's Index making a new low in early 2008, as shown in Figure 11-4.

U.S. DOLLAR INDEX CASH . . monthly OHLC plot

Figure 11-4: The long-term bear market in the U.S. dollar index.

The U.S. dollar index trades on the Chicago Mercantile Exchange. Here are the particulars of the index:

- A minimum tick is 0.004 and is worth $5.
- Futures contracts expire in March, June, September, and December.
- The overall value of a contract is 1,000 times the value of the index in dollars.

✔ Delivery is physical, meaning that you receive dollars based on the value of the index on the second business day prior to the third Wednesday during the month of the expiring contract. On the last trading day, trading ceases at 10:16 a.m.

✔ Delivery day is the third Wednesday of the contract month.

✔ No trading limits are placed on the U.S. dollar index. Trading hours are from 8:05 a.m. to 3:00 p.m., with overnight trading from 7 to 10 p.m.

The U.S. dollar index was modified at the inception of the euro and is weighted in a way that's similar to the Fed's trade weighted index, as follows (expressed in percentages):

✔ **Euro's weight:** 57.6 percent

✔ **Japanese yen:** 13.6 percent

✔ **British pound:** 11.9 percent

✔ **Canadian dollar:** 9.1 percent

✔ **Swedish krona:** 4.2 percent

✔ **Swiss franc:** 3.6 percent

The U.S. dollar index is best used as an indicator of trends in the currency markets.

The U.S. dollar index isn't as good of a trading vehicle as the individual currencies. The best way to trade the index is by using currency mutual funds or exchange-traded funds (ETFs). To trade the dollar's uptrend use the Powershares U.S. Dollar Bull ETF (UUP). For downtrends use the Powershares U.S. Dollar Bear ETF (UDN). The Profunds Rising Dollar Fund (RDPIX) and Falling Dollar Fund (FDPIX) are two mutual funds that follow the general trend of the dollar. As a rule, though, I prefer to trade the individual currency ETFs. See Chapter 5 or visit www.joe-duarte.com for more details on how to use ETFs to trade currencies.

I know this book isn't about trading mutual funds or ETFs, but one of the secrets of trading success is understanding what kind of a person you are. If you're overwhelmed by the big expensive trading rig you need to make any money in forex and upset (I know I am) because you can't take a coffee or bathroom break for fear the market will move against you and in the blink of an eye you'll end up with a margin call, then you need to consider using these funds. By using the funds, you are, in essence, taking away a good portion of the problems that you can face by directly trading currencies. The funds are priced only once a day. If you check the dollar index a few times during the day, then you have a pretty good idea as to how your fund is going to close that day.

Trading Foreign Currency

Trading currencies can be exciting and lucrative. For me, it's a great market because of the way politics affect the trends. Elections, strikes, and sudden developments, both good and bad, can lead to significant trading profits — if you stand ready to trade.

Trading the euro against the dollar

The euro is a convenient currency because it encompasses the policies and the economic activity and political environment of a volatile but predictable part of the world — Europe.

France, Italy, and Germany, the largest members of the European Union (EU), normally operate under high budget deficits and tend to keep their interest rates more stable than the United States, where the free-market approach and a usually vigilant Federal Reserve make more frequent adjustments on interest rates. The general tendency of the Fed is to make the dollar trend for very long periods of time in one general direction.

Aside from the technical analysis, here are some general tendencies of the euro on which you need to keep tabs:

- The European Central Bank is almost fanatical about inflation, given Germany's history of hyperinflation in the first half of the 20th century and the repercussions of that period, namely the rise of Hitler. That means that the European Central Bank raises interest rates more easily than it lowers them.

- The European Central Bank's actions become important when all other factors are equal, meaning politics are equally stable or unstable in the United States and Europe, and the two economies are growing. For example, if the U.S. economy is slowing down, money slowly starts to drift away from the dollar. In the past, that meant money would move toward the Japanese yen; however, because the market knows that Japan's central bank will sell yen, the default currency when the dollar weakens is often now the euro.

- The flip side is that the market often sells the euro during political problems in the region, especially when the European economy is slowing and the economy in the United Kingdom (UK), which often moves along with the U.S. economy, is showing signs of strength.

As usual, you want to closely monitor major currencies and the crossrates. It's okay to form an opinion and have some expectations, but the final and only truth that should make you trade is what the charts are showing you. The direction that counts is the one in which the market is heading.

The UK pound sterling

The pound is active against the dollar and the euro, offering good opportunities to trade both pairs (GBP/USD and USD/GBP; see the section "Dabbling in da forex lingo," earlier in this chapter). The United Kingdom is a pivotal nation because it bridges the economical, geographical, and ideological divide between the United States and Europe.

Economically, the United Kingdom is more free-market oriented than Europe, and it tends to share a more common set of views with the United States. At the same time, the United Kingdom can't totally disassociate itself from Europe, given its history and its geography.

The upshot is a currency that is affected by politics at home and on the two continents to which its destiny is so closely related.

Because the United Kingdom is an oil producer, the pound can be affected more directly by oil prices than other currencies. The relationship between oil and the pound is fading, however, because production in the United Kingdom's North Sea oil fields is steadily decreasing.

The Japanese yen

The Japanese yen is a manipulated currency, which basically means it is kept low artificially by the Japanese government.

The combination of low interest rates, the lasting economic effects from the bursting of the Japanese real-estate bubble, and the collapse of the stock market and the banking system in Japan have forced its government to keep the yen's value low by selling it in the open market when it reaches a certain level.

The main purpose of maintaining a weak currency is to keep the Japanese export machinery operational. Over the long term, however, a weaker currency will continue to hurt Japan's chance of achieving a lasting recovery.

The most useful time to trade the yen is when political and potential military problems are taking place in Asia. China's rise as a global power can eventually lead to a major and uncontrolled weakening of the yen. The best way to trade the yen is not against the dollar but rather to use crossrate analysis, especially against the euro and the Swiss franc.

The Swiss franc

The Swiss franc is considered a *reserve currency*, or one that is reliable and tends to hold its value when others don't. It also is a currency to which traders and other investors flow during times of global crisis. Its strength is based on three traditional expectations in the market:

✔ **Reliable economic fundamentals:** Switzerland has a history of low inflation and current account surpluses. It also is a country whose banking system is well known for holding the deposits of extremely wealthy and stable clients.

✔ **Gold reserves:** The Swiss franc still is backed by gold, because Switzerland's gold reserves significantly exceed the amount of currency it has placed in circulation. Switzerland has the fourth largest holding of gold in the world. Relative to Gross Domestic Product (GDP), the level of international reserves — with or without gold — is far ahead of all other countries.

✔ **Little political influence:** Switzerland's political neutrality enables it to set a monetary policy that operates (essentially) in a vacuum and thus enables its central bank to concentrate its effort on price stability. In December 1999, the Swiss National Bank changed the way it manages monetary policy, from one that traditionally targeted the money supply to one that targets inflation. The bank's goal is a 2 percent annual inflation rate.

The two major factors to keep an eye on when trading the franc are

✔ **Economic data:** The franc can be affected by several key economic reports, including

  • The release of Swiss M3, the broadest measure of money supply

  • The release of Swiss CPI

  • Unemployment data

  • Balance of payments, GDP, and industrial production

✔ **Crossrates:** Changes in interest rates in the EU or the United Kingdom can alter crossrates and have an effect on the U.S. dollar. For example, if the euro or the pound rises and the Swiss franc weakens against them, the franc also is likely to move with regards to the dollar, thus offering traders like you three potential trading vehicles. The general tendency is for a sudden move in EUR/USD — which can be triggered by a major fundamental factor, such as an unexpected change in government, a terrorist attack, or a major economic release — to cause an equally sharp move in USD/CHF in the opposite direction.

The panic response

The Swiss franc often is a financial instrument of refuge for wealthy individuals, corporations, and traders. After the events of September 11, 2001, and the July 2005 bombings in the London Underground, the Swiss franc was the immediate beneficiary of the *flight to quality trade,* as traders acted on reflex, at least initially, and moved money toward traditional safe havens. The U.S. dollar used to be more of a safe haven prior to September 11, 2001, but that distinction has changed. The markets have adjusted their expectations based on the fact that even though no more major attacks have occurred in the United States, the United States nevertheless remains the primary target of Al-Qaeda. Whenever a major terrorist attack occurs, the markets always react as though the attack may be followed by a strike on the United States. Besides the Swiss franc, other safe havens include U.S. Treasury Bonds, U.S. Treasury Bills, and Eurodollars.

Arbitrage Opportunities and Sanity Requirements

The 24-hour trading day in spot currency markets — and its potential for activity whenever any major event occurs and develops — offers great opportunities for *arbitrage,* or trading both on the long and short side by using different currencies. Arbitrage is a sophisticated strategy that you can use when you become experienced at trading.

Here are some basic arbitrage rules to keep in mind:

- ✔ **Currencies move in response to news events.** Keeping a calendar of economic releases for Europe, the United States, the United Kingdom, Japan, and Switzerland is a good habit to get into. When a major economic release is outside the realm of expectations, currencies will move, and you can be poised in those situations to make large sums of money in short periods of time.

- ✔ **Major events, such as September 11, 2001, hurricanes, and other natural disasters also make the currencies move.** I'm not trying to be morbid, but trading on bad news is a fact of life. As a trader, you can make bad-news decisions that are profitable if you're watching for them.

- ✔ **Keep an eye on crossrates and bond markets.** These areas move together, and they often move in opposite directions. After you become comfortable with currencies, you may want to consider setting up trades in interest-rate futures and currencies, which can serve as either a hedge or a profit-making opportunity.

✔ **Research your opportunities in the options markets, and develop a program that includes options.** Currency and interest-rate futures offer option opportunities. By using currency and/or interest-rate options, you can protect your currency positions at a fraction of the cost of owning the direct contract or lot.

✔ **Use the hypothetical trading systems.** Available on the Internet, you can use these Web tools to try different strategies or dissect new charting setups. ActionForex.com has some good demos. Get comfortable with the way the currency markets work first, however, before you risk any large sums of money.

✔ **Beware of using mini accounts.** Although mini accounts enable you to trade forex for $300 or less, such trades are a good way to get hurt, given the speed at which these markets can move. Instead, you need to be well capitalized before you make your move into this trading arena.

✔ **Don't give up your day job unless you're a truly gifted trader.** Most people are not gifted traders, and they need to use the currency markets only as part of an overall strategy to build wealth steadily and to protect their overall investment program and goals.

Don't try to trade around the clock. Much of the action in currencies takes place overnight. Europe and Asian trading in currencies can be extremely powerful, and any open position that was profitable when you went to bed can be wiped out by morning. Use your stops wisely, and close out any positions that make you uncomfortable when you're done for the day.

Chapter 12

Stocking Up on Indexes

- -

- -

Stock-index futures came of age October 19, 1987. That's when a major stock market crash was fueled by something known as *portfolio insurance,* or the sale of futures contracts to protect losses in individual stock positions. The most important and lasting influence of the 1987 crash was that the world was awakened to a new era of investing — the era of the one market — in which stock-index futures and the stock market became a single entity.

I remember October 19, 1987, vividly. I had no money and no investments at that time. Boy, was I lucky. But market activity on that day and during the ensuing months was responsible for turning me into a financial-market junky and enabling me not only to save for my retirement but also to earn a living doing something that is exciting and enjoyable — trading and teaching others how to trade.

My first real-life experience with money in a stock-market crash came in 1990, when Saddam Hussein invaded Kuwait. My next experiences came in 1997 and 1998 when the Asian currency crisis hit the markets. Each step of the way, I remember watching the relationship between the cash market and stock-index futures. That interplay sets up the potential strategies for specu-lation and for hedging that I describe to you in this chapter.

You don't need to trade every major index contract in the world to be suc-cessful; you just need to find one or two with which you're comfortable — the ones that enable you to implement your strategies. In this chapter, I focus on the Standard & Poor's 500 (S&P 500) Stock Index futures, a well-known contract that is central to the markets. Any of the lessons that I describe with respect to the S&P 500 can, however, be applied to just about any contract.

Seeing What Stock-Index Futures Have to Offer

Stock-index futures are futures contracts based on indexes that are composed of stocks. For example, the S&P 500 futures contract is based on the popular market benchmark of the same name — the S&P 500 Stock Index, a group of 500 commonly traded stocks (see the section "The S&P 500 futures [SP]," later in this chapter).

When you trade stock-index futures, you're betting on the direction of the contract's value, and not on the individual stocks that make up the index. In a sense, by focusing on the value and general trend of the stocks as a group, you're blocking out a good deal of the noise that often is associated with the daily gyrations in the prices of the individual stocks.

Stock-index futures are an integral part of the stock market's daily activity. Currently more than 70 stock-index futures contracts are traded on at least 20 exchanges around the world. As a percentage of the total number of futures contracts traded, stock-index futures are by far the largest category of futures contracts traded. That dominance clearly speaks of the major role that stock-index futures play in risk management for the entire stock market.

I can think of several major reasons for trading stock-index futures. Here are some of the more common ones:

- **Speculation:** When you speculate, you're making an educated guess about the direction of a market. I hope you gather from reading this and other chapters of this book that an educated guess is based on careful examination of market history, trends, and key external events that can affect the prices of financial assets. When you speculate, you can deliver trading profits to your accounts by going long or short on index futures or betting on prices rising or falling, respectively.

- **Hedging:** A *hedge* is when you use stock-index futures and options to protect either an individual security in your portfolio or, in some cases, the entire portfolio from losing value. For example, if you own a large number of blue-chip, dividend-paying stocks, and you're getting some nice income from them, you have to think long and hard about selling them. Yet, in a bear market, your stock portfolio is going to decrease in value. By using stock-index futures and options, you can sell the market short and protect the overall value of your portfolio, while continuing to receive your dividends.

✔ **Tax consequences:** Gains in the futures markets are taxed at a lower rate than stock-market capital gains. At the top rate, short-term gains (because that's what futures traders deal with, primarily) in stocks are taxed at a 39.6 percent rate. Capital gains from successful futures trading are blended by the IRS as follows:

- The IRS has a complex set of rules for taxing gains in the futures markets with specific forms with which you must become familiar, such as IRS Form 4797 Part II for securities or Form 6781 for commodities. I could devote at least a third of a chapter to tax rules, but space restrictions won't allow it, so that means that you need to check with your accountant *before* you start trading.

- The flip side is that you can deduct your losses and get preferential treatment on your gains if you form the right kind of corporation and set up retirement plans and other kinds of shelters. These factors may vary depending on the state in which you reside, and they may change over time as new tax laws are written. Again, be sure to check with your accountant.

- The IRS also taxes stock-index futures at a different rate than commodities, such as soybeans. Short-term gains in the former are taxed up to 35 percent, while short-term gains in the latter average out to 23 percent.

  For example, for every $10,000 you make in short-term gains as a result of trading individual stocks, you may have to pay as much as $3,960 in taxes, based on laws in effect in 2007, but when you trade stock-index futures, every $10,000 short-term gain can be taxed for only $2,784. The $2,784 is based on the blending formula used by the IRS. Again, check with your accountant for the numbers that apply to you and your tax bracket. Keeping abreast of tax changes is important. When a new president and Congress take office in 2009, tax changes are almost certain to come, and investors who got a nice ride from the Bush administration may again become targets for the government's never-ending appetite for money.

✔ **Lower commission rates:** Many futures brokerages offer lower commission rates. This practice is not as widespread as it was before online discount brokers for stocks became a mainstay of the business. But you still can find low commission rates in the futures markets, a factor that becomes more important as you trade large blocks or quantities of stocks.

✔ **Time factors:** If something happens overnight when the stock market is closed, and you want to hedge your risk, you can trade futures on Globex while Wall Street sleeps. Globex is a 24-hour electronic trading system for a wide variety of futures contracts (see Chapter 3).

Contracting with the Future: Looking into Fair Value

Fair value is the theoretically correct value for a futures contract at a particular point in time. You calculate fair value by using a formula that includes the current index level, index dividends, number of days to contract expiration, and interest rates. Without getting caught up in the details, the important thing for you to remember about fair value is that it's a benchmark that can be a helpful tool for your analysis of the markets.

For example, when a stock-index futures contract trades below its fair value, it's trading at a *discount*. When it trades above fair value, it's trading at a *premium*.

Knowing the fair value is most helpful in gauging where the market is headed. Because stock-index futures prices are related to spot-index prices, changes in fair value can trigger price changes.

If the spread between the index and cash widens or shrinks far enough, you'll see a rise in activity from computer-trading programs. Here's how it works:

- ✔ If the futures contract is too far below fair value, the index (cash) is sold and the futures contract is bought.

- ✔ If the futures contract is too high versus above its fair value, the futures contract is sold and the index (cash) is bought.

- ✔ If enough sell programs hit the market hard enough over an extended period of time, you can see a *crash,* a situation where market prices fall dramatically.

- ✔ If enough buy programs kick in, the market tends to rally.

Fair value is the number that the television stock analysts refer to when discussing the action in futures before the market opens.

Major Stock-Index Futures Contracts

You can trade many different stock-index contracts, but they all share the same basic characteristics. I describe many of these general issues in the section that follows, and I address any particular differences with descriptions of other individual contracts throughout the rest of this section.

The S&P 500 futures (SP)

The biggest stock-index futures contract is the S&P 500, which trades on the Chicago Mercantile Exchange (CME). This index is made up of the 500 largest stocks in the United States. It's a weighted index, which means that component companies that have bigger market capitalizations, or market values, can have a much larger impact on the movements of the index than components with smaller market capitalizations. For example, a stock like IBM has a larger market capitalization than the stock of a smaller company in the index, such as retailer Costco.

Some of the particulars about the S&P 500 Index include the following:

- **Composition:** The S&P 500 is made up of 400 industrial companies, 40 financial companies, 40 utilities, and 20 transportation companies, offering a fairly diversified view of the U.S. economy.

- **Valuation:** The S&P 500 Index is valued in ticks worth 0.1 index points or $25.

- **Contracts:** S&P 500 Index futures contracts are worth 250 times the value of the index. That means that when the index value is at 1,250, a contract is worth $250 \times \$1,250$, or $312,500. A move of a full point is worth $250.

- **Trading times:** Regular trading hours for S&P 500 Index futures are from 8:30 a.m. to 3:15 p.m., but S&P 500 Index futures contracts are another example of how 24-hour-a-day trading enables traders to respond to economic news and releases in the pre-market and aftermarket sessions. The evening session starts 15 minutes after the close (at 3:30 p.m.) and continues in the overnight until 8:15 a.m. on Globex.

- **Contract limits:** Individual contract holders are limited to no more than 20,000 net long or short contracts at any one time.

- **Price limits:** Price limits should not be confused with circuit breakers (see next list item). *Price limits* halt trading above or below the price specified by the limit. A price limit is how far the S&P 500 Index can rise or fall in a single trading session. The limits are set on a quarterly basis. If the index experiences major declines or increases beyond these limits, a procedure is in place to halt trading. You can find the price limits detailed on the CME's Web site (www.cme.com).

- **Circuit breakers:** Circuit breakers halt trading briefly in a coordinated manner between exchanges. The limits that trigger circuit breakers are calculated and agreed upon on a quarterly basis by the different exchanges.

  The *collar rule* addresses price swings related to program trades that move the Dow Industrial Average more than 2 percent by requiring index arbitrage orders, or orders that bet on the spread between the futures and cash of stock indexes, to be stabilizing. That means that traders using these methods can't pile on orders on the sell or the buy side in an attempt to exaggerate the gains or losses for the market. In effect, what this rule does is decrease the chance for huge gains or losses as a result of futures trading. Details can be found at the Web site for the Securities and Exchange Commission (SEC — www.sec.gov). For this overview chapter, it's good to know that the collar rule exists and that it can have an effect on trading.

✓ **Final settlement:** For all stock-index futures, settlement on the CME is based on a Special Opening Quotations (SOQ) price, which is calculated based on the opening prices for each of the stocks in an index on the day that the contract expires. Don't confuse the SOQ with the opening index value, which is calculated right after the opening. *Note:* Some stocks may take a while to establish opening prices.

✓ **Margin requirements:** Margin values for S&P 500 Index contracts are variable. In March 2008 the initial margin for the S&P 500 contract - was $22,500, and the maintenance margin at $18,000.

✓ **Cash settlement:** Stock-index futures are settled with cash, a practice known as, you guessed it, *cash settlement.* That means if you hold your contract until expiration, you have to either pay or receive the amount of money the contract is worth as determined by the SOQ price (see the previous "Final settlement" list item). Cash settlement applies to all stock-index futures.

Overnight and pre-market trading can be thin and dangerous, especially during slow seasons in the stock market, such as summer, fall, and around the winter holidays.

The NASDAQ-100 Futures Index (ND)

The NASDAQ-100 Futures Index contract is similar to the S&P 500 Index futures contract. Here's what you need to know about it:

✓ **Composition:** The NASDAQ-100 Stock Index is made up of the 100 largest stocks traded on the NASDAQ system, including large technology and biotech stocks.

✓ **Valuation:** The ND is valued in minimum ticks of 0.25 that are worth $25.

✓ **Contract limits:** No more than 10,000 net long or short contracts can be held by any individual at any one time.

✓ **Margin requirements:** Margins required for NASDAQ-100 Index futures are similar to the S&P 500 Index futures. In March 2008, the initial margin for the ND contract was $16,250, and the maintenance margin was $13,000.

Minimizing your contract

The e-mini S&P 500 (ES) contract and the e-mini NASDAQ 100 (NQ) are among the most popular stock-index futures contracts, because they enable you to trade the market's trend with only a fifth of the requirement. The e-mini S&P is a favorite of day traders because of its high intraday volatility and major price swings on a daily basis. The mini contracts are marketed to small investors, and they offer some advantages. However, they also carry significant risks, because they're volatile and still have fairly high margin requirements.

The mini contract can be very volatile and can move even more aggressively during extremely volatile market environments. Here are some particulars about the e-mini contracts:

- **Composition:** The ES and NQ e-mini contracts are based on the same makeup as the respective S&P 500 and NASDAQ 100 index contracts.

- **Valuation:** One tick on ES is 0.25 of an index point and is worth $12.50. One tick on NQ is 0.50 of an index point and is worth $10.

- **Contracts:** The value of an ES contract is $50 multiplied by the value of the S&P 500 Index. The value of an NQ contract is $20 multiplied by the value of the NASDAQ-100 Index.

- **Trading times:** The e-mini contracts trade nearly 24 hours per day, with a 30-minute maintenance break in trading from 4:30 to 5:00 p.m. daily.

- **Monthly identifiers:** Monthly identifiers for both mini contracts are *H* for March, *M* for June, *U* for September, and *Z* for December.

- **Margin requirements:** Margins for the ES and NQ contracts are less than for the normal-sized contracts. As of November 2007, the ES requires $4,500 for initial margin and $3,600 for maintenance, and the NQ requires $3,250 and $2,600, respectively.

The day-trading margin is less than the margin to hold an overnight position in S&P 500 e-mini futures. Traders, though, are obligated to pay for the difference between the margins for entry and exit points, which means that if you lose, you're likely to pay up in a big way at the end of the day.

When you own normal-sized contracts and e-mini contracts in one or the other of the underlying indexes, position limits apply to both positions, meaning that each of the contracts is counted as an individual part of the overall position, and the combined number of contracts can't exceed the 20,000 contract limit for the S&P 500-based index and the 10,000 contract limit for the NASDAQ-100-based index.

Formulating Trading Strategies

Now that you know the basics of some of the futures contracts that you can trade, the next step is to put this information to use in formulating strategies. As with any other futures trading, you may want to try some of these in paper trading or by using an online trading simulator. It's always better to get the feel of trading a contract before jumping in with real money.

You can apply every technique described in this book to trading stock-index futures. Moving averages, RSI, MACD, the Swing Rule, pattern recognition, support/resistance levels, and many others (see Chapter 8) — with or without fundamental analysis — all work, and if you apply them properly, you're likely be fairly successful.

Using futures rather than stocks

At the beginning of this chapter, I note that stock-index futures can be used for hedging or for speculating. Here is a good example of how you can use them as a substitute for individual stocks.

Assume that you have a $500,000 portfolio of Treasury bonds (T-bonds) that are paying you a fairly decent return of 5 percent to 6 percent. You aren't planning to sell any of them because you want to hold on to those decent yields as long as possible. Based on your knowledge of technical analysis, market sentiment, and your analysis of the economy (see Chapters 6, 7, and 9), suppose that you're looking at a scenario which in the past has led to a stock market rally, and you'd like to take advantage of that opportunity.

One way to do so is to sell $40,000 of your portfolio and split it in half. For simplicity's sake, assume that the margin, or the amount that you will have to fork over for one S&P 500 futures contract, is $20,000. With that you buy one S&P 500 futures contract, where the margin is roughly $20,000 (Amount 1), while you keep the remaining $20,000 (Amount 2) in your margin account to give you some flexibility, such as leveraging your position with options, considering other strategies, and for protecting you if you're wrong and get a margin call.

Amount 1 ($20,000) should provide enough in your margin account for you to buy one S&P contract, and at the July 15, 2005, closing price of 1230.80, it would give you control of roughly $307,700.

With Amount 2 (the other $20,000), you can invest in and collect interest on Treasury bills and look for other opportunities, perhaps in the options markets, as you look to either hedge your S&P 500 contract or to leverage it further, depending on market conditions.

This strategy isn't without risk, but again, it isn't irresponsible either, and it's sensible if your goal is to take advantage of what you think is a coming rally in the stock market. By using stock indexes with a portion of your bond portfolio, you are

- ✔ **Simplifying your exposure to stocks:** You don't have to go out and buy 10 or 15 individual stocks to diversify your stock portfolio by using the stock indexes.

- ✔ **Still leaving most of your money in income-yielding T-bonds:** In other words, you're still guaranteed a reliable rate of return.

- ✔ **Taking prudent risks:** If you act responsibly, monitor your position, and follow sound trading rules (see Chapter 17), including prudent profit taking, position hedging, and cutting any sudden and unexpected losses, your risks remain tolerable, even if the market goes against you.

- ✔ **Benefiting financially:** The flip side of risk is that if you're correct, you may make a large sum of money in a relatively short period of time.

Protecting your stock portfolio

Another good hedge involves a well-diversified stock portfolio of dividend-paying stocks and stock-index futures. Using the $500,000 example again, assume your portfolio is made up of stocks rather than bonds.

You can see in Figure 12-1 that the S&P 500 Cash Index makes a new high in March, but the relative strength indicator (RSI) fails to match it. That clear divergence is enough cause for concern for you to start monitoring all your high-yield, dividend-paying stocks. Even though you find that they're actually holding on pretty well, you're still not sure what will happen if the market starts selling off. You have no guarantee that even low-volatility stocks won't be sold in a significant price correction.

You have several possible decisions to make. You can

- ✔ Take profits on your stock portfolio.

- ✔ Sell call options or buy put options on each of your individual stocks. Call options essentially are bets that the underlying stock is going higher. Put options are bets that the underlying stock is going to fall. If you sell a call option, you collect a premium that cushions any losses. If you buy a put option, the appreciation of the value of the put (if your stock falls) cushions any losses. See Chapter 4 for more about the basics of options.

- ✔ Look to the futures market for a good way to hedge your stocks.

Option strategies on individual stocks may be a good way to go unless you have 10 or 20 positions to hedge, which can take most of your time to monitor and manage.

Figure 12-1:
The 12-
month S&P
500 Cash
Index and
RSI.

The idea is to understand that the futures and spot markets are linked, which is what became widely known through the unfortunate circumstances surrounding the market crash in 1987. Since then, this relationship has become widely accepted.

In the example that follows, I look at two charts of the S&P 500. Figure 12-1 is a chart of the S&P 500 Cash Index. Figure 12-2 is a chart of the S&P 500 Index futures. Both are from the same date, July 15, 2005. The object is to find out how futures and cash indexes work in tandem and how you can use this relationship to protect your stock portfolio. For better reference, you need to realize that the futures chart offers a zoomed-in view of the time period.

Using the RSI and cash market in Figure 12-1 as your guide, here is the anatomy of a hedge trade for your stock portfolio, using the S&P 500 Stock Index futures:

- **The indicators:** The RSI's lack of confirmation in the cash market was a caution signal and should have alerted you to a potential change in trend.

- **The trend-line analysis:** The trend line on the cash index confirmed a major market break. The break below Trend Line 1 by the S&P 500 Cash Index in Figure 12-1 confirmed your expectations and was your signal to do one of the following:

  - Short one S&P futures contract

  - Buy an S&P futures put option

Notice how RSI kept falling despite the attempted rally in the S&P 500. The descending trend line above the S&P 500 exhibited resistance in the market, and the failure at the trend line led to another leg down for the S&P 500.

Likewise, note how the RSI bottomed along with the market and how the S&P in the cash and futures contracts broke back above the uptrend line. If you played this trade correctly, you made some money and protected your portfolio (or both).

And notice how the action in the S&P futures was closely mirroring the action in the cash index. If you covered your futures short position in April, you didn't have to do much more to manage your stock portfolio because the market rallied for another two months after that.

The tendency of most traders would be to stay too long in the trading position that I just described — as the market was making a bottom in April. That's what the markets do to fool you. Futures traders don't have the same amount of time to make decisions as someone who's trading only stocks. If you played this trade correctly, you made money. If you weren't sure about what to do, you could have covered the risk to your short position in the futures contract by setting up an options straddle so you could sell the put as the market reversed and ride out the call as the market rallied.

A straddle is when you buy both a put and a call, and it's best used when you're not sure which way the market will break. A successfully executed straddle means that you must sell one side of the straddle (the put or the call). Yet it's not always obvious which side should be sold, as sometimes it's best to take profits on the winning side while you wait for the market to turn around before you sell the losing side. Check out Chapter 4.

Swinging with the rule

A little-used strategy that you sometimes can use to help you know when to take profits is called the *swing rule*. In the example used in the previous section, the swing rule works well, but you need to take a close look at some six-month indicators. Looking at Figure 12-2, which shows the S&P 500 Index futures, note the "Swing line" label, right at the 1,200 level. A *swing line* is a line that you can draw across the dome formed by the price changes in the futures contract from February to March. As you can tell, the price made a full swing (up and over) during that time frame, ending up right about where it started before it rallied for a few weeks.

To calculate the swing rule, you take the top price of that dome, which is roughly 1,240, and subtract the bottom, or the level across which you drew the swing line (roughly 1,200) to get a 40-point swing. Swing lines serve as guides to how much you can allow the market to fall before you consider taking at least partial profits. Don't get too bogged down on the exact numbers. This is not an exact rule, but it does help you to get fairly close to good target approximations.

In this case, the swing rule works perfectly because the market bottoms near 1,160, just about 40 points below the swing line at 1,200.

Figure 12-2:
The S&P 500 September futures.

Speculating with stock-index futures

Aside from hedging, you can simply speculate with futures contracts just by using technical and fundamental analyses (see Chapters 6 and 7).

Stock-index futures are almost guaranteed to move in response to economic indicators. You can set up positions with both futures and options as you wait for the news to hit. In the last several years, the monthly employment report, which is issued the first Friday of every month, has been an excellent mover for stock-index futures.

Using Your Head to Be Successful

If you're disciplined, you stand a much better chance of being more successful — or even extremely successful. The following sections offer some suggestions for keeping your head together.

Get real

You can't win every time, and you can't have the same success as a pit trader. Pit traders and retail investors use different time frames and strategies, so it's unrealistic to expect the same kinds of results.

Most pros will tell you that a large portion of their trades break even, lose a little, or gain a little, and that they hit home runs only about 30 percent of the time. So if you don't develop a trading plan and prepare yourself for the reality of the game, you're not going to enjoy it.

Limit your risk

Professional traders rely on a few standards, and although the figures change slightly, the principles of those standards remain firm:

- Risk no more than 5 percent of your equity on any one trade.

- Limit your losses to no more than 5 percent per trade. This is a dynamic process. Adjust your 5 percent loss limit to your current equity level. That means that as your equity rises, the amount risked also gets larger, and as your equity falls, so does the amount risked. That's how you stay in the business, by letting your winners run and keeping a short leash on your losers.

Become a contract specialist

The more you know about a particular type of contract, the better off you are. Here are some actions you can take to become a specialist:

- **Figure out how many days a particular contract tends to spend rising or falling along a Bollinger band.** Bollinger bands are flexible bands of price support and resistance levels described fully in Chapter 7. You can use them to get an idea about when a contract is likely to turn around. This tool is particularly useful when you're swing trading near a top or bottom. Although the Bollinger band trends won't be exact, as long as you know that the index usually turns five to ten days after moving along the band, you can start to follow the index more closely and watch for trading opportunities.

- **Try different sets and combinations of moving averages.** Watching various moving averages, one with the other, you can find out which contracts trade better, for example, with a five-day exponential average, and which ones work best with a nonexponential moving average.

- ✔ **Try different oscillators and combinations of them.** By trying them out, you can find out which ones work best with each index that you trade. The RSI oscillator works better with some futures contracts, while the MACD and other oscillators work better with others.

- ✔ **Check out the charts from the past.** Don't be afraid to go back months or even years to look at charts of what some indexes have done in the past. Patterns shown in the charts tend to repeat time and again, which is why pattern recognition becomes so useful.

- ✔ **Try different option parameters with your index trading.** Find the ones that tend to work best for you and your time frame. Experiment with different strike prices, and consider paper trading with straddles and with individual options. See Chapter 4 for more of the basics of options. Also see *Options For Dummies* (Wiley).

Don't trade when your mind is elsewhere

If you're not up to trading on any given day, that's fine. But if you turn on your screen when your mind is in the clouds and you start making trades, you're going to get hurt. Trust me when I tell you that even if you have only a $5,000 account and you're trading only one contract at a time, a $500 loss amounts to about 10 percent of your entire account. In the futures market, that kind of pitfall can take all of about five minutes' worth of action.

Never be afraid of selling too soon

If you set your targets and they get hit almost immediately after a news release, follow your rules. Your objective got hit; take the money and run. By the same token, don't get greedy. If you're looking at a nice profit, take it before it turns into a loss.

Never let yourself get a margin call

I'll probably get hit by my editor for saying this too many times, but you can't say it, read it, or hear it enough: *Never* let yourself get a margin call. Set loss limits, no matter what. In the rare case that you do get a margin call even though you've set up good stops, the markets must have done something remarkable. Meet your margin call. Figure out why you got it. And keep an eye on the market, because other opportunities may soon arise.

Part IV
Commodity Futures

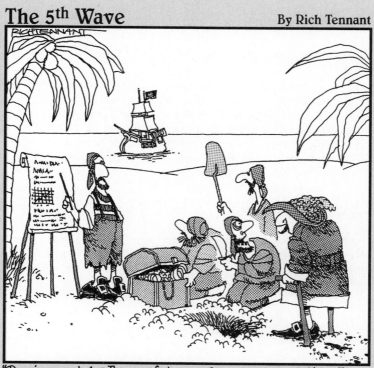

"Precious metals? Energy futures? Currency speculation? I say
we stick the money in the ground like always, and then feed
this guy to the sharks."

In this part . . .

I discuss the increasingly important commodity markets in this part. As China and India grow their economies, these areas of the futures markets should continue to be increasingly prominent. Supply rules the roost in all markets, but in these it is even more important. You jump right in with the kings of the hill — oil and energy futures. Then you get into some metal without the leather as you look at gold, copper, and other precious and industrial metals. Finally, I take you down on the farm to fill you in on livestock and agricultural futures.

Chapter 13

Getting Slick and Slimy: Understanding Energy Futures

I never realized that I was going to become an expert in energy until I wrote a book entitled *Successful Energy Sector Investing* (Prima-Random House, 2002). I also never thought that crude oil would touch $100 per barrel in my lifetime either. But on January 2, 2008, it did — briefly — and by February 7, 2008, the price had moved to $105. Anything is possible. No one can ever predict what any market will eventually do with any certainty. But you can do a lot to prepare yourself as a trader, especially in the energy sector.

I can't tell you everything I know about oil in one chapter. Here I provide you with a good summary of the way professionals think about and execute their trades in the energy markets, and the way I make recommendations on energy stocks and exchange-traded mutual funds (ETFs, see Chapter 5), as well as covering and analyzing important stories regarding the oil markets on my Web site (www.joe-duarte.com).

One thing is almost certain, however: The energy markets will be a major focal point of the financial markets and the global economy for many more years. And the key to understanding energy trading is to understand oil, natural gas, gasoline, and heating oil futures.

The emphasis in this chapter is on the entire energy complex from a speculator's standpoint, concentrating on the practical. The goal is to understand how you can use a combination of three factors — supply and demand, geopolitics, and technical analysis — to reach sensible decisions about making good energy market trades.

In this chapter, when I refer to interest rates I'm referring to both the U.S. Federal Reserve adjusted rates and the bond-market rates unless I specify otherwise.

Some Easy Background Info

Trading in energy futures began in 1979, and it's centralized at the New York Mercantile Exchange (NYMEX), the world's largest physical commodity futures exchange. The 132-year-old NYMEX trades futures and options contracts for crude oil, natural gas, heating oil, gasoline, coal, electricity, and propane. The NYMEX also is home to trading in metals (see Chapter 14).

Trading is conducted on the NYMEX in two divisions:

- ✔ **The NYMEX division,** which trades energy, platinum, and palladium
- ✔ **The COMEX division,** which trades the rest of the metals

For smaller traders, NYMEX offers e-mini contracts for oil and natural gas that also trade on the Globex network of the Chicago Mercantile Exchange (CME).

The NYMEX Web site, www.nymex.com, offers a good deal of information and is worth a visit. The calendars and margin requirements, which are listed individually for each contract, are especially useful to traders.

Next to interest rates, energy — especially oil — is the center of the universe not only for industry but also for the financial markets.

Completing the Circle of Life: Oil and the Bond Market

Much of what happens in the world — from your mortgage rate to how easily you find a job — depends on what I like to call the *Circle of Life* formed by energy prices and interest rates. For the sake of simplicity, I use the term *oil* interchangeably with the term *energy* in the rest of this chapter unless I note otherwise.

This relationship is important because it ties together the two most important aspects of the global economy: energy (the fuel for growth) and interest rates (the catalyst that powers borrowed money to do things). Sometimes the price of oil leads to a rise in interest rates, both in the bond market and through the actions of central banks, and at other times the opposite happens. In this chapter, the term *interest rates* means both types unless I specify one or the other. The relationship depends on where the economic cycle of supply and demand and the political current happen to be at the time. After September 11, 2001, traditional relationships changed somewhat but not completely.

Here are two examples. In mid-2005, one of the major reasons for the Fed to continue to raise interest rates, according to speeches made by Fed governors and Fed Chief Alan Greenspan, was that the rise in oil prices was creating inflation. At the same time, the bond market was struggling with the possibility that high-energy prices were increasing the chances of a recession.

As a result, the Fed kept raising interest rates, and the bond market was stuck in a trading range with rates slowly creeping higher.

If you fast forward to 2008, the economy of the United States was slowing, as a result of the credit crisis created by the subprime mortgage crisis. Yet oil prices kept moving higher. In this instance, the markets were struggling with the potential for supply shortages of crude oil, along with geopolitical issues, as the Middle East conflict was heating up, and demand for oil from China remained stable.

The Federal Reserve kept lowering interest rates in this latter instance, because they were more concerned about the slowing in the economy than the potential inflationary pressures of higher oil prices.

Here's the basic concept. If oil prices rise high enough, one of two scenarios happens: The Fed starts worrying about either inflation or an economic slowdown because oil prices are so high that people can't buy enough of other items.

If inflation is the dominant theory at the Fed, the central bank will raise interest rates. If a slowing economy is more likely, the Fed will start lowering interest rates. The bond market eventually will catch up with whatever the Fed does, and sometimes leads the action of the Fed.

Watching the bond market

You're probably wondering how you can determine — or at least make an educated guess about — how the Fed will act. You can often find your best clue by monitoring the bond market. If bond-market interest rates begin to rise along with oil prices, it's a sign that the bond market is growing concerned about high oil prices triggering inflation. If bond-market rates rise high enough, the Fed is likely to increase bank interest rates. If rates start falling in the bond market, then bond traders are expecting a slowing of the economy, and the Fed is likely to reduce interest rates. As I note in the preceding section, though, the Fed sometimes makes the first move by raising interest rates, and the bond market follows.

This explanation isn't infallible, but it holds true a fair amount of the time. In 2004 and 2005, then-Federal Reserve Chairman Alan Greenspan called persistently low bond-market interest rates combined with the Fed's continuously high interest rates a "conundrum."

Nevertheless, when oil prices rise along with bond yields and/or interest rates from the Fed, you must look for an *inflection point,* such as where bond yields and overall interest rates have gone high enough to lead to a break in the price of oil, because traders have started factoring in the fact that oil prices have risen to a point where they're becoming a hindrance to economic growth.

The bond market's responses to the actions of the Federal Reserve aren't guaranteed. The bond market acts on its own initiative, meaning that if the Fed lowers interest rates, such as the Fed Funds and/or the Discount rate, the bond market will sell off if it senses inflation, and market interest rates will rise. Such a scenario developed in early 2008 when the Fed had to lower interest rates, but persistently high oil prices and overall demand for commodities continued to fuel inflationary fears.

Looking for classic signs as oil prices rise

The overall markets are likely to project certain signs as oil prices rise and traders start gauging the effect of the increases on the economy, including

- **Decreasing traffic in stores and malls (and on the highways, for that matter):** By August 2005, as oil prices were reaching all-time record highs, retailers began blaming a slowing of sales on high gasoline prices. Also look for how many people are actually buying products, as opposed to window shopping or just hanging around the mall.

- **Decreasing consumer confidence:** By August 2005, consumer confidence was skidding. Plenty of reasons could be cited for falling consumer confidence and rising gasoline prices. Hurricane Katrina did significant amounts of damage to the Gulf of Mexico's coastline in the United States and rendered the city of New Orleans nearly useless. The port of New Orleans, a major import hub for oil and export hub for agricultural products, closed for days. And the oil and gas production and refining infrastructure of the area, which accounts for 20 percent of the gasoline and natural gas used in the United States, shut down and took several months to get back on line.

✔ **Crazy headlines:** Look for increasing emphasis on oil prices on the evening news and in the media that don't normally cater to business news. A perfect example was the call from Congress for a windfall profit tax on oil companies and repeated calls for hearings on price gouging by gas stations and fuel retailers.

These scenarios can take a long time to develop. You have to be very patient and let the charts guide your trading. In this case of the U.S. economic slow-down, nothing really hit the skids until the subprime mortgage crisis became evident in 2007; by late in the year more and more people were losing their jobs. More interesting is that even when all these negative things in the economy became obvious, at least as of March 2008, oil prices were still acting fairly well, with West Texas Light Sweet Crude oil trading at $105 per barrel.

Here's a key to the relationship between oil prices and the economy in general: At some point, interest rates will rise enough to cool off the demand for oil. When the economy reaches that point, oil prices will start to fall and, at some point after that, traders and bond yields will begin to factor in a slower economy. The other side of the coin is that the Organization of Petroleum Exporting Countries (OPEC), if nimble enough, may be able to slow the rate of descent of prices by attempting to reduce production. This factor can be difficult to interpret because OPEC is infamous for routinely cheating on production quotas.

The Fed's main goals are to keep prices steady and keep everyone employed, but achieving them is nearly impossible. That means the Fed will make mistakes and create inefficiencies in the market that are key to traders making a profit. As a trader, one thing you definitely know is that the Fed will act. As a result, oil always is on the move, and that creates opportunities for you to trade. You have to throw ideology out the door. Regardless of the party you vote for or what you believe, in the oil market it's what you see that can make you money.

Check out Figure 13-1 (later in this chapter), which shows the relationship between interest rates in the bond market and oil prices. In a classic sense, this is the way things are supposed to work:

✔ Oil prices and interest rates generally move in the same direction when viewed over long periods of time. Keep in mind that this relationship involves a wide band of movement and that I'm discussing only the very big picture, in the classic sense. The important point to remember is that rising oil prices can lead to inflation, and inflation eventually will lead to higher interest rates, both in the bond market and from the central banks. See Chapters 2, 6, and 10 for more about bonds, inflation, and the economy.

✔ At some point, if classic (historical) relationships hold up in the future, oil prices and interest rates will rise enough so that the economy also begins to slow. A slowing economy then tends to dampen demand for oil and prices retreat.

The preceding describes a classic relationship that was well established before the emergence of China, India, and other emerging markets as major consumers of oil. As China's economy continued to grow in the post 9/11 world, the relationship between supply and demand in the world markets was distorted. Prior to China's accelerated expansion, the United States and Europe were the major oil consumption regions of the world, with little competition. Thus, when those economies slowed down, oil prices would eventually fall. The future is less certain, as it's unclear whether the demand from China and the emerging markets will be enough to make the classic relationship between oil and interest rates a moot point. My guess is that the relationship will not become useless, but that it could take a lot longer before the endpoint, where high interest rates lead to falling oil prices, is reached.

Note that oil prices made a new high in March 2005, but interest rates in the bond market didn't. At that point in time, you needed to be thinking that a top in oil prices was possible because interest rates in the bond market didn't make a new high along with oil prices. Even though you may not have been right, you nevertheless needed to think about it.

Examining the Peak Oil Concept

Peak oil is the concept that the world's oil production has peaked or will peak, and that after it does production levels will never again be as high.

The peak oil idea is controversial, but it's increasingly plausible given the state of the global oil industry. The most important factors affecting this theory are as follows:

✔ Countries such as Venezuela, Iran, and Nigeria, all of which are OPEC members, aren't necessarily friendly to the United States and other industrialized nations. Turbulent political situations can reduce oil production in these and other countries, as can any potential production problems having to do with how much oil is available for extraction at any one point.

✔ Poor maintenance of key facilities and equipment and questionable reserve data, in essence lies about how much oil is really in the ground, are reportedly rampant throughout OPEC nations; Indonesia's production has already been in decline for years. Indonesia is a net importer of oil, despite being an oil-producing nation. Another example is Venezuela where thousands of oil wells, with potential extractable reserves in the ground, are in such states of disrepair that they are no longer usable.

✔ Traditional non-OPEC sources of oil, such as the North Sea and Mexico, are also showing signs of declining production. The eventual loss of production from key fields in Mexico will likely affect the U.S. economy at some point. This is because many of these fields have been producing for decades and have just run out of the easy-to-extract reserves.

What I think about peak oil doesn't matter, because somewhere in the back of just about every oil trader's mind is the thought that the world may just be running out of oil — a thought that now maintains an essentially permanent influence on the oil markets. Needless to say, the concept of peak oil

✔ Gathered steam after the events of September 11, 2001, and became well established in many corridors of trading during the mega bull market in oil that ensued and that remains in place well into early 2008.

✔ Received support in July 2005 when Saudi Arabia told the world that in ten years, its production wouldn't be able to keep up with global demand if demand continued to grow at rates that were prevalent at the time.

By 2008, some startling statistics were circulating. According to several key opinions, world oil production may, in essence, have either peaked already or will peak sometime in the next 10–20 years. If that's true, the world as you know it will certainly change. In fact, according to a CIBC World markets report published in February 2008, it will take 4 million barrels per day of new oil to keep up with the oil demand of the next few years — and that's if you take into account what's already been lost in places such as Mexico, Indonesia, Venezuela, and the United States.

So if the report, and the work of Matthew Simmons in his book *Twilight In The Desert: The Coming Saudi Oil Shock and the World Economy* (Wiley, 2006), are right, peak oil may already be under way. Simmons did a literature review of hundreds of papers with relationship to Saudi Arabia's oil supply and concluded that the Saudis don't have near as much oil in the ground as they say they do, and that they have had shoddy maintenance of their existing fields that can still produce. If he is correct, that would mean that peak oil may be closer than the overall estimates, which seem to agree on 2010 or 2011 as the key dates.

The Post-9/11 Mega Bull Market in Energy

The world changed after September 11, 2001. The invasions of Afghanistan and Iraq were only a small part of what happened, at least in terms of the financial markets.

Just prior to September 11, 2001, the United States was scrambling to recover from the economic weakness caused by the bursting of the Internet bubble. However, the attacks on the World Trade Center derailed the fragile economic improvements and plunged the country into a deep psychological and logistical nightmare in which businesses closed their doors and job losses began to mount.

Here's what happened:

- **The U.S. dollar went into a multiyear bear market.** Money left the United States as the Fed lowered interest rates, making the dollar less attractive. Politically, the world also viewed the United States as unstable, unpredictable, and vulnerable because of the attacks. As with any bear market, there were periods after 2001 when the dollar rallied. But the rallies did not last. In February and March 2008, the U.S. dollar, as measured by the U.S. Dollar Index, made new all time lows.

- **Oil and natural gas entered once-in-a-lifetime secular bull markets.** However, the natural gas bull lost steam much earlier than the bull in crude oil because new production sources, such as the Barnett Shale deposit near and under the city of Fort Worth, Texas, came online. A *secular bull market* is one that lasts years to decades. Traders almost immediately started bidding up the price of oil, initially because of the connection of the terrorists who attacked the United States to Saudi Arabia, the world's largest oil producer. However, as time passed, a new dynamic developed as money began to flow into China.

  In other words, as the United States appeared to be entering a period of uncertainty, traders began looking for places where economic growth wasn't as affected by what happened on September 11, 2001. These traders found China, whose currency was pegged to the dollar.

  As the dollar fell in value, the Chinese yuan remained weak, increasing the demand for Chinese products and revving up the Chinese economy, which relied heavily on exports to other countries, especially Europe and the United States. As more foreign money flowed into China for those exports, the Chinese economy became more and more able to produce goods and export them to the entire world. The upshot of all this economic rotation was a faster rate of increase in global oil demand, just at a time when production was starting to plateau.

- **Long-term interest rates entered a downward sloping and wide trading range.** The yield on the U.S. ten-year Treasury note initially rose, because traders began to price in the likely collapse of the U.S. economy, and because China and oil-rich countries recycled their new found riches into U.S. Treasury bonds. Although by 2003 the U.S. economy wasn't as strong as it would have been had September 11, 2001, not occurred, it clearly wasn't going to collapse.

  As the economy stabilized, interest rates began to rise. Note, though, that the dollar didn't bottom out until 2005, a full two years after bond yields started to rise, and so did oil demand.

The key is not to be in a big hurry to see these events unfold, and not to be too rigid in our expectations or interpretations. That's because these relationships can take significant amounts of time to reach points at which they become evident. Sometimes it takes a large number of interest-rate increases and a long period of rising bond yields to turn a major currency like the dollar around. Don't forget that the politics and general stability of a country play big roles in how strong its currency will be. In the post-September 11, 2001, period, the markets weren't immediately convinced that the United States would be able to survive the attack and remain a major world power.

As of 2008, those who bet against the United States in the immediate post-9/11 period as a military power were proved to be wrong. Despite large amounts of political controversy and conflict, the United States remained a major world power. The irony is that even though the 9/11 attacks did not destroy the United States and its economy, an internal attack on the U.S. economy in the form of fraud, greed, and bad policy did deliver a significant blow, as the subprime mortgage crisis unfolded. In essence, the ensuing credit crunch was a bloodless coup as U.S. unemployment began to rise, record numbers of home foreclosures developed, and the U.S. dollar continued to fall.

Understanding Supply and Demand

Wanna know a secret? Although most people think that demand is what makes prices change, supply rules in the energy markets. As the U.S. economy slowed during the months that followed the World Trade Center attack, the Chinese economy picked up steam, and its demand for oil increased.

The increased Chinese demand, however, wasn't enough to boost oil prices immediately. That boost didn't become noticeable for several months. Instead, the markets correctly began to price in the possibility of attacks on the oil-producing infrastructure and the increasing challenges of getting oil out of the Middle East. More important, the market again correctly factored the loss of Iraq's oil supply into the markets as the United States attacked Iraq.

Now in 2008, the market faces a different set of dynamics. Iraqi oil is starting to flow back into the market, but it may not be enough to compensate for the loss of production in Mexico, Venezuela, the North Sea, and other areas that will likely crop up in the next few years.

Keep these important tidbits about the oil markets in mind:

- ✔ The world runs on oil, and any threat to the oil supply leads to rising prices.

- ✔ As an oil trader, your primary goal is to consider the effects of events on supply and to correlate those effects with your charts.

- ✔ Demand fluctuates, but supply is finite. Weeks are necessary to ramp up supply or to turn it back down. Refineries are a bottleneck in the system. So even if plenty of oil is sitting in storage, if the refineries can't turn it into gasoline or heating oil, the supply of those products is impaired.

Playing the Sensible Market

The energy markets make sense, regardless of whether you believe in the concept of peak oil.

Real companies have huge trading desks with hundreds of traders all betting on the price of oil. Banks and brokers join oil, trucking, and airline companies in using the oil markets on a daily basis to hedge their future price risks and for pure speculation. Even Goldman Sachs and Merrill Lynch got into the oil storage and distribution business in the early part of the 21st century in the wake of September 11, 2001.

In other words, the oil market is about real people trying to figure out how much oil they're going to need to run their businesses in the next few months to years, regardless of whether they're suppliers or users.

Charting refinery capacity in the United States

The United States hasn't built a new refinery since the 1970s. The combination of environmental concerns, red tape and paperwork, costs in the billions of dollars, and the multiyear time frame needed to finish a new refinery are prohibitive and have prevented any new oil-refining capacity from coming online. In essence, the United States is now in a position in which domestic refinery capacity can't meet any increase in demand for oil or oil products. That means that now more than ever, the United States depends on foreign resources for its oil and refined products.

Damage to refining and shipping capabilities caused by Hurricanes Katrina and Rita brought the U.S. refinery issue to the forefront as gasoline prices skyrocketed. The markets and consumers also reacted as prices reached a level that was high enough to decrease consumption and lead to lower prices.

The net effect of the post-September 11, 2001, bull market in oil, though, was to reset fuel prices at a higher level than prior to that date. I don't think gasoline prices will ever dip below $.50 again, barring some truly extraordinary event.

Stock prices are built mostly on analysts' drivel, such as price/earnings ratios and new paradigms, such as the nonsense that sank the Internet stocks. Oil, gasoline, heating oil, and natural gas prices, on the other hand, are based more on real-life circumstances and aren't usually influenced by the kind of fiction spawned by slick Wall Street analysts penning negative e-mails about the stocks they push onto the public.

Supply rules the energy markets, and here are the basics:

- ✔ OPEC supplies 30 to 40 percent of the world's oil. Russia, the next-biggest supplier, and other non-OPEC producers like Mexico, Norway, and the United Kingdom make up the rest of the world's supply. The United States also is an oil and natural gas producer, with Alaska and the Gulf of Mexico being the largest affected areas. The United States ranks above Mexico and Canada in proven oil reserves. The total oil reserves in the United States are roughly one tenth of those in Saudi Arabia. Still, as time passes and exploration becomes more difficult for both geologic and political reasons, the dynamics of the oil market will change, and likely for the worse, with the potential for higher prices and supply disruptions rising.

- ✔ From a practical standpoint, supply is made up of what comes out of the ground, what can be refined, and what can be delivered, both before it gets to the refinery and after it's refined into gasoline, heating oil, diesel, and other fuels.

- ✔ The potential for supply disruption can occur at any of several steps along the route from extraction through the point of sale, and each step has its own unique chance of causing price-increasing supply screw-ups.

- ✔ Worker strikes, hurricanes and all other kinds of natural disasters, accidents, spills, sabotage, and even market manipulation by OPEC and other producers all end up affecting supply, not demand.

- ✔ Oil without a doubt is a political tool. The Venezuelan government of Hugo Chavez didn't like President George W. Bush, so it repeatedly threatened to cut shipments of oil to the United States during the Bush years in the White House. Sabotage of oil pipelines was a major weapon in Iraq in the early days of the U.S. invasion. It remains to see what will happen when a new U.S. president is elected and takes office in 2009 and how the war in Iraq will eventually evolve.

The one constant in supply, especially in the United States, is that not enough refinery capacity is available to keep up with any more than normal demand. That means when winters are extremely cold, refineries are a key bottleneck in the oil-delivery system.

In the new world, with China, India, and the United States gobbling up increasing supplies of oil, oil markets in general have to deal with the reality that supplies are going to be tighter than they were a few short years ago. That's why prices stayed high in spite of the fact that the war in Iraq settled into a less hectic rhythm and why even if prices fall from levels above $70–$80 per barrel, the days of $10 oil aren't likely to return in the near future unless the global economy collapses.

Handling Seasonal Cycles

Energy demand, especially for heating oil, gasoline, and natural gas, is extremely seasonal in nature, and if you look at your own life, you can easily understand how these cycles work.

In winter, you heat your house. If you live on the East Coast of the United States, that means you use heating oil. Everywhere else you burn natural gas and sometimes coal. Some areas rely on nuclear energy. Likewise, during summer you drive your car or fly off somewhere to go on vacation.

Traders anticipate the ebb and flow of these cycles and factor them into their bets. A good number of traders work for companies, energy and otherwise, that use the futures market either to have fuel delivered to them for resale or for their own use. Others use energy futures to hedge the cost of the energy they need to run their businesses. Still others are speculating and trying to make a buck.

All cycles are variable and describe the oil markets in broad strokes only, so you should never expect the course of the oil business to be perfect each time you trade. You will, however, be a better trader if you remain aware of these cycles and watch for their presence. In general, crude oil futures

✔ Experience a lull in the spring months when refineries convert production from heating oil to gasoline. When that happens, the price of heating oil starts to fall, and gasoline prices firm up.

✔ Swing up and down during the summer based on gasoline supplies. As the end of the summer nears, another pause occurs when refineries switch over from gasoline back to heating oil production.

This broad cycle became unreliable after September 11, 2001, because prices bucked the cyclical trends and pretty much went higher.

Bear in mind, though, that a seasonal tendency for price action does exist. For example, you don't generally want to look to trade long on gasoline in winter. Instead you want to focus on heating oil during cold-weather months. At the same time, you need to consider natural gas as a potential short sale during the spring and early summer.

Preparing for the Weekly Cycle

A more useful cycle hinges on what happens on Wednesday mornings — or on Thursday mornings after three-day weekends. That's when the American Petroleum Institute (API) and the U.S. Energy Information Agency (EIA) release their weekly supply data reports.

Analysts all pony up their estimates for the reports usually on Monday and Tuesday. They're all focusing on supply, not demand, and they want to know whether inventories are *building* (increasing in supply) or *drawing down* (decreasing in supply).

Making trades based on the API and EIA supply data is a good idea to consider because you can generate some nice short-term profits if you play them right.

The markets focus mainly on the report from the EIA because it's a government agency that *requires* companies to provide their supply statistics. The API uses data supplied on a volunteer basis. Thus the API data tends to be less exact because of its information-gathering system.

Analysts almost never get it right. That means that the market usually jumps up or down after the data comes out. I do just about everything I possibly can to rearrange my schedule so I can be in front of my trading screen when that report comes out.

A great time for a coffee break is at 10:30 a.m. eastern time on Wednesdays so you can watch for the energy supply data. Setting up some potential trades ahead of the release of the reports can help you get a jump on executing them based on the new supply data. Wednesdays can be the most profitable day of the week in the energy pits.

Checking other sources before Wednesday

On Monday and Tuesday, I start scanning news sources for analysts' opinions about the oil market. Doing so gives me a good idea about what may happen if the market is priced wrong regarding current supply levels.

Some good stuff to read before the release of the reports include the commodities column at MarketWatch.com (`www.marketwatch.com`). It provides a good summary of expectations. Reuters (`www.reuters.com`) and Bloomberg (`www.bloomberg.com`) also provide good summaries of what the market is setting itself up for when the data comes out. If your broker gives you access to good news data, Dow Jones Newswires is about as good as any source to get the same data. Dow Jones Newswires is a subscription service accessible online, usually through brokers and financial-service institutions.

How to react to the report

Making trades based on the supply reports isn't an exercise in being exact, because analysts usually are clueless about what's coming up. What you want to look for are instances when they all agree one way or another. For example, if they're all leaning toward a *build* (increased supply) of crude, be ready for the market to go higher if the report even hints of a supply shortage. The same is true for when the market gets set up for a *drawdown* (decreased supply) — be ready for the market to go lower if the report hints of more abundant supplies. Here are a couple of tips for trading the supply reports:

✔ **Be careful when the report comes out.** Give the market some time before you jump in. The first few trades can be volatile. After a minute or two, your real-time chart should start to show you the way the market is headed.

✔ **Consider some option strategies.** As with other reports, a straddle (see Chapter 4) is a good potential strategy to consider. Other hedging techniques, such as holding some long positions in blue-chip oil stocks and selling the futures, or buying puts on the futures, also may work.

If the supply data surprises the markets in a big way, the move can be huge, and prices are likely to gap up as the figure is released. In this case, you may be looking at one of the following three scenarios:

✔ **You're already out of the market.** If you aren't already in the market, you miss a chance to make some money. However, don't go chasing prices trying to get into the market. You'll end up being sorry.

✔ **You have an established position.** You take advantage of the data being in your favor by ratcheting up your sell stops so you can take as much profit as possible if the market happens to turn on you. If you're using a broker, hopefully you gave him instructions on what to do in this situation; otherwise, you'd better have his number on speed dial and hope you're one of his favorite clients.

✔ **Your position gets stopped out.** If you were in the market but were stopped out because you guessed wrong, be glad you're out. Reassess your position and wait for a better opportunity. When you get stopped out, it means that the stop-loss order you placed to limit your losses was triggered as prices dropped to the level you specified.

Forecasting Oil Prices by Using Oil Stocks

One of the most reliable methods of forecasting futures prices is to use the action in oil stocks. John Murphy is one of the most prominent promoters of this dynamic, and I've found his approach a very useful starting point.

Changes in oil stocks tend to precede the moves in oil prices and should also confirm them. Sometimes oil stocks also will move along with or just after crude oil futures.

Although oil stock prices may sound unpredictable, as a new bull market in oil starts, oil stocks will normally start rising along with crude prices either before or right after crude oil futures start rising.

Much of the time, although not always, oil stocks will rise or fall before the price of crude oil rises or falls.

Similarly, as the falling trend line of a bear market in oil takes hold, oil stocks will either break sometime before, along with, or just after crude oil futures. Figure 13-1 provides a good example of the dynamic, using information from Exxon Mobil, the oil (XOI) and oil service (OSX) indexes, and December 2005 crude oil futures.

Take note of how

✔ The price of Exxon Mobil stock (bottom-left chart) bottomed out before the XOI index (top-left chart) took off.

✔ The XOI index began to rally at a much steeper rate of rise than the December 2005 crude oil futures (CLZ5) contract. Some of the steeper rise results from the fact that the volume of trading in the December 2005 contracts didn't pick up until 2003 and then really started booming in 2004. Nevertheless, oil stocks clearly began to rally before the futures.

✔ Oil service stocks (OSX top right chart) kept pace with the XOI and Exxon.

✔ Exxon stopped rallying in February 2005, and oil futures(bottom-right chart) and the rest of the oil stocks continued to move higher. Every time oil futures made a new high, Exxon didn't confirm them — a classic technical divergence that requires confirmation. Figure 13-1 shows a classic double-top pattern in Exxon. A *double top* is when the market reaches a price that's similar to a previous price and then rolls over. A double top is a sign of failing price momentum. Notice how the double top in Exxon was followed by a breakdown in the price of oil, which on November 1 dropped below $60.

Figure 13-1:
The relationship between Exxon Mobil, the XOI and OSX indexes, and December 2005 crude oil futures. Top row: Amex Oil Index (XOI, left), Philadelphia Oil Service Index (OSX, right). Bottom row: Exxon Mobil stock (XOM, left), crude oil futures (right).

Figure 13-2 is an enlarged version of Figure 13-1, and it shows in greater detail how the double top in Exxon coincided with the breakdown in the price of the December crude oil contract and how the break in the stock preceded the break in the futures. Be sure to check out these points in Figure 13-2:

- ✔ **Relative strength indicator (RSI) for Exxon and for CLZ5:** Lower highs are present on both charts; however, the Exxon chart also shows clear overhead resistance on the stock's price, a sign that sellers are waiting to unload as soon as Exxon nears $64 per share.

- ✔ **How the crude futures chart continues to make new highs:** The RSI oscillator for crude futures also is cause for concern for the same reason — because it also fails to confirm the new high in crude, a sign of a momentum failure.

When the price of Exxon stock no longer confirms the new high in crude oil, you need to start being careful and monitoring the momentum and trend indicators so you can prepare to sell your crude futures position. In other words, Exxon, in this case, flashed a correct warning sign that oil prices were likely to fall.

Figure 13-2: The relationship between Exxon Mobil (XOM) and December crude oil futures (CLZ5) from February to October 2005 (Exxon Mobil on the left, crude oil futures on the right)

As a futures trader, the situation shown in Figure 13-2 gave you little choice but to continue to trade crude futures on the long side. However, in this case, because Exxon was warning you and the RSI oscillator wasn't confirming the rallies, you need to be very careful and use tight stop-loss points or consider trading only with options to curb your risk.

Burning the Midnight Oil

Crude oil trades around the world, but New York's Mercantile Exchange (NYMEX) is considered the hub of global oil trading.

Light, sweet crude is high-grade, low-sulfur crude oil that's more easily refined than thicker oils. It also yields better products. When it isn't going by that name, it's called West Texas Intermediate. High-sulfur crude, such as that which comes from Venezuela and certain Saudi Arabian wells, requires special refineries that process only the heavier crudes.

NYMEX also provides trading platforms for futures contracts based on the following:

✔ Dubai crude oil. This contract is a futures contract for Dubai crude oil.

✔ The differential between the light, sweet crude oil futures contract and Canadian Bow River crude at Hardisty, Alberta.

- ✔ The differentials between the light, sweet crude oil futures contract and four domestic grades of crude oil, including Light Louisiana Sweet, West Texas Intermediate-Midland, West Texas Sour, and Mars Blend.
- ✔ Brent North Sea crude oil.
- ✔ Oil options.

Crude oil is the world's most actively traded commodity, and the NYMEX contract for light, sweet crude is the most liquid of all crude oil contracts. The NYMEX Web site (www.nymex.com) is well worth a visit.

Here are the particulars of a crude oil contract:

- ✔ **Contract:** Each crude oil contract contains 1,000 barrels of oil that will be delivered to Cushing, Oklahoma.

   The e-mini contract trades on the CME Globex electronic platform are cleared at NYMEX and hold 500 barrels of light, sweet crude.

- ✔ **Valuation:** A barrel of oil holds 42 gallons and trades in U.S. dollars per barrel worldwide. The minimum tick of $0.01 (1 cent) is equal to $10 per contract.

- ✔ **Trading:** NYMEX offers both open-cry trading during regular hours and electronic, Web-based trading after hours. Open outcry trading hours are from 10 a.m. to 2:30 p.m. After-hours futures trading takes place on the NYMEX ACCESS, an Internet-based trading platform, starting at 3:15 p.m. Monday through Thursday and ending at 9:50 a.m. the following day. Sunday trading starts at 6 p.m.

- ✔ **Margins:** The initial crude oil contract margin for nonmembers as of January 2008 was $7,088 (with the maintenance margin for customers at $5,250).

- ✔ **Settlement:** Contract settlement is physical, and delivery takes place at Cushing, Oklahoma, or similar pipeline or transfer facilities.

You can find contract listings and termination dates at www.nymex.com.

Getting the Lead Out with Gasoline

Gasoline has become a hugely important contract for several reasons. It's the largest-selling refined product sold in the United States and accounts for almost half of the nation's oil consumption. Two important factors that you need to know about the gasoline futures contract are that

- ✔ **Refinery capacity is limited.** As the global economy continues to grow, the global demand for gasoline also is rising. As is true in the United States, the number of cars in China also is growing, contributing to this increased global demand. For many of the same reasons, environmental and otherwise, gasoline demand outpaced refinery capacity for a good portion of 2005.

✔ **International competition for oil and geopolitical problems in South America are on the rise.** Although a bit more subtle, the importance of Venezuela as a major exporter of oil and gasoline to the United States is becoming a major global market factor. As rhetoric grew more intense between Venezuelan president Hugo Chavez and the United States in 2005, so did the risk of Venezuela cutting off exports.

The situation between the Chavez government and the United States is rather fluid. Much of it may be due to the personality conflict between Chavez and President Bush, who will leave office in 2009. So things can theoretically change.

Chavez, though, has pursued the development of alternative markets for Venezuela's oil products, including having made deals with China and several countries in South America. Indeed, Chavez has made production, exploration, and refinery deals with Russia, Brazil, India, Iran, and Cuba. At some point, if Chavez is successful, the United States may indeed encounter supply problems. I'd expect that the United States can buy oil and gasoline from alternative sources. The key is that prices are likely to be higher because of the logistics involved.

Contract specifications

You needed a $7,425 initial margin per contract to trade a gasoline futures contract and $5,500 to trade gasoline futures in February 2008.

A contract gives you control of 1,000 barrels or 42,000 gallons of unleaded gasoline. A 25-cent move in the per-gallon price of gasoline is worth $10,500 per contract, and that amount is the limit move. Each tick of $0.0001 (1/100th cent) is worth $4.20 per contract. Delivery is physical to the New York harbor.

Trading strategies

Keep the following general tendencies in mind when trading gasoline contracts, but understand that they're not guaranteed to occur or to follow any particular script.

Gasoline prices tend to move along with prices for crude oil; however, gasoline prices aren't guaranteed to mirror crude prices, because they move according to their own supply and demand scenario.

Gasoline prices tend to be the highest during summer months when demand is highest. Prices tend to rally for the July, August, and September gasoline futures contracts during April and May. Figure 13-4 shows the start of the rally in the September contract at the beginning of May. The figure also exhibits choppiness in the market as expectations for less driving are incorporated into gasoline prices. This chart is particularly important, because it shows the consistency of the overall seasonal pattern. In 2005, gasoline supplies were below historical stockpiles because of an overall tightness in the market and problems experienced within the refinery industry.

You also need to take note within Figure 13-4 that although Hurricane Katrina pushed gasoline futures prices above $2, the seasonal pattern held. Aside from the usual decrease in demand caused by seasonal factors, in this case, the market was essentially flooded with gasoline imports from Europe, and President Bush also suspended the need for refining a multitude of different grades of gasoline that are normally produced to meet clean-air standards. The combination of these three individual variables led to the decline in gasoline prices.

Keeping the Chill Out with Heating Oil

The price of heating oil has a tendency to rise as the winter months approach. As is true with all energy commodities, supply is the key, and chart watching is as important as keeping up with supply when trading heating oil futures.

After gasoline, *heating oil*, which also is known as *No. 2 fuel oil*, makes up about 25 percent of the yield from a barrel of crude oil. Here are the particulars of trading heating oil futures:

- ✔ **Contract:** Heating oil futures trade in the same units as gasoline: 1,000 barrels of 42 gallons each, or a total of 42,000 gallons. The contract is based on delivery to New York harbor, the principal cash-market trading center.

- ✔ **Margins:** Margins for heating oil are quite high, and they're based on a tiered structure designed to give a more precise assessment of risk. Each tier consists of at least one futures month, and all the months within a given tier are consecutive. In general, as of February 2008, the Group 1 margin for nonmembers was $6,750, with maintenance margins at $5,500.

    If you trade *nearby contracts,* contracts that expire in months that are in close proximity to the current month, your margin will be higher, because the volatility and the chance for profit is higher, and you're being charged a premium for that.

- ✔ **Valuation:** The price relationship of each tick is identical to gasoline, with 1/100th of a cent equaling $4.20 per contract.

The airline industry, refiners, and others in the oil business use the heating oil futures contract to hedge diesel-fuel and jet-fuel prices, which ultimately means that you're trading against a savvy group of adversaries when you trade heating oil contracts.

Figures 13-3 and 13-4 also show the general tendency of heating oil to rally with oil, gasoline, and natural gas prices. During the time frame depicted in the figures, the contract started to show some price compression in late August and had joined gasoline in diverging from crude oil prices, which suggested that a big move was coming.

Looking for confirmation from different markets is important. As Figures 13-3 and 13-4 show, the energy complex was running into trouble. Crude oil topped out first, followed by gasoline, heating oil, and finally natural gas.

Figure 13 3: Gasoline and crude oil futures show the effect of Hurricane Katrina.

Figure 13-4: Heating oil and natural gas futures after Hurricane Katrina.

Getting Natural with Gas

Natural gas is an increasingly popular fuel. Its reputation for burning cleaner than crude oil and coal has made it the number-one choice of environmentalists and a commodity with a rising demand profile.

Russia has the world's largest natural gas reserves. The United States has roughly a tenth of the reserves of Russia, and Iran has the second-largest natural gas reserves. Yet, domestic production in the United States has increased significantly since crude oil prices have been on the rise.

Natural gas supplies about 25 percent of the energy used in the United States and is increasingly important in generating electricity, especially during the summer months, because of air conditioning.

Natural gas contracts have nine margin tiers, with initial margin requirements differing and changing from time to time. Check out `nymex.com` for current figures when you're considering trading. Tier 1 margins in February 2008 were $6,750 and $5,000, respectively, for initial and maintenance for retail customers.

A natural gas contract gives you control of 10,000 million British thermal units (mmBtu), and a $0.1-cent move is equal to $10 per contract.

Aside from the usual supply-and-demand dynamics, natural gas is subject to pressures from the hurricane season, because many major natural gas rigs are located in the Gulf of Mexico. Figure 13-4 shows how natural gas prices held up better than heating oil and gasoline during the week and weekend leading up to the climactic run toward land of Hurricane Katrina.

You can trade natural gas and crude oil via exchange-traded mutual funds. For crude oil, use the U.S. Oil Fund (USO), and for natural gas, use the U.S. Natural Gas Fund (UNG).

Natural gas is extremely volatile, so you should be very well versed in technical analysis before you try to trade it, even through UNG. A good idea is to do a fair number of paper trades before you tackle natural gas trading in the real world.

Getting in Tune with Sentiment and the Energy Markets

Sentiment is an unclear concept. To some, it can mean sadness; to others, it means great joy. In the financial markets, it means greed and fear. Greed usually comes with market tops, and fear usually is the hallmark of market bottoms. These diverging concepts are, of course, what make up the contrarian thesis of investing. (For more information about contrarian thinking, see Chapter 9.)

In the summer of 2005, when oil prices had risen by roughly 50 percent from the previous summer, many attributed the huge rise in prices to a three-pronged combination of refinery problems, significant weather changes, and steady economic growth, compounded by event fear and fanned by the flames of the greatest extension of a bull market in oil that started after September 11, 2001. It was in this context that I started carefully tracking market sentiment.

When I appeared on CNBC on August 24, 2005, the first question I answered was, "How high can oil go?" My response was that $60 or $70 was possible, but that I wasn't sure. I also said that the market had been going up for some time and that it was due for a pause.

When I returned to my office after the interview, the network pundits were talking to Professor Michael Economides, author of *The Color of Oil* (Round Oak Publishing, 2000), and he was predicting $100 oil, although he didn't say by when. All day long on CNBC and elsewhere in the financial media, coverage of the oil markets was rather dramatic, and so were the perceptions of what was coming.

The next day oil prices fell more than a dollar, and the headline "SCREAMS AT THE PUMP" appeared on the Drudge Report a few days later, signifying that life in the oil markets was about to become even more interesting.

By August 26, 2005, the market was trying to decide what effect Hurricane Katrina was going to have. The market close on that Friday was inconclusive, but by Sunday, August 28, it became clear that Katrina was a major storm and that the oil infrastructure in New Orleans and the Gulf Coast area, which is responsible for a major portion of the energy supply and distribution of the United States, was in peril.

Although oil had traded above $70 per barrel as the storm was brewing overnight August 28, not enough data was available to support prices at that level. As the storm hit on the morning of August 29, damage reports began trickling in, and by August 30, oil finally burst above $70 per barrel during a regular trading session.

As the news of the storm trickled in, and the damage assessment became clear, the oil market took on an entirely new, extremely serious tone that was certain to suddenly make the American public keenly aware of daily price fluctuations.

By the end of trading August 30, crude oil futures for October closed at $69.85, just shy of $70, but nevertheless, still at an all-time record high.

On September 17, I appeared on the *Financial Sense News Hour* radio show with Jim Puplava, and Jim and I both agreed that oil prices were looking as if they were making a top. Few other analysts were on that side of the trade at the time. I submitted an article to Rigzone.com in which I reported the conversation Jim and I had, and I forwarded the article to CNBC, which was interested enough to call me back for an interview.

I was back on CNBC the week after I made the call on the Jim Puplava show, and told them that if oil fell below $56, it could go to $40. During the next several weeks, the oil market dropped from the $70 area to around $60 by November 1, when Republicans were agreeing with the Democrats in Congress and starting to discuss adding a windfall tax to oil companies for making too much money, another sign that prices could fall farther.

A second storm, Hurricane Rita, also hit the Gulf region just a few weeks after Katrina, but the damage, although significant, wasn't as bad.

As history shows, the U.S. economy recovered, but the price of oil, after a brief fall, continued its bull market.

What was apparent in November 2005 was that at least 50 percent of the oil and natural gas production infrastructure in the Gulf of Mexico was off-line, although refinery capacity was steadily coming back online. The United States was running on imported gasoline from Europe, yet prices still were going lower and people were still calling for $100-per-barrel oil.

Some Final Thoughts about Oil

I'll end this chapter with a list of some final thoughts to illustrate several points that you need to know about the oil markets in the winter of 2008:

- ✔ **The bull market in oil was nearly seven years old.** If you count September 11, 2001, (or shortly thereafter) as its date of birth, that means the bull market was getting old, even by secular or long-term bull market standards, which are measured in years and sometimes decades. No one knows how long a bull market of this magnitude can last. But one thing is nearly certain, this one has been quite amazing, and theoretically has the potential to last several more years, although there are likely to be periods of significant declines along the way to higher prices.

✓ **The prevailing wisdom in August 2005 was that oil prices couldn't go anywhere but up.** The world, after all, was running out of oil, and the global economy could never slow down. At the start of 2008, the global economy was slowing, and demand was about to slow, so prices should have fallen. But they didn't fall. In 2005, prices pulled back and the bull market resumed. In 2008, prices finally closed at new records, well above $100.

In other words, no matter what the news and the experts are saying, always trade with the trend. Develop a sense of when the market can turn, and don't be afraid to put your money where your mouth is. Don't let what you want to see happen get in the way of what's happening. And don't let what you want to happen get in the way of your trading. The market will almost always prove you wrong until you throw in the towel on your beliefs and what your analysis is telling you. Then if you're not careful, it will swallow you whole.

Chapter 14

Getting Metallic Without Getting Heavy

In This Chapter

▶ Pricing the heavy-metal economy

▶ Exploring the fundamentals of gold markets

▶ Finding the trading line for silver

▶ Going platinum (just not blonde)

▶ Following the trends and markets in copper and other industrial metals

▶ Strategizing for trades in copper futures

*W*hen I think of heavy metal, I think of loud music, long hair, and fast guitar licks. And if you look hard enough, you may even see me at one of those increasingly popular 1980s' metal reunion tours during the summer because I like to see those old boys still strut their stuff.

The other side of heavy metal has nothing to do with music, but it's still quite industrial and can be just as profitable as record sales and concert grosses. Indeed, metal futures (you knew I'd get around to it, didn't you?) experienced a significant revival because the global economy, largely influenced by aggressive growth in China, has brought the luster back into what was a largely faded area of the futures markets.

Metals divide into two major categories: precious and industrial. The markets of the two different classes look at the same side of the economy but from different angles. Although precious metals are thought of as hedges against inflation, price changes in the industrial metals category usually are precursors to the start and often the end of economic cycles.

From a trading standpoint, especially from that of a beginner's, the best way to get started in the metals markets is to become familiar with the gold and copper markets. They're the two most economically sensitive of all the metals.

In this chapter, I focus on gold and copper, but I also tie in enough information about silver, platinum, and the other industrial metals to understand how the markets for each of them work.

Tuning In to the Economy

The prices of precious and industrial metals are linked to economic activity. Gold steals all the headlines, but the industrial metals do much of the work. Here's what I mean: Rising economic activity leads to increasing demand for industrial metals. When industrial activity reaches the point where demand starts to outstrip supply, inflationary pressures start to build in the system. At that point, gold prices can start to rise.

Industrial metal prices are sensitive to demand. Copper prices, especially, can be a leading indicator of an increase in economic activity, given the widespread use of the metal in housing, electronics, and commercial construction. The flip side is that the copper market can start to sag, and prices can start to drop several months ahead of data such as Gross Domestic Product numbers (see the section "Getting into Metal without the Leather: Trading Copper," later in this chapter).

The key word here is *can*. With most of the world's supply of gold in the hands of central banks — whose main goal is fighting inflation — the managers of those central banks know that speculators see rising gold prices as a sign of inflation. When gold rallies tend to get out of hand, central banks start selling the metal from their huge stockpiles, and prices eventually fall.

No one really knows whether central banks are heavy buyers of gold when the price starts to fall; however, central banks can plausibly become gold buyers of last resort when the fears of deflation hit the market or prices continually decline.

The fact that central banks tend to be gold sellers during rallies doesn't mean gold prices can't rally for significant periods of time. It just means that central banks are a formidable market opponent of the everyday trader and that the days of straight-up advances in gold where smart speculators make or break their lifetime's fortune, although still possible, aren't as likely as they once were.

And just so you don't go around thinking that I'm pushing conspiracy theories, you can check out all kinds of extreme and sensible commentaries on central banks and gold anywhere on the Internet.

A good commentary at Financial Sense.com (`www.financialsense.com/fsu/editorials/2004/0308.html`) summarizes a fully disclosed five-year plan of gold sales by central banks.

The highlights are simple. The central banks

- ✔ Acknowledge that gold is "an important element of global monetary reserves."
- ✔ Set limits of sales over the five-year period of the program to no more than 500 tons per year and no more than 2,500 tons over the entire five-year period.
- ✔ Won't sell more gold than they have in reserve.
- ✔ Review the agreement in five years.

The bottom line is that gold is a tricky market because of central banks and the role they play in it. On the other hand, industrial metals such as copper offer more transparency in their pricing patterns because of their close relationship with economic expectations and economic activity.

From an investment standpoint, gold still is central to the world's monetary system — no longer because it's a standard for payments, but rather because it's the most strategic holding common to the world's central banks and often serves as a tool to cool off the world's view of inflation.

When you invest in gold, you're swimming against the tide. The world's central banks hold 25 percent of all the gold ever mined. According to the World Gold Council, in 2003, central banks held ten times the amount of gold that was mined in that year — 33,000 metric tons housed in vaults versus 3,200 metric tons mined. I'm not saying that you need to avoid gold completely; I'm simply noting that the average investor is up against gargantuan market-making opponents in the world's central banks.

Gold Market Fundamentals

South Africa is the world's largest producer of gold, accounting for 25 percent or more of all global production and 50 percent of the accessible reserves. Russia, the United States, Canada, Australia, and Brazil make up the rest of the top-tier producers.

The all-time high in gold prices was set in January 1980, when the price of the October contract hit $1,026 per ounce as the spot-market price rallied to $875. By February 2008 gold had moved back over $1,000 for a brief spell as the weakness in the U.S. dollar and inflationary pressures from China pushed prices upward. In March, gold prices crashed and burned also, taking prices back down below $1,000. The decline started minutes after Federal Reserve Chairman Ben Bernanke lowered interest rates, but changed the Fed's message to the markets highlighting the central bank's concern about inflation.

Here are two key factors to keep in mind about the gold market:

- **Two major influences have an effect on gold prices.** They are

    - **Major political upheaval:** Political crises tend to be the major reason for gold prices to rise.

    - **Inflation:** The influence of inflation on gold prices is much less intense than it was in the past because of the management of gold prices by the central banks.

- **The most reliable influence in the gold market is its relationship to the U.S. dollar.** Figures 14-1 and 14-2 show how the trends of gold and the U.S. dollar reversed after the events of September 11, 2001, and how they accelerated after the U.S.'s subprime mortgage crisis. The Federal Reserve (the Fed) lowered interest rates in both cases, in effect printing money and decreasing the value of the dollar, which brought the gold bugs out of hibernation.

Gold prices and the U.S. dollar tend to move in reverse of each other. This relationship isn't a perfect one, but it's worth looking for and tends to hold up well over long periods of time.

The price of gold can be confusing, so here's a quick primer. The international benchmark price for gold is the *London Price Fix,* which is set in U.S. dollars and is quoted in troy ounces twice daily as the a.m. fix and the p.m. fix. The London exchange summarizes global gold trading as these composite prices.

Gold trades around the world on major exchanges in China, the United Kingdom (UK), and the United States. India and China are countries with expanding demand for gold.

Figure 14-1: Gold bottoms near September 11, 2001, and accelerates its advance in 2007 as the U.S. dollar weakens.

GOLD NEAREST FUTURES . . monthly OHLC plot

Gold blasts to new highs on the U.S. Dollar weakness after the subprime mortgage crisis.

Gold bottoms near 9-11-2001 and starts a long-term rally.

Figure 14-2: The U.S. dollar breaks down after September 11, 2001, and again breaks to new lows as the subprime mortgage crisis hit.

U.S. DOLLAR INDEX NEAREST FUTURES . . monthly OHLC plot

Spot gold and gold futures trade on the New York Mercantile Exchange (NYMEX). Gold futures also trade on the Chicago Board of Trade (CBOT) and have relatively low margin requirements for speculators. That means gold can be an attractive market for small accounts. As of November 2007, initial margin was $3,375, and maintenance was $3,375. The full contract margins at CBOT were $2,309 and $1,710.

Mini contracts are smaller versions of the original contract. The mini contract for gold futures also trades on CBOT. As of November 2007, mini-sized gold margins were $770 and $570 for initial and maintenance. In the case of gold, a mini contract contains 33.2 troy ounces of gold, compared with a full-size contract that holds 100 troy ounces. The margin requirements are smaller, but the general characteristics and fundamentals of the market remain the same.

You can find several reliable information sources for gold on the Internet. Two I like to use are the World Gold Council (www.gold.org) and Kitco.com (www.kitco.com).

When trading gold and gold futures, you need to watch the following:

✔ **Actions taken by central banks around the world:** Central banks tend to be net sellers. As a general rule, they either sell or stay out of the markets. See "Tuning In to the Economy," earlier in this chapter.

The Fed, the European Central Bank, the Bank of England, and the National Bank of Switzerland usually are major players in the gold market, but any central bank is a potential seller, especially during periods of heightened inflationary expectations.

- ✔ **The geopolitical situation:** Asia, the Middle East, and South America are global regions full of potential instability. The chance for terrorist attacks is rising on a daily basis and is likely to become something that remains a big influence from time to time during the next several decades.

- ✔ **Wars:** Wars can lead to volatility in the price of gold. The expectation for higher prices during wars is often not met, given the frequency of major regional conflicts around the world and the frequent selling by central banks.

- ✔ **General weakness of the dollar and other major global currencies:** The general relationship is for gold to rise when the dollar weakens. As with other traditional relationships, this rule isn't set in stone but rather is a tendency caused by central-bank intervention in the gold and currency markets. This relationship is as reliable as any in the financial markets and is worth understanding and monitoring.

  In 2007, the U.S. dollar fell to a new low as measured by the U.S. Dollar Index. The dollar fell to a level not seen since the 1970s.

  At the same time, the price of gold moved above $800 per ounce. Noticeably, the price of crude oil was nearing $100 per barrel at the same time. The combination of higher oil prices, higher gold prices, and a lower dollar was confirmation that the financial markets were betting on inflation.

- ✔ **Inflation:** If the Fed starts talking seriously about inflation and starts raising interest rates aggressively, the gold market is likely to respond with higher prices. For a major rally in gold to develop, the markets have to start believing that central banks can no longer control inflation. That hadn't happened since the 1970s. In 2005, though, the Fed and other global central banks began talking more seriously about inflation. When they did, gold prices began showing some rising power. This accelerated in 2007 when all the world's central banks had to pump large amounts of liquidity into the money markets as the liquidity crisis spawned by the subprime mortgage crisis spread throughout the world.

- ✔ **Technical analysis indicators:** They can keep you on the right side of the trade. As with other markets (see Chapter 7 for an overview of technical analysis), moving averages, trend lines, and oscillators such as the MACD and RSI work with gold prices and need to be an integral part of your gold trading.

Getting into the habit of looking at long-term commodity charts on a weekly basis makes you better able to deal with any titanic shifts in the long-term trend, such as what occurred September 11, 2001. Figures 14-1 and 14-2 clearly mark two inflection points in the gold market's key reversal and subsequent multiyear bull run.

Lining the Markets with Silver

Silver is a *hybrid metal* because it's used for industrial purposes and as a precious metal in jewelry. The silver market is extremely volatile and can be difficult to trade.

Mexico and the United States are the largest producers of silver. Silver mines usually can't operate profitably when market prices fall below $8 per ounce. As a result, when prices fall below that level, production of silver wanes considerably, with much of it coming as a byproduct of copper, lead, and zinc mining processes.

When trading silver, you need to know these nuts and bolts:

- One silver contract contains 5,000 troy ounces, with a 1 cent move being worth $50.

- The modern-day trading range for silver is from 35 cents during the Great Depression up to $50 per ounce when the Hunt brothers tried to corner the silver market in the late 1970s.

- When copper, lead, and zinc prices rise (especially because of decreased production), the price of silver is likely to rally because much of the world's silver is a byproduct of mining and processing the other three metals.

Catalyzing Platinum

The platinum market is heavily influenced by Japan, where it's the precious metal of choice. Although a precious metal, platinum also has hybrid qualities. In fact, it's more often used as the key component in making catalytic converters for cars.

The relative economic strengths in Japan, in the automobile market and in the medical and dental fields — where platinum is also in demand — are the major influences on the price of platinum.

Platinum trades on the NYMEX in contracts containing 100 troy ounces. It can be thinly traded, though, and is best avoided by beginning traders. As with gold, South Africa is the world's largest producer, with Russia second and, due to some recent finds, North America third. Platinum usually trades at a higher price than gold, because supply is much smaller — only 80 tons of the metal reach the market in any given year. For example, on October 28, 2005, platinum futures closed at $941 per troy ounce while gold futures closed at $474. As with any other market, you can apply the usual method of finding out about the fundamentals combined with technical analysis.

Industrializing Your Metals

Technical indicators are the key to predicting future trends in industrial metals, so you need to be on the lookout for the early clues before a trend changes.

The most important industrial metals (copper, aluminum, zinc, nickel, lead, and palladium) start to rally when the market senses that demand is starting to increase, or they start to fall back when the market senses supplies starting to stabilize. In general terms, then, trends in the industrial metals markets start to turn at these transition points. As a trader, you can't get caught in the expectations game, though. You need to wait for the markets to make their moves; you don't get a prize for being the first trader to buy something.

Although gold still is an important asset, the industrial metals complex is a better place for speculators to trade because it's where supply and demand information and easily measured economic fundamentals (with good correlation to prices) are available and tested by price action and overall response in the markets.

Getting into Metal Without the Leather: Trading Copper

Copper is the third most-used metal in the world, and it's found virtually everywhere around the globe. The most active copper mines are in the United States, Chile, Mexico, Australia, Indonesia, Zaire, and Zambia.

A beginning trader may be tempted to dive into the gold market, but some good reasons exist for considering copper first, especially its close connection to the economic cycle and the housing market.

Generally, I like to trade markets that have a good correlation to a sector of the stock market where I have access to company earnings and where industry executives are required by law to provide the market with truthful information by using widely disseminated means such as television and major media outlets. You can see what I mean in the next section.

Before that, though, you need to know a few things about copper before you start trading it, and these things have nothing to do with leather, smoke-filled stages, or headbanging. The keys to trading copper that I tell you about in this list set the stage for the more-involved data that follow.

- ✔ **Uses:** The major uses for copper are in

  - Construction and housing for plumbing and wiring

  - High technology for wiring

  - Semiconductor-related industries for wiring

- ✔ **Markets:** Copper trades at the COMEX, which is a division of the NYMEX in New York, and at the London Metals Exchange. The London contract trades several times more than the U.S. contract in terms of volume, but both are liquid and active contracts.

- ✔ **Contracts:** The COMEX contract is for 25,000 pounds of copper, and the London contract is for 55,000 pounds. New York prices are quoted in dollars and cents per pound, but London prices are quoted in dollars and cents per ton. Thus, a 1-cent move in New York is worth $250, and a $1 move in London in worth $25.

You can use stock prices and trends as predictors of industrial metal prices.

Setting up your copper-trading strategy

Figuring out key relationships within any market is your first step when analyzing it from a technical standpoint. One of my favorites is the relationship between the copper market and the stock of Phelps Dodge, and in turn, its relationship with the bond and housing markets. These interrelationships are as important as any you can find in the futures market, primarily because all the pieces depend on one another for a complete picture of their respective markets to emerge. Here's why:

- ✔ **Phelps Dodge was a leading smelter and producer of copper.** As a result, the stock had an excellent record of predicting the trend in market for the metal. The key to the success of the relationship is that stock investors start betting on the future trend of earnings for the company based on their expectations for copper demand, and thus, its connection to the company's earnings in 2007. Freeport McMoRan (NYSE: FCX), another mining company that also mines for gold, bought Phelps Dodge. The addition of gold into the mix made me look for another bellwether. The truth is that I finally found two stocks that could serve the same purpose. One is Freeport McMoRan (NYSE: FCX), and the other is Southern Copper Corporation (NYSE: PCU). Together, these two stocks were almost as good as Phelps Dodge. What's important is that you look at the copper stocks as well as the price of copper. The upcoming Figures 14-3 and 14-4 update the relationship between the stocks of the copper producers and the price of copper.

- ✔ **The housing market has a good correlation to the price action of housing stocks.** The key is the information provided in monthly housing reports, especially housing starts and building permits. These two reports are the lifeline of the whole equation, because the Fed looks at them closely as it tries to figure out what to do with interest rates.

The housing stock that you use for this purpose needs to be one that behaves similarly in each cycle. I usually use Centex (NYSE symbol: CTX) or Toll Brothers (NYSE symbol: TOL), because they're large capitalization stocks that service significant portions of the housing market. Toll Brothers is an upscale builder that usually is one of the last to top out because it serves richer customers who can last longer. Centex is a good cross-section builder that also works on commercial properties.

✔ **The bond market takes its cues from inflationary indications.** For example, if housing prices rise too rapidly, and signs of bottlenecks appear in commodities markets for copper and lumber, the bond market starts to sell off and interest rates rise.

Charting the course

Putting copper market interrelationships together requires you to keep a close watch on charts of the components that I explain in the preceding section, including copper futures, shares of Phelps Dodge Corporation, housing starts and building permits, and the bond market.

Figures 14-3 and 14-4 show good examples of how these relationships worked with Phelps Dodge, and the historical significance of the relationship is worth chronicling. Notice the general trends of the metal (Figure 14-3) and the stock (Figure 14-4) and how they usually change directions within a close time frame of each other. Phelps Dodge topped in March while the metal was drifting lower. Soon after, though, the metal made a new low, and both rallied starting in May and heading into August.

Figure 14-3:
Six-month chart of copper futures for the September 2005 contract.

HIGH GRADE COPPER NEAREST FUTURES . . monthly OHLC plot

Figure 14-4:
Six-month chart of stock prices for Phelps Dodge Corporation in 2005.

In Figure 14-5, you can see how housing starts started drifting lower in the spring of 2005 after hitting a high point in January. The slowing of housing starts correlates well with an intermediate-term top seen in the price of Phelps Dodge stock. Notice that as housing starts stabilized, Phelps Dodge and copper each staged yet another rally that reached new highs as it extended into August.

HOUSING STARTS

Annual rate in millions of units, seasonally adjusted

Figure 14-5:
Housing starts from January 2002 to July 2005.

According to Figure 14-7 (later in this section), Centex, a good representative of the housing sector, rallied a full two years before Phelps Dodge took off on its own rally. The reason the rally in Centex led to the rally in Phelps Dodge shows up in Figure 14-6. Copper prices were forming a base in the late 1990s, but only when the market started to price in the fact that demand for the metal would likely outstrip supply did the rally in Phelps Dodge begin.

Figure 14-7 shows something very important: Centex (right), a major U.S. homebuilder, began to falter at the same time housing starts began to drift. This move is more obvious in Figure 14-8, which shows the U.S. ten-year Treasury note yield rising dramatically on August 6, 2005, in response to a strong U.S. employment report. Note that on the day of the big move up in interest rates, Centex fell apart.

By August 16, Phelps Dodge also had fallen, but then something interesting happened in September and October. Hurricanes Katrina and Rita hit the U.S. Gulf coast, leading to massive housing and commercial building destruction. As a result, the market started pricing in a rebound in new construction, driving prices higher.

At the same time, during this period, China's economy, as measured by gross domestic product (GDP), continued to grow at a 9.4 percent clip as the U.S. economy grew at a faster-than-expected rate, and copper prices moved to a slightly new high as the market factored in a rise in demand for copper in the wake of the rebuilding.

Figure 14-6:
Long-term view of copper prices.

Figure 14-7:
A decades-long view of the prices of Phelps Dodge and Centex.

Figure 14-8:
A huge one-day backup in bond yields drove interest rates up and housing stocks down.

In the following section, I discuss the relationship between copper and the global economy as the U.S. economy began to slow and the Chinese economy didn't. This situation led to a slowing in the advance for the price of copper, while some of the demand for the metal slowed due to the weakness in the United States. However, the strength in China was good enough to keep things going.

My point is that markets react to circumstances as well as perception. A major top in copper was building as the housing market began to respond to higher interest rates, but an intangible set of events — in this case, the hurricanes — and the persistent growth of the Chinese and American economies led to a new leg up in prices. These circumstances give more credence to the relationship between interest rates, the price of copper, and the housing market.

Organizing the charts

I find it useful to organize the way I look at my charts on a timeline, and you may benefit from organizing the way you look at charts, too. Here are the steps that I take:

1. **Look at daily charts.**

   Starting with a glimpse of daily charts helps you to get the current picture straight.

2. **Look at longer-term charts.**

   I like to take a step back and view charts spanning years so I can put the current picture (from Step 1) in the right perspective. Orienting the short-term with longer-term charts helps you decide whether the current trading activity is within the long-term trend or a counter-trend move.

3. **Look at shorter-term charts.**

   By shorter-term, I mean checking out charts that span either a few days or maybe even only an intraday time period (hours or even minutes) with an eye on optimizing my entry and exit points.

Use a charting program that enables you to look at more than one chart at a time.

Here's what you need to watch for when viewing your charts:

- **Interest-rate trends:** Interest-rate trends are your leading indicator, because the housing market thrives on low interest rates. The big move up in rates in early 2005 wasn't the top in copper, but it was enough to take the wind out of the rally's sails for quite some time.

- **Differing timelines:** By looking at the same chart using at least three different timelines, you focus in on a much clearer picture of what's happening in the market. With practice, you can compile the trio of timeline data in only a few minutes.

- **Overall trends:** Using a long-term chart like the one in Figure 14-5 as your guide, you can check out a market's overall trend. You need to plan your trades based on the primary long-term trend. For example, if copper is in a three-year uptrend, you can expect pullbacks. You can short the pullbacks whenever they look like they're going to last. However, as a trader, your main focus needs to be on trading the long side until an irrefutable break to the downside occurs. When that break occurs, you need to turn your sights to short selling, all the time knowing that you'll eventually get short-term opportunities to go long.

An example of such a potential break came in November 2007, where the copper market failed to keep up with the advance in PCU. When the commodity fails to keep up with the bellwether stock, it can be a sign of trouble ahead. The two may not finally agree for a long time. The chart of the stock, for example, may feature a double top that closely corresponds to the time frame where the third peak of the triple top occurred in copper.

✔ **Economic News:** You need to keep abreast of the news. In November 2007, the triple top in copper came as the U.S. economy was showing significant signs of a potential slowing due to the persistent problems in the housing sector. It was also a time when oil prices were near $100 per barrel, and China was in the midst of an energy crisis because its domestic oil companies were having a hard time keeping up with demand.

✔ **Trend lines:** Never ignore a sustained move above or below a multiyear trend line. Watch trend lines closely. Figure 14-6 shows a new bull market forming in copper, starting in 2003 as the multiyear downtrend line was broken. So just as Pink Floyd sings, "How can you have any pudding if you don't eat your meat?" — if you trade futures, keep this in mind: If you don't read your charts, you'll miss important turning points in the market.

✔ **Divergence in your charts:** Make sure copper stocks and copper futures are moving in the same general direction. If they're not, you have a *technical divergence,* a situation that can result in one of two scenarios:

- Futures will turn in the direction of the stocks.
- Stocks will turn in the direction of the futures.

Figures 14-3 and 14-4 show a small divergence between Phelps Dodge and the September futures contract. Although they bottomed in May, the move in copper was stronger than the one in the stock. It took until June for the full reversal in Phelps Dodge to confirm the rally in the futures.

Making sure fundamentals are on your side

Success in the futures market depends on how well you know the market in which you're trading, technically and fundamentally. The economically sensitive metal markets are too difficult to trade without using both technical and fundamental analyses.

Here are some key tips on how you can make sense of technical and fundamental information:

- ✔ **Check housing starts.** This key report shows you whether the current trend in copper is sustainable. For example, housing starts were flat in June 2005, a factor that was reflected in the July 19 report, which you can view at *The Wall Street Journal* online, www.wsj.com, when you subscribe.

- ✔ **Look beyond the headlines.** The full text of the June housing report contained some important details about single-family home starts being down 2.5 percent from the May report. However, the number of building permits still was rising, so that particular number held up the market. Still, as the newspapers flaunted the never-ending housing boom, the June report was cautionary.

- ✔ **Check supply and demand.** You need to know what supply-and-demand indicators like the Purchasing Manager's (ISM) reports are saying.

A good way to get a grip on supply and demand is to see which industries are reporting growth and which aren't from the ISM report, which also is available in full on *The Wall Street Journal* Web site. The July 2005 report was released August 5, 2005, just a few days after the Fed started to set the stage for a more aggressive stance toward higher interest rates and just before the housing stocks began to show signs of weakness. The list of industry sectors that the July ISM report said were growing included Instruments and Photographic Equipment; Food; Wood and Wood Products; Electronic Components and Equipment; Leather; Miscellaneous; Industrial and Commercial Equipment and Computers; Transportation and Equipment; Furniture; Chemicals; *Fabricated Metals;* and Textiles.

The sectors that the July ISM said were decreasing in activity included Printing and Publishing; Glass, Stone, and Aggregate; *Primary Metals;* Apparel; Rubber and Plastic Products; and Paper.

A quick glance at these sectors shows these factors:

- • Several housing-related sectors were growing, especially the fabricated metals, such as steel, textiles, and wood, which are used in furniture. Indeed, furniture also was growing. The overall picture for housing, however, was mixed.

- • Primary metals, copper included, were one of the weak sectors.

At a point in the copper market like the one described in the preceding list, you want to be careful, watch the charts, and wait for the next month's report to confirm your suspicions that the trend may slow.

Getting a handle on the Fed

You must maintain a continued awareness of when the Fed's board of governors and open market committee are meeting.

Nothing happens to interest rates without the Fed getting into the game. So you have to keep an eye on the central bank to watch for clues about whether the Fed is happy with current rates. Remember, the Fed, by design, is paranoid about inflation, and the central banks, as members of the Fed, can control gold prices, thus making the markets wonder about inflation. However, the Fed and the central banks can't sweep rising housing and commodity prices under the rug, so they have to do something about them.

In early 2005, the Fed was getting annoyed with the housing market. Fed Chairman Alan Greenspan had described regional bubbles in selected markets and expressed mixed feelings about them. In July, Greenspan pointed to "signs of froth in some local markets where home prices seem to have risen to unsustainable levels."

The Fed's governors like to make speeches or leak key concepts to the press. And that's clearly what happened in 2005 just before the employment report was to be released August 6, 2005.

On August 3, 2005 (a Wednesday), Greg Ip, a reporter for *The Wall Street Journal* with a pretty good pipeline into the Fed, wrote: "As the Federal Reserve prepares to raise short-term interest rates again next week, officials there increasingly believe the bond market, which sets long-term rates, is diluting their efforts to tighten credit and contain inflation." And it got even scarier: "Some policy makers worry that bond yields are being kept in check by overly complacent investor sentiment, which could rapidly dissipate, pushing up mortgage rates and shaking the housing market. Indeed, some Fed officials see similarities between the attitudes of bond investors today and of stock investors in the late 1990s."

As the subprime mortgage crisis unfolded in 2007, the Federal Reserve was reluctant to predict a recession, but it was talking about a "significant" slowing in the growth rate of the U.S. economy. The Fed was also concerned about the inflationary effects of having had to ease interest rates and increase the liquidity available to banks due to the slowing in the housing sector. In fact, at the time the Federal Reserve was in a box. It knew it could cause an inflationary spiral by lowering interest rates, but it also knew if it didn't it could cause a recession.

When the Fed is in a box, you want to watch the U.S. dollar and the gold markets. In 2007, it paid off quite well because the dollar fell, and gold rallied, giving you and me two good opportunities. One was to short the dollar, and the other was to go long on gold.

Getting beyond gold and copper

Other metals besides gold and copper trade in the futures markets. After you master — or at least become familiar with — the gold and copper markets, you can try your hand at aluminum, zinc, nickel, lead, and tin.

Most of them are more thinly traded than gold and copper, with the exception of aluminum, which can be very liquid.

The major influences are similar to the economic fundamentals for gold and copper: strikes and wars, individual metal stocks released regularly by the exchanges, and inflation.

Pulling it together

After you determine the long-term trend and check for potential land mines (such as the Fed clearly telling the markets that interest rates are going way up and for a long time), you need to core down your technical analysis toward the short term by doing the following:

- ✔ Use trend lines, moving averages, and oscillators (see Chapters 7 and 8) to look for clear and precise entry points above key resistance when going long and below critical support levels when going short.

- ✔ Always confirm your trades with at least two technical oscillators, such as MACD and RSI, before diving in.

- ✔ Set sell stops or buy-to-cover stops, depending on the direction of your trade, by referring to moving averages or percentages as your guidelines.

Never lose more than 5 percent on any given trade, and you'll stay in the game.

Chapter 15

Getting to the Meat of the Markets: Livestock and More

*I*f you're like I was before I began trading, the first image of futures trading that comes to mind is something like pork bellies or orange juice. You probably start chuckling and shake your head, saying, "No way man . . . not for me . . . no sir."

Then there's the Hollywood take on commodities traders. They're usually portrayed as not-too-smart, greedy fellows, looking for an edge and a quick buck.

In the movie *Trading Places,* Eddie Murphy and Dan Akroyd turn the tables on two old scoundrels played by Ralph Bellamy and Don Ameche, who are gaming the orange-juice market with inside information before the release of the monthly data hits the wires.

Although the movie is entertaining and the two old buggers get what they deserve, it unfortunately paints a lopsided picture of the futures market. Some traders in the futures markets might very well seriously consider trading on insider information. But given the tight surveillance of the markets and the potential for being caught, finding out just how the markets work and whether you're cut out to trade probably is the best route for you to take.

Trading, after all, is a serious business, and the meat markets are basically about how much you and I have to pay to eat. If you look at it from that standpoint, you start taking it a bit more seriously.

Meat markets are as much about farmers, producers, and other industry-related traders using the markets to hedge their bets against potentially negative outside influences — weather, herds that catch plagues, and even fad diets like the low-carb craze that took hold in the last decade — as they are about people like you and me who look at charts and real-time quotes and try to make money by trading meat.

This chapter is meant to provide a good overview of basic trading strategies in the meat markets. Some excellent and more in-depth information can be found at these Web sites:

- The Chicago Merchantile Exchange (CME) at www.cme.com/files/LivestockFund.pdf)

- Ohio State University at www-agecon.ag.ohio-state.edu/people/roe.30/livehome.htm

The best free charting for cattle futures is available from Barchart.com at www.barchart.com, which is a good place to start looking at the meat markets and becoming familiar with the action that takes place before deciding whether you want to trade in them.

Exploring Meat-Market Supply and Demand, Cycles, and Seasonality

Like all commodities markets, meat markets are based on supply. However, a more equitable relationship exists with demand in the meat markets than in other commodities markets where supply is key. The two major temporal factors to understand about the meat markets are the longer meat cycle, which is different for cattle than it is for hogs, and the more reliable — although not perfect by any means — aspect of seasonality.

The meat market goes through several phases where herds are built up and subsequently sold. When farmers increase the number of cattle in their herds, it's called the *accumulation phase,* and when they thin the herd for selling, it's called the *liquidation phase.* For hogs, the spectrum starts with *expansion* and ends with *contraction.*

The time that passes from accumulation to liquidation and from expansion to contraction is called the *livestock cycle.* Historically, the cycle for cattle usually lasted 10 to 12 years, and for hogs, it usually was around 4 years. The actual length of the cycle is measured either from one *trough,* or the low point in inventory, to the next, or from one *peak,* or high point in inventory, to the next. The time that it takes for female swine to reach breeding age has a direct effect on the hog expansion phase.

Seasonality, on the other hand, can be short term or have more of an intermediate duration. During summer months, the demand for certain cuts of beef that can be grilled outside tends to increase. The same is true of the demand for turkeys at Thanksgiving time. When consumers are flocking to one kind of meat at specific times, prices can be affected, and the market reacts and adjusts. For example, some specific times that affect specific meat markets include

- **January through March:** These three months tend to be strong ones for feeder livestock prices because grain prices tend to be lower during the same period. *Feeder cattle* are steers, castrated males, and heifers, or females that have not calved. These animals weigh anywhere from 600 to 800 pounds when they arrive at the feedlot, with a goal of reaching 1,000 to 1,300 pounds before they're slaughtered.

- **April through August:** The spring and summer usually are weak months for feeder prices.

- **September through December:** These four months are a second season of strength in feeder prices; however, the January through March period historically has been the stronger of the two periods.

Feeder cattle and oat prices sometimes move before live cattle prices. So reliable is this tendency that some traders actually describe this relationship as "Feeders are the leaders."

Corn, a mainstay in livestock feed, is increasingly being used in the production of ethanol to fuel motor vehicles. This trend is a significant pricing component in both the grain and meat markets. These markets are likely to ebb and flow accordingly over the next several years, depending on how prevalent ethanol becomes as a fuel in the United States. In late 2007, ethanol's popularity was waning as major infrastructure problems for the industry, as well as the impact on the environment and the world's fuel and food supply, was a hot political topic.

Understanding Your Steak

Here's a quick-and-dirty overview of the cattle business to get you rolling in the right direction.

Despite increasingly frequent scares about mad cow disease, the steak that everyone loves to eat starts off with a *cow/calf operation,* which in short is a cattle-breeding business that consists of a plot of land that holds a few bulls, some kind of feed, and an average of 42 cows, according to government statistics provided by the United States Department of Agriculture (USDA). The cow/calf operations are where natural or artificial insemination takes its course and calves are born.

The breeding process

Producers breed cattle in the late summer or early fall because nine months are required to birth a calf. Most of the cattle production in the United States takes place in Kansas, Nebraska, Colorado, Oklahoma, Texas, Iowa, Minnesota, and Montana. Many of these areas of the country endure tough winters, so birthing calves in spring gives them a better chance for survival.

Calves spend six months or so with their mothers and then are either released into the feedlot or undergo *backgrounding,* a period where smaller animals catch up in size and weight, essentially a process by which they are fed until they grow to 600 to 800 pounds, which is considered large enough to enter the feedlot and become *feeder cattle,* the beef that humans consume.

Feedlots are where feeder cattle — calves, or steers and heifers — are fattened up. *Cattle hotels* are commercial feedlots that account for only about 5 percent of all lots that are involved in raising feeder cattle, but they produce 80 percent of the cattle sold. Feedlots sometimes buy cattle for their clientele or charge farmers a fee to custom feed their stock.

Commercial operations offer farmers convenient services, such as boarding and feeding cattle, and often serve as middlemen by setting up deals between farmers and slaughterhouses. In other words, commercial operations fatten up herds and use their industry contacts with packing plants to sell their client/farmer's herds. Sometimes commercial operations combine smaller herds from several farms into one feedlot and then sell them to the slaughterhouses.

Feeder cattle are fed a high-energy diet consisting of grain, protein supplements, and roughage. Putting on weight fast is the idea. The grain portion these cattle are fed usually is made up of corn, milo, or wheat if the price is low enough. Usually, the protein supplement includes soybeans, cottonseed, or linseed meal. The roughage usually is alfalfa hay or even sugar beet pulp, depending on market prices.

The packing plant

When feedlot animals reach specific weights, they are sold to the packing plant. The packing plant is where live cattle and hogs are sent to be slaughtered. Packers sell the meat and byproducts, including the hides, bones, and glands, to different customers, including retailers, such as grocery stores and manufacturers of clothing and furniture.

The feeder cattle contract

Feeder cattle contracts are made up of feeder cattle, the precursor to live cattle, and are the province of the feedlot operator. See the previous section, "The breeding process," for details about feeder cattle, and the next section for details on live cattle.

The prices of feeder cattle contracts are dependent on two major raw materials: the number of animals on the feedlot and the price of grain.

Feedlot operators increase the number of animals based on the demand for feeder cattle, which is dependent on the demand for live cattle. Corn and other grain prices influence the costs of maintaining an animal on the feedlot. Cheap grain prices usually correlate well with higher feeder cattle prices when you trade this contract. Low supplies of grain stocks, on the other hand, usually lead to weak feeder prices. Here are some of the specifics of feeder cattle contracts:

- ✔ **Composition:** This contract holds 50,000 pounds of feeder cattle, with specifications calling for a 750-pound steer, such that each contract holds an average of 60 animals.
- ✔ **Valuation:** Prices are quoted in either cents per pound or dollars per hundredweight.
- ✔ **Settlement:** Delivery is cash settled and is based on an index, with the final price being the price of the index on the contract's last day.
- ✔ **Price limits:** The price limit is equal to the live contract limit, which is 300 points or 3 cents per pound, or $3 per hundredweight, above or below the closing price for the previous day.

The CME live cattle contract

The main difference between the live cattle contract and the feeder cattle contract is that the animals in the live cattle contract are ready for slaughter.

Buyers of live cattle usually are meat packers who sell the meat and byproducts. In general, prices for live cattle tend to rise from January to March, start falling in April, bottom out in July, and then remain below average until October.

This shifting of prices results from the pattern of cattle slaughter. According to USDA data, the number of cattle slaughtered peaks during the period from June through August, making a second but lower peak in October, and then declining into February, when the cycle starts rising again until the June/August top.

Live cattle contracts are much like feeder cattle contracts, with the same daily limits (300 points, 3 cents per pound, or $3 per hundredweight) above or below the previous day's close, but each contract consists of 40,000 pounds of slaughter-ready animals.

Beef prices are susceptible to mad cow disease and other health-related stories — such as being linked to cancer and heart disease — as well as product recalls due to bacterial contamination. Other issues that occasionally appear in the press with regard to the meat market include the use of illegal immigrants as part of the workforce in meat processing plants and farms. These stories can remain in the headlines for several days or weeks. During those periods, avoiding the beef market is often the best alternative for inexperienced traders. The flip side is that those kinds of stories can also provide trading opportunities. As you understand more about trading these markets, you can adjust your tactics to accommodate these instances.

Understanding Your Pork Chop

The hog market is similar in many ways to the cattle market, but it has some important distinctions:

- Pork demand rises in spring because of Easter and in winter because of the holiday season.

- Hog prices tend to rise in January and peak in May and June, rolling over in July and falling into fall and the holiday season.

- During the period of rising hog prices, the number of slaughters decreases.

Living a hog's life

Similar to cattle, hogs being raised for the market go through significant stages that traders need to track. The two basic stages are pre-slaughter and post-slaughter. The pre-slaughter stage is known as the *farrow-to-finish operation,* which encompasses the entire process from breeding and rearing a hog to slaughter because the hog stays on the same farm from birth to finish.

When hogs reach 220 to 240 pounds, which takes about six months, they're sent to market. Unlike beef, a significant amount of pork is processed into smoked, canned, or frozen ham.

Pork bellies

As a frustrated baseball announcer, I love a good slice of bacon, so I thought I'd do the next best thing by shouting out the title of this section as if it were Sammy Sosa striding up to the plate.

Pork bellies, though, are not a laughing matter. Indeed, they are the part of the hog from which bacon is derived. Hogs are cash settled, based on a USDA-calculated index.

Here are the basics of what you need to know about pork-belly contracts:

- **Contracts:** Pork-belly contracts are traded in lots of 40,000 pounds, compared with 40,000 pounds for the live-hog contract.

- **Valuation:** When trading hogs and pork bellies, a 1-cent move in hogs is worth plus or minus $400 per contract, while a 1-cent move in pork bellies is worth $400 per contract.

- **Market makeup:** Speculators make up 85 percent of the trading volume in pork bellies.

Pork bellies are among the most treacherous of futures contracts. The combination of a big move with just a penny's movement in the price and the volatile nature of the contract in general make the pork-belly contract one that you need to be extremely careful about when you trade it.

Matching Technicals with Fundamentals

If you're a livestock producer, you have to be thinking about hedging techniques because you have real cattle that you must deliver to the market at some point. Thus, futures markets offer you a great opportunity to reduce your risk, and fundamentals combined with technical analysis can help you set up your hedging trades.

Figure 15-1 shows a fairly classic six-month chart for feeder cattle prices. Note how prices rallied in the early part of the year and started to roll over during the summer months.

As a speculator, you want to understand the market from a hedger's point of view, but you need to focus on these keys to the cattle market:

- **Understanding the seasonal cycle:** Livestock prices tend to be cyclical in nature, but more important, you want to confirm that the cycle is working the way it usually does. In the case of the chart in Figure 15-1, you'd be correct in playing the long side of the market during the early part of the year.

- ✔ **Using technical analysis:** You're not out on the farm, so you must trust the price action. Trend lines, moving averages, and oscillators are useful in trending markets, such as the one shown in Figure 15-1. See Chapter 7 for a full overview of technical analysis.

- ✔ **Keeping your strategies fluid:** As with other contracts, you need to keep up with government reports that are scheduled for release and hedge your regular positions by buying options or by selling futures contracts if you're long.

- ✔ **Following your trading rules:** If you set a sell stop or a buy-to-cover stop on a short position, don't change it other than to keep ratcheting it up or down as your position becomes more profitable. And when your rules say the time is right, don't hesitate to take those profits.

If you get stopped out, you either saved yourself a lot of trouble or didn't give yourself enough room. That dilemma is easily remedied. Go back and check the usual price range of the commodity for the specific time frame in which you're trading. If you're trading 15-minute bars and the commodity tends to move one to two ticks during that period, then set your stop just outside of or close to the normal movement. That way, if you get stopped out, it was because of an abnormal movement by the market against your position, and you've likely saved yourself from an even bigger loss.

Figure 15-1: Feeder cattle futures for August 2005.

Watching for the Major Meat-Market Reports

As with virtually all other commodities markets, given their connection to supply and demand, meat-market traders need to keep an eye on their own distinct set of key reports. The CME and your broker have calendars that warn you when these key reports are going to be released. You need to take seriously the reports I describe in the sections that follow because they're the most important inside influence on prices. Many times the information in one of them is enough to change the overall trend of the particular market for extended periods.

Of course, some reports are more important than others, but you're asking for trouble if you either have an open position or you're trying to set one up without knowing what to expect when one of these potential bombshells hits the street.

Counting cattle

Released every month by the USDA's National Agricultural Statistics Service (NASS), the Cattle-on-Feed Report usually moves the market and is made up of these three parts:

- ✔ **Cattle on feed:** This part of the report focuses on the actual number of cattle in the feedlots.

- ✔ **Placements:** This part of the report focuses on the number of new animals placed into feedlots during the previous month. This number is an important predictor of future supply, because an animal placed in a feedlot can be market-ready in 120 to 160 days.

- ✔ **Marketings:** This part of the report focuses on the number of animals taken out of the feedlots. This number is a hazier piece of data because it can be affected by an individual operator's feeding methods and particular animal-specific idiosyncrasies.

  For example, depending on demand and how well a particular animal grows, feedlot operators can vary their marketings from month to month.

Posting pig-related data

The Hogs and Pigs Survey, which is released quarterly by NASS, reports pig crop data from 16 major hog-producing states and is the most important report for the hog and pork-belly markets. Information in it can lead to limit moves that can last for several days whenever surprises are reported.

This report definitely is a market mover, but it can be wrong — although you won't be able to verify whether it's right or wrong for six months or so.

Here are the nuts and bolts of the Hogs and Pigs Survey:

- ✔ **Total numbers of pigs:** This figure is the *pig crop,* and it shows where the market volume is at the time the report is released.

- ✔ **Breeding herd numbers:** This figure tells you the total number of hogs not sent to slaughter that are to be kept for breeding purposes.

- ✔ **Farrowing intentions:** This number provides an indication of breeding levels expected in the future.

- ✔ **Market hogs:** This number is the portion of the report that gives you the number of hogs that are being taken to market.

Other meat-market reports to watch

If you want your research to be complete, take note of these reports:

- ✔ **Cattle Inventory Report:** This report is released in January and July and provides the number of mature animals and the number of calves in the annual crop.

- ✔ **Cold Storage Report:** This report is a monthly release that tells you how much meat is stored in the freezers, including beef, chicken, and pork. It usually moves the pork-belly markets more than anything else.

- ✔ **Out of Town Report:** This report is released after the markets close every Tuesday and, like the Cold Storage Report, is aimed mostly at pork-belly traders. It measures whether pork bellies were put into freezers or taken out of storage. Rising numbers of bellies going into freezers is bearish. Falling numbers of bellies in storage is bullish.

- ✔ **Daily Slaughter Levels:** This report measures the daily activity of meat packers.

Interpreting Key Report Data

Reports in March and June 2005 affected the ebb and flow of the August 2005 pork-belly contract by starting a recovery in the market and pointing to two trading opportunities you can use to catch this kind of market bottom.

Figure 15-2 shows the pork-belly contract for August 2005 and how it broke above the first trend line and marked a trading bottom and how a second trend line marked a break in the downtrend. The first break in the market occurred soon after the release of the March Cold Storage Report from the USDA, usda.mannlib.cornell.edu/reports/nassr/other/pcs-bb/ 2005/, which contained the following line:

> "Total red meat supplies in freezers were down 1 percent from last month, but up 4 percent from last year. Frozen pork supplies were up 9 percent from last month and up 14 percent from the previous year. Stocks of pork bellies were up 19 percent from last month and up 32 percent from last year."

This reported glut of pork was not worked off until June when the government's Cold Storage Report indicated:

> "Frozen pork supplies were down 9 percent from May, but up 24 percent from the previous year. Stocks of pork bellies were down 9 percent from last month, but up 97 percent from last year."

By July:

> "Frozen pork supplies were down 4 percent from last month, but up 32 percent from the previous year. Stocks of pork bellies were down 14 percent from last month, but up 90 percent from last year."

That was three months of sequential decreases in the amount of pork in storage, which was good enough for the market to make a bottom. The chart in Figure 15-2 clearly shows how a series of reports can influence the sensible, supply-and-demand driven pork-belly market.

Notice the following key technical developments on the charts in Figure 15-2:

- ✔ Open interest (line on bottom of chart above volume bars) rose as selling accelerated, which is a bearish sign because it shows more people are selling.

- ✔ Open interest declined as the pork-belly contract started to bottom, which is bullish because it shows selling is losing strength.

Figure 15-2:
Pork bellies
respond to
key reports.

Labels on chart: Cold storage report shows huge rise in bellies; Trading bottom; Belly glut improving; Down trend broken

Outside Influences that Affect Meat Prices

An important set of background factors can affect meat prices. Some are short-term influences, but others have been in the pipeline for some time and can suddenly be felt when a certain catalyst hits the news, such as an article that shows that beef is not as healthy for consumption as it was thought to be.

Some longer-term and softer influences on meat prices are

- ✔ **Population changes:** If a demographic shift occurs in which more children are born, more baby food will be sold, which tends to be more vegetable based.

- ✔ **Income changes:** The overall economy affects the kinds of food people buy and whether they will go out to a restaurant and order higher-priced items, such as steaks.

- ✔ **Prices of substitutes:** Higher beef and pork prices are likely to lead to increased use of chicken; that is, until the price of chicken gets too high and the potential for a shift back to pork and beef increases.

- ✔ **Prices of complements:** With a sudden increase in the price of barbecue sauce, you can see a decreased demand for beef or pork.

- ✔ **Changing consumer tastes:** This anomaly can be described as the classic Atkins diet effect. Pork, beef, and chicken prices rose when the low-carb craze swept the United States. If a soybean-based diet was to catch on in the same way, you'd likely see a similar phenomenon in soybean prices, while you'd likely see the reverse in meat prices.

Some shorter-term but more constant influences on meat prices are

- **Weather:** A tough winter can lead to big animal losses, which, in turn, can affect supply for extended periods of time. Cold winters also tend to make animals eat more but gain less weight. So even if no animal deaths occur, the time to market can be delayed because producers need more time to fatten up animals, in effect delaying their time to market. A glut in the market can then result at a later time, lowering prices after the initial rise caused by the short-term shortage.

- **Grain prices:** Generally speaking, high feed prices result in liquidation, and low feed prices result in accumulation. The liquidation/accumulation ratio also is affected by the kind of prices producers get for their finished products. If meat prices are high, producers can spend more money on feed and pass along the added price.

A *forced liquidation,* a period where large numbers of animals are sent to market because of droughts or periods of high feed prices, can lead to a longer-term boom in prices. For example, in 1996, all-time high prices in corn led to forced liquidation of both corn stores and herds. Cattle prices fell, only to rebound strongly after the excess supply was taken off the market.

Chapter 16

The Bumpy Truth About Agricultural Markets

*T*he agricultural markets have staged a resurgence over the last few years, as the use of corn for the manufacture of ethanol has led to price increases and political controversy over the grain's role in global agriculture. As with most booms, there will eventually be a bust, and the heady gains of the recent past will meet with significant price declines. Still, good trading means that you go with the trend, and because what goes up must come down, when the boom busts, you are likely to get good opportunities to trade these markets on the short side.

During the first 70 years of futures trading, agriculture was dominant given its Japanese origin in the rice markets. However, in the 1980s and 1990s, as the stock market captured the public's imagination, these markets became the province of insiders, such as grain producers, farmers, and professionals.

Obviously, things have changed as corn trading patterns have recently shown. There are some key factors that are likely to keep these markets near the headlines for a significant portion of the future:

✔ Weather patterns and climate change continue to add volatility and intensity to the grain markets. and Politics center on environmental concerns as well as the use of crops for food or fuel, while are also an important influence.

✔ Fossil-fuel prices are also increasingly influential as they raise the cost of grain production, transportation of grains to markets, and the choices consumers make in their food purchases.

For entry-level futures traders, the most important agricultural contracts are the corn and soybean contracts. They are the most actively traded and quoted agriculture contracts, so I devote much of this chapter to them.

After you gain a basic understanding of the concepts of seasonality and crop cycles and how external factors influence them, adapting to other contracts becomes relatively easy. In addition to the two major grain contracts, I also briefly touch on coffee, sugar, and lumbers futures in this chapter.

Staying Out of Trouble Down on the Farm

From a real-world economic standpoint, futures contracts in the agricultural markets are important. However, they're not for the fainthearted because of their volatility, the thinness of trading that sometimes accompanies them, and the dependence of prices on the influence of the weather.

Indeed, trading grains and softs can be very challenging, especially during periods of volatile weather. If recent history is any indication, this will become a rule more than an exception, especially during hurricane season. *Softs,* by the way, is the name given to a group of commodities that includes cocoa, sugar, cotton, orange juice, and lumber. Here are some characteristics of trading grains and softs that you need to know to stay out of the doghouse and the poorhouse:

- ✔ **Thinly traded contracts:** Grain contracts and softs are not traded as much as stock-index or financial contracts, which leaves traders open to the effects of *decreased liquidity.* Liquidity is an important term referring to the availability of money in the markets. Decreased liquidity, in turn, can lead to wide price swings in short periods of time, which make trading difficult. See Chapters 7 and 8 for information on technical analysis and details on trading gaps.

- ✔ **Low liquidity:** A lack of cash in these markets can lead to lots of chart gaps and limit moves.

Before you trade any agricultural futures, you need a refined understanding of the fundamentals of the particular sector and market in which you're trading. For example, at the very least, you need to know about growing and harvesting seasons, geopolitical risks in the growing area, and how the weather affects the crop. In other words, these contracts are better left for serious and experienced traders because they're more adept at collecting information, putting it in the proper context, and managing risk. I'm not saying that you shouldn't trade these markets. I'm just saying that they're not the best ones to start with. As you gain more experience with the general aspects of futures trading, you'll be able to do more in these areas.

Corn, soybeans, and other agricultural futures are excellent contracts to allow someone else to trade for you, either through a commodity fund that specializes in these markets or an advisor with a good record who knows what he's doing.

Consider trading commodities through an exchange-traded fund (ETF). I like the PowerSharesDB Commodity Index Tracking Fund (DBC). It isn't a perfect way to trade the grains, but it does include corn and wheat as part of the components. The ETF buys futures and U.S. Treasury bills and tracks the Deutsche Bank Commodity index. Other index components include oil, heating oil, gold, and aluminum. For a more direct way to trade grains through ETFs, you can use the PowerShares DB Agricultural Fund (DBA). I go into more detail on using ETFs to trade commodities and futures in Chapter 5.

Agriculture 101: Getting a Handle on the Crop Year

You need to know what the crop year is to be able to understand grain trading. The *crop year* is the time from one crop to the next. It starts with planting and ends with harvesting. During that time, crops are going through what the U.S. Department of Agriculture and Joint Agricultural Weather facility call the moisture- and temperature-dependent stages of development.

What happens between planting and harvest tends to affect the prices of the crops the most. For example, the weather is a major factor. Drought, flooding, and freezing are the major events. Other external events, such as shipping problems, can also affect delivery at key times, such as when Hurricane Katrina hit the port of New Orleans, from which much of the Midwest's grain makes its way out of the United States.

Think of the supply of grain brought to market as a rationed situation. By that I mean that although grains are used year round, most of them are replenished only one time during the year. As a result, prices are affected by a combination of current supplies and future supply expectations. The way a grain market perceives future and current supplies and the way that traders predict the effect of internal and external factors on prices is a major set of variables to consider. In other words, in all markets there is a certain fudge factor, or an intangible influence on prices.

Think of it along these terms. In futures markets, as in all markets, perception is as much a part of pricing as reality. The markets are efficient, and that means they react to the information that they have available instantaneously, which leads to short-term price volatility. As with the hog and pig report I discuss in Chapter 15, data in a single quarterly report may be significantly off the mark as slaughter approaches, and thus the reality in any market, grains and softs included, can be different than the original report indicates. So you need to know that markets can retrace major moves as better information becomes available.

As with most other commodities, trading in corn and soybeans is all about supply.

Except during times of extraordinary circumstances, such as dietary fads or major external, political, climactic, or geological events, demand stays within a fairly predictable range. Under normal circumstances, demand fluctuates within certain bands based on the number of people and animals to be fed at any given time. Consequently, the market focuses on anything that affects how much grain will be available to feed them from year to year.

That doesn't mean that demand isn't important. For example, the markets are used to a certain amount of demand for soybeans from China every year; however, if China's weather changes dramatically and its domestic crop suffers, global demand for soybeans will increase, thus having a direct effect on the markets. Assuming that U.S. supply remains stable in a year that China's weather changes, you're likely to have an increase in prices caused by the increased demand.

Likewise, if the supply of soybeans is decreased because of a crop plague in the United States — which supplies most of the world's soybeans — and global demand remains the same, prices are likely to rise.

The situation is similar in virtually all markets; changes in supply tend to affect prices more strongly than changes in demand. See Chapter 13 for more details about how supply rules the markets.

 In general, high levels of current supplies and/or expectations of high supply levels in the future usually lead to lower prices. Conversely, low levels of current supplies and/or expectations of future shortages usually lead to higher prices.

Weathering the highs and lows of weather

Weather has the greatest influence on crops, and significant weather developments affect crop markets. Globally, weather is important in grain and seed markets. Some basic points to keep in mind about the weather include

- ✔ Spring weather in the United States (or anywhere for that matter) affects planting season. Too much rain can delay planting.

- ✔ Summer weather affects crop development. Crops need rain to develop appropriately. Droughts play havoc with crop development.

✔ During the North American winter, agricultural market watchers and traders concentrate on the weather in South America because it's summer there. Likewise, dormant winter wheat in North America needs enough snowfall to protect the crop from *winterkill,* or freezing because not enough snow is on the ground to insulate the crop.

✔ A wet harvest can cause delays and decrease crop yields.

All these factors can raise prices.

The U.S. Department of Agriculture (USDA) Weather Bulletin, `www.usda. gov/oce/waob/jawf/wwcb.html`, is an excellent resource for information about weather trends and potential developments. You can subscribe to the report for $60 per year. The USDA releases it on Wednesdays. Subscribing to these reports may not be worthwhile unless you're a farmer who's looking into the small details. As a trader, especially one using charts, you'll be reacting to the market's response anyway.

Weather markets, or periods when crops are being affected by droughts, floods, or freezing temperatures, create possibly the most volatile types of markets, and they're risky to boot. Droughts or unusual snowfall or rainfall patterns are among the more common events that trigger weather markets.

Looking for Goldilocks: The key stages of grain development

Prices for grain and soybean futures can move significantly during three key time frames when seasonal and logistical expectations are the result of the cultivation and growing cycles. At these three times of year, weather conditions mustn't be too hot, too cold, too dry, or too wet. Like Goldilocks and her porridge, conditions have to be "just right" during

✔ **Planting season:** When it's time to plant, rainfall is the major influence. Too much rain means a late planting season that can lead to smaller, lower-quality crops, which in turn can lead to higher prices. A wet planting season offers traders an opportunity to trade on the long side.

✔ **Pollination or growing season:** Rain and heat are the keys when seeds are pollinating and growing. Too much heat and too little rain lead to lower levels of pollination, which again can lead to smaller crops. Cold temperatures and too much water can have the same effect.

✔ **Maturation and harvest season:** When plants are maturing and harvest is near, too much heat and too much rain can mean poor crops from difficult field conditions and the spread of fungus among crops.

Cataloging Grains and Beans

The grain complex has multiple components, including soybeans, soybean meal, soybean oil, Canola, palm oil, corn, oats, and wheat. I concentrate on the soybean and corn markets because they're the most heavily traded and offer the best opportunity for small accounts and beginning traders. However, you can apply what you find out about these grains and how these markets work to develop an understanding of other grain markets and to set up strategies.

One caveat is that individual markets have their own subtle sets of parameters, and you'll have to figure them out as you expand your trading horizons.

The soybean complex

The *soybean complex* is made up of three separate futures contracts for delivery of soybeans, soybean meal, and soybean oil. Soybeans are legumes, not grains, but they're traded and cataloged as part of the grain complex. Don't let this weird stuff confuse you. Markets and traders are efficient, and they look for convenience. Besides, can you imagine somebody on TV talking about legume futures? Egads!

Until 2004, the United States was the largest soybean producer with about a 50 percent market share. Until 1980, the United States held an 80 percent share, but the Carter administration's grain embargo, a political maneuver in 1980 that was designed to protest the Russian invasion of Afghanistan, cost the U.S. farming industry dearly.

Currently, South America produces most of the other half of the world's soybeans, with China making up the rest.

Soybeans are the protein source used most by humans and animals around the world. The primary uses of soybeans are for meal for animal feed and oil for human consumption.

Soybean contracts

The soybean contract trades on the Chicago Board of Trade (CBOT). Here are the particulars of a soybean contract:

- ✔ **Contract:** A contract is 5,000 bushels, and prices for soybeans are quoted in dollars and cents per bushel.

- ✔ **Valuation:** A 1-cent move in the price of soybeans is worth $50 per contract, with daily price movements shifting as much as 50 cents per day.

- ✔ **Limits:** Trading limits in soybeans are variable based on prevailing market conditions. As of April 2008, the limit was 50 cents per day ($2,500 per contract) with no limits in the spot month.

- ✔ **Margins:** As of April 2008, the initial speculative margin requirement was $5,400 per contract, and the maintenance margin requirement was $4,000 per contract.

Soybean meal contracts

Soybean meal (what's left after the extraction of oil from soybeans) can be fed to cattle, hogs, and poultry. A 60-pound bushel of soybeans yields 48 pounds of meal. Forty percent of U.S. meal production is exported. The rest is used domestically. Here are the particulars of the soybean meal contract:

- ✔ **Contract:** A soybean meal contract is 100 short tons (200,000 pounds), with a (short) ton equal to 2,000 pounds. Prices are quoted in dollars and cents per ton.

- ✔ **Valuation:** A $1 move in the per-ton price of soybean meal is worth $100 per contract.

- ✔ **Limits:** Price movements are limited to $20 per day, which is also variable, again depending on market conditions. If the market closes at the limit, the limit is raised for the next three days to accommodate traders. Although this tactic may seem a bit strange, remember that the role of the futures markets, especially in key commodities such as grains, is to enable commerce to take place — capitalism at its finest. If market conditions are such that limits need to be expanded, the exchanges are more than happy to accommodate the markets.

- ✔ **Margins:** As of April 2008, the initial margin requirement was $2,700, and the maintenance margin was $2,000.

Soybean oil contracts

Soybean oil is the third major soybean product for which futures contracts are bought and sold. A bushel of soybeans produces 11 pounds of oil, and soybean oil competes with olive oil and other edible oils. Soybean oil is extracted by a multistep process that involves steaming, pressing, and percolating (similar to brewing coffee) the beans. If you're really into how soybean oil is extracted, plenty of background info can be found on the Internet. Have at it! Here are the basics of what you need to know:

- ✔ **Contract:** A soybean oil contract is 60,000 pounds. Prices are quoted in cents per pounds.

- ✔ **Valuation:** Be careful trading soybean oil. A 1-cent move is equal to 100 points, which is worth $600 per contract.

✔ **Limits:** Trading limits are set at 1 cent, but they can be adjusted because soybean trading can be very volatile due to the weather and other external factors. Thus, trading limits are variable, meaning that they can be changed if prices continue to be very volatile over a period of time. See Chapter 3 for more about trading limits.

✔ **Margins:** As of April 2008, the initial margin requirement was $2,025, and the maintenance margin requirement was $1,500.

Getting corny

Corn is the most active commodity among grain contracts, and it is the major crop grown in the United States. American farmers grow about 50 percent of the world's corn supply, and 70 percent of U.S. production is consumed domestically.

Corn futures are known as *feed corn,* or corn that's fed to livestock — not the same stuff that you and I eat at summer picnics or find behind the Jolly Green Giant label. Here are the particulars of corn futures:

✔ **Contract:** A contract holds 5,000 bushels, and a 1/4-cent move is worth $12.50 per contract. Prices are quoted in cents and ¼ cents.

✔ **Limits:** The daily limit is 20 cents, or $1,000. There are no limits in the spot month.

✔ **Margins:** As of April 2008, the initial margin requirement for speculators was $2,025 per contract, and the maintenance margin requirement was $1,500 per contract.

The CBOT's Web site (www.cbot.com) can provide you with a great deal of useful background information, charts, and even trade summaries. I highly recommend a good review of the data there.

Culling Some Good Fundamental Data

Although charts are the most useful tools for trading futures, getting a grip on the fundamental expectations of price movements in the particular contract you're trading is important. The fundamentals, of course, are background information, and you need to be aware that even the best guesses can be wrong. The key is to gauge what the expectations are for the market and then find out what prices actually do.

Getting a handle on the reports

You can find plenty of good fundamental information at the USDA's Web site at www.usda.gov. Here is a good sequence of data and market factors to keep in mind for getting a handle on a market's supply and demand:

- **Beginning stocks:** The *beginning stock* is the amount of grain that's left over from the previous year, as reported by the government.

- **Production:** *Production* is the estimated amount of a crop that will be harvested during the current year.

- **Weekly Weather and Crop Report:** The USDA releases a weekly Crop Progress Report that updates the crop and weather conditions. This report usually is released on Wednesday. See the earlier section, "Weathering the highs and lows of weather," for data included in this key report.

- **Import data:** The United States is a grain exporter, so this data rarely is significant. If that ever changes — permanently or temporarily, the markets will let everyone know.

- **Total supply:** The *total supply* is the sum of beginning stocks, production, and imports.

- **Crush:** (No, I'm not talking about your favorite orange or grape soda — although a grape soda would taste great right about now.) *Crush* refers to the amount of demand being exhibited by *crushers,* or businesses that buy raw soybeans and make them into meal and oil.

- **Exports:** Two export reports are released each week. They are

    - Export inspections — released on Monday after the market closes

    - Export sales — released on Thursday before the market opens

- **Currency trends:** Trends in the currency markets, especially those of the dollar, can affect export reports.

- **Seeds and residual:** Usually 3 to 4 percent of the crop is held for seeding the next year's crop. *Seeds* are important because they're the next season's planting stock. *Residuals* are the portions of soybean oil that are not used in food-related processes. Soybean oil also is used as an additive in pesticides and has biochemical uses, including medications. It's also used as grain spray to prevent dust from settling on stored crops.

- **Total demand:** *Total demand* is the sum of exports, seeds, crush, and the residual figure.

- **Ending carryover stock:** Ending carryover stock is a big number that tends to move the markets. It's the total supply minus total demand.

Don't forget the Deliverable Stocks of Grain report

The Deliverable Stocks of Grain report is an interesting report that merits its own section. Every Tuesday the CBOT tallies the number of bushels of corn, wheat, soybeans, and oats stored in elevators that are licensed to deliver grains in relation to trades made on the CBOT.

This report is important because the information contained in it is a good way to determine whether enough grain is in storage for delivery. If not, the market experiences a short squeeze because traders with short positions don't have any way to make good on their deliveries. They have to buy futures contracts to make good on their bets. A *short squeeze* happens when large numbers of traders have open short positions, or bets that the market will fall. If the market goes against those short positions, traders have to buy contracts to prevent their losses from getting worse. When large numbers of short positions must cover their positions at the same time, the market rallies.

The Deliverable Stocks of Grain report is issued as a Microsoft Excel spreadsheet and can be found on the CBOT Web site. The best way to use it is to keep track of deliverable stocks and watch how the data are trending over a period of time. In fact, you can view several reports and then construct your own chart on the figures so that the trend becomes visible. Otherwise, you must rely on the market's reaction to the release.

Gauging Spring Crop Risks

The *risk premium* is the influence of future expectations of supply on current prices, and it's the basis for price fluctuations in the futures markets. As mentioned in the section "Looking for Goldilocks: The key stages of grain development," earlier in this chapter, crops are most vulnerable during planting, pollination, and harvesting. During these stages, the markets begin to apply a risk premium to prices. This kind of pricing can be an emotional rather than rational process, which is why prices can fluctuate wildly on weather reports, fires, and reports of diseases and insect infestations in the fields.

Corn and soybeans are planted in spring, so they tend to compete for acreage, which makes the price relationship between the two important. In other words, how much acreage farmers decide to devote to each crop is a significant influence on prices.

You need to realize that risk is around every corner during each stage of the crop year. Any external news event, such as flooding, drought, crop plagues, late freezes, or even the accidental introduction of a foreign beetle that flourishes as crops emerge, can shake the markets.

A perfect example of crop risk and its effect on the markets was associated with the rise of orange juice prices in October 2005. Aside from the damage to Florida orange orchards from Hurricane Wilma, an increase was reported in *canker,* a bacterial infection of citrus fruit trees that's spread by wind. Any citrus tree within 1,900 feet of an infected tree had to be cut down.

Planting risk premiums tend to be higher than pollination risk premiums because of the market's fear that the crop won't ever be planted. Pollination risk tends to be less because after the crop is planted, chances are greater that at least some of the crop will emerge and thus be pollinated. The third risk comes at harvest time, when traders begin to fear that crops will wither in the field because of bad weather or other events.

As the market begins pricing in *risk premiums,* futures contracts in corn and soybeans tend to rise during the months of March and April because of the following:

- ✔ Corn planting starts in late March and usually is completed by late May. March and April tend to be months during which corn tends to rally.

- ✔ Soybeans usually are planted in mid-March through May. March and April can be good rally months for soybeans.

Pollination and harvest risks come into play as the year progresses:

- ✔ Corn pollinates in late June or early July. June can be a strong month for corn.

- ✔ Soybean pollination usually takes place in August. August beans can experience a small rally.

- ✔ October and November are harvest months. Rallies during these months usually are not very profitable, because harvest usually takes place and, barring truly extraordinary circumstances, supply and demand find a balance.

During the summer of 1973, the Russians made large purchases of grains. *Supply fear* (the fear that planting, pollination, or harvesting won't be successful) truly gripped the market, and the resulting rally was violent, but it didn't last long. In the absence of major problems with planting, pollination, or harvesting, grain prices responded by falling back to their mainstream trend lines, which is rather simple technical analysis.

During May and June, you need to tailor your trades toward going long in corn and soybeans; however, after August, you need to be looking to go short so you can capitalize on the normal trends of the market. The key word is "looking," because external factors like the weather can cause the market to deviate from general seasonal tendencies.

The bumps, rallies, and valleys of the grain markets are only tendencies. Before deciding to make a trade, be sure to

✔ Find out from your charts whether the market actually is following seasonal patterns that have tended to happen in the past. In 2005, trading was difficult in the corn market, but it was easier in soybeans because the market tended to trend for longer periods.

✔ Look for evidence that confirms what prices are telling you. In the case of corn in 2005, open interest started to rise in conjunction with prices, which is as good a confirmation of a rising trend as there is. Rising open interest means that more buyers are coming into the market. Compare the open interest in soybeans with that of corn, and you can see that the open interest rate for corn actually was flat. Corn contracts had no life in them at that time.

Agriculture 102: Getting Soft

Coffee, sugar, orange juice, and cocoa are known as the *softs*. Some call them the breakfast category of futures. They can deliver some profitable moves if you take the time to become familiar with the standard stuff that goes on in the softs markets.

In contrast to grains and beans, much of the action in softs goes on overseas and often in remote regions of the world, especially in places that from time to time are politically unstable. As a result, trading the softs can be more volatile.

Having coffee at the exchange

Coffee trades in the United States and in London, with the United States trading the largest amount. Coffee is the most active contract at the Intercontinental Exchange (ICE)/New York Board of Trade.

Coffee is all about supply, and the 2001 International Coffee Agreement (ICA), a product of the International Coffee Organization, is meant to provide guidelines with regard to managing the global coffee supply and to encourage consumption. Like all such agreements, the ICA isn't foolproof. It can be circumvented and thus can create controversy in the markets.

 Coffee supplies can be affected by smuggling and by quantities of coffee that are not a part of the quota system and arrangements agreed upon by the ICA. Prices can fall whenever the market is hit with data or rumors suggesting that smuggling is on the rise. For general details and news on coffee, visit the ICA's Web site at www.ico.org/.

Coffee is produced in two classes, Arabica and Robusta, and thus two coffee contracts are traded. These two classes of coffee can trend differently during short periods of time, but they tend to trade along the same long-term trend line.

Arabica

Arabica beans account for 60 percent of the world's coffee supply. Arabica is a cool-temperature, high-altitude crop. Brazil and Columbia combined produce a third of the world's Arabica coffee. Costa Rica, Mexico, Guatemala, Honduras, and El Salvador also are major producers of Arabica, and Indonesia, Uganda, and Vietnam produce the rest.

Arabica is the more important of the two coffee classes when analyzing the North American markets. Supply, as is usual with commodities, is the key. Weather, blights, moves by big retailers, and political events in Africa, Asia, Brazil, and South America, in general, can cause volatility in the coffee markets.

Robusta

Robusta is a less mild variety of coffee that comes from Africa and Asia. Robusta trades in London and is most often used as instant coffee because of its stronger flavor.

Trading coffee

Coffee trading is centered on the New York ICE/New York Board of Trade for Arabica and the Euronext for Robusta. Euronext consolidated the futures markets in Belgium, France, The Netherlands, and Portugal. Here are the particulars for coffee trading:

- **Contract:** The contract size for coffee in New York is 37,500 pounds of Arabica, and it trades at the ICE/NYBOT. Robusta coffee futures trade at Euronext. A Robusta contract contains 5 tons of coffee.

- **Valuation:** A 1-cent move is worth $375 per contract for Arabica. The minimum tick is $1 per ton for Robusta.

- **Limits:** No limits are in place for Robusta.

- **Trading hours:** - Trading hours in New York for Robusta as listed at ICE/NYBOT are "8:30 a.m. to 12:30 p.m.; pre-open commences at 8:20 a.m.; closing period commences at 12:28 p.m. (electronic trading hours: 1:30 a.m.–3:15 p.m. ET)."

Staying sweet with sugar

Sugar is another breakfast commodity, and it's another volatile commodity that is best left for more experienced traders. As with all commodities, you have to understand the basics of the industry, the key reports that move the market, and how to apply technical analysis to trading. Unlike coffee, most sugar-producing countries produce much of the sugar that they use and then export the rest.

Cuba, India, Thailand, and Brazil are major sugar cane producers. Russia and the European Union are the major sugar beet producers. Russia, Europe, the United States, China, and Japan are the biggest importers, and Cuba, Australia, Thailand, and Brazil are the biggest exporters.

The two sugar contracts are

- ✔ **#14,** which has subsidy-supported sugar.
- ✔ **#11,** which has free-market sugar. The free-market sugar contract is the one to trade. A contract is for 112,000 pounds, and a 1-cent move is worth $1,120.

Sugar trades on the stock-to-usage ratio, which is the level of supplies compared to demand. Sugar traders talk about tightness, which means the state of the supply/demand scenario. A ratio of 20 to 30 percent is low and usually leads to higher prices.

Traders also watch for candy sales and the price of corn because of competition from high-fructose corn syrup, which competes with sugar as a commercial sweetener.

Building a rapport with lumber

Lumber is another so-called soft. Why that is, I can't tell you. Some traders think that it's lumped in with the rest of the softs because another place can't be found for it.

Lumber is used in homebuilding, and the price can be volatile. In some cases, lumber prices peak or trough before housing busts or booms, respectively. Several months can elapse before a glut or a major shortage finds its way from the futures markets to the housing industry.

The lumber contract calls for 80,000 board feet (construction grade two by fours) manufactured in the Pacific Northwest or Canada. Prices are quoted in dollars and cents per board foot. A $1 movement in price equals $80 in the contract. Lumber is another thinly traded contract that you can work your way toward trading as you gain more experience.

Part V
The Trading Plan

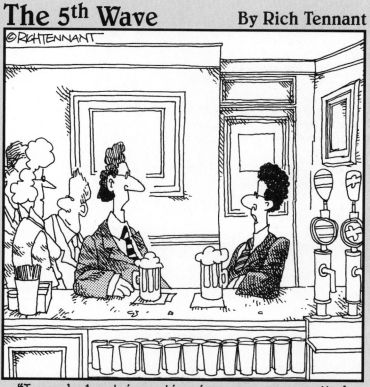

The 5th Wave   By Rich Tennant

"I read about investing in a company called Unihandle Ohio, but I'm uneasy about a stock that's listed on the NASDAQ as UhOh."

In this part . . .

In Part V, you're getting serious — down to brass tacks. You can't trade without getting organized, so I show you how to set realistic goals and expectations, take inventory of your finances, figure out how to best choose a broker, develop a trading plan, and work through a futures trade in real time.

Chapter 17

Trading with a Plan Today So You Can Do It Again Tomorrow

In this chapter I help you decide whether you or someone else will do your trading, and I explain how you can go about setting up your trading infrastructure.

Deciding just who will do your trading is as important a decision as you can make because your success or failure, or how fast you get to your goals, can depend on how you decide to make your trades. Each side of the aisle has advantages and disadvantages, and much of deciding whether to trade for yourself or have someone do it for you depends on your personality, how much hand-holding you need, and what your expectations are.

If you decide to make your own trades, you must fully commit your time and efforts to the enterprise. In a very real sense, you're starting a new business, and any casual notion you have that becoming a trader will be an easy, effortless road to riches is the way to disaster.

The decisions you make have a direct and usually quick bearing on how much money you make or lose while trading.

Financing Your Habit

The most difficult question that you must answer about trading has to do with where you're going to get the money to trade futures.

A simple rule: If you have to borrow money, you shouldn't trade futures or anything else. Money for trading needs to be money that you can afford to lose, period.

You may have to develop a savings plan over several years to finance your new endeavor. As a result, you may need to make changes in your spending habits, such as missing a vacation, driving a more modest car, or eating at less fancy restaurants.

Regardless of how you do it, the best way to trade futures is with your own money. When it's your money that you're trading, you're more likely to be extremely careful about what you do with it.

Although most discount brokers enable you to open a self-managed futures trading account for $5,000, most Certified Trading Advisors (CTAs) require a minimum of $50,000, with the range usually being anywhere from $25,000 up to several million dollars. See the next section for more details about choosing a broker or CTA.

Deciding Who's Going to Do the Trading

After you've made up your mind to trade futures, you need to decide who's going to do the actual trading. The choice is pretty simple; either you or someone else will do it, but that also means you have to decide whether to use an advisor, a broker, or a managed account.

Choosing has its subtleties. Keep in mind that when a broker is doing your trading — depending on your agreement — he or she may have to call you and ask your permission to trade on your behalf. That can delay your ability to make short-term profits. Conversely, you may choose to give your broker full trading authority and discretion to make trades for you. If you do, then you have to abide by the results of the broker's decisions, which means you may face some conflict down the line if your broker is either unscrupulous or not very talented.

A *managed account* is akin to a mutual fund. It is a pooled amount of money that is managed by an individual or a group. Those managers don't have to ask for permission to trade your money because they trade the entire pool simultaneously, and shareholders make or lose money depending on the results of the pool's trades and the number of shares they respectively hold.

The main advantage of letting someone else do the trading is that you can spend time finding out how to trade while your account grows, assuming that you find a good firm or broker to manage your account. The main disadvantage is that you have little control of your money. If you need control, you'll probably be miserable.

Here are your basic trading options:

✔ Manage the account yourself based on your own analysis.

✔ Manage the account yourself based on advice from newsletters, publications, or even a broker.

✔ Have a CTA manage the account.

✔ Buy an interest in a limited-partnership pool managed by a professional CTA. Limited-partnership pools also are known as futures funds.

Other advantages of managed futures, either individual accounts or trading pools, are as follows:

✔ Good CTAs have more experience than novice traders and therefore have a better chance of making money.

✔ Trading pools have more money to invest than individuals and thus can establish better positions in the market.

✔ Trading pools can pay lower commissions when they trade and thus save you money on costs.

✔ Trading pools are structured as limited partnerships or LLCs, entities that limit your risk. They spread risk across all the partners, with the managing partner or the manager/management firm assuming the largest part of the risk. You're liable only for losses or any required restitution for fraud and so on, and your liability is limited to the percentage of the partnership that you own. So if you own 2 percent of the shares, and the partnership goes belly up, you're at risk of losing only an amount commensurate with what you put in.

Some managed futures funds guarantee the return of your initial investment if you remain with the fund for a set number of years. The disadvantages of that option are that your return from these funds may be lower, and you usually must hold the fund until maturity, so your money's tied up in the fund, regardless of how well it's doing.

The disadvantages of managed futures accounts are

- ✔ Higher fees, loss of control of your money, and the general illiquidity associated with them.

- ✔ The fact that you have to part with (or give up control of) your money for an extended period of time and be willing to weather some volatility during that holding period.

The Commodity Futures Trading Commission (CFTC) provides an excellent summary of what a CTA is and how the commodities trading system functions at www.cftc.gov/opa/backgrounder/opacpocta.htm.

Choosing a CTA

A CTA is a professional money manager who must register with the CFTC and undergo a rigorous FBI background check before being allowed to trade other people's money. A knowledgeable CTA can manage your futures trades. You can find a CTA either through a broker or by subscribing to services such as Managed Accounts Reports (MAR; www.marhedge.com), which can become expensive.

Reviewing the CTA's track record

After you get a few names of potential CTAs, review their disclosure documents, which by law have to present all their vital information and their track records. Track records (also by law) have to be presented in a way that is easy enough for you to understand, regardless of whether the advisor has made money. They include comparisons with benchmarks such as the S&P 500 and the Lehman Brothers Long-Term Government Bond Index.

The track record also has to show

- ✔ How much money was being managed

- ✔ How much money per month came from trading

- ✔ How much came from new deposits or was lost to withdrawals from the fund

- ✔ Amounts of fees charged by the fund

- ✔ Amounts of fees paid by the fund

- ✔ Earnings from interest

- ✔ Net return on investment after all fees and trading were taken into account

Be careful in how you look at the posted returns of CTA candidates. Here's an example: Suppose you have two advisors, X and Y, and advisor X's three years of returns are +10 percent, +40 percent, and –20 percent, while advisor Y's returns for the same three years are +15 percent, +10 percent, and + percent. At first glance, you're probably inclined to think that X is the better of the two, but if you do the math, you'll see that if you gave them each $1,000, after three years, X would have $1,232, while Y would have $1,328.

Other CTA characteristics to watch for

Use this checklist to make your best choice of CTAs. Above all, make sure that you match the CTA to your risk tolerance.

- ✔ **Check how long the CTA has been in business.** The longer the advisor has been in business, the better he is likely to be, because he's a survivor.

- ✔ **Find the CTA's largest drawdown or the biggest loss he's ever had.** The two important things to find out are how bad the loss was and how long it took the CTA to get the money back after the loss.

- ✔ **Evaluate the returns of prospective CTAs based on risk.** The CTA who has a lower return but took less risk may be a better choice because he or she is likely to provide more stable returns, and you may sleep better.

- ✔ **Check out the stability of the business.** Make sure that plenty of signs point to the CTA having a stable business and a stable methodology. Look for consistent, but not necessarily high, returns.

- ✔ **Ask about risk management.** Look for reasonable answers with regard to money management and risk aversion.

- ✔ **Look for conflicts of interest.** Is the CTA getting paid by certain brokers to use their services? Is that costing you money? What kind of fees is the CTA collecting from other sources as fees and commissions?

Considering a trading manager

Another possible suggestion is employing a trading manager or a middleman when you're trying to choose a CTA. If you're overwhelmed by the thought of having to plow through hundreds of documents while screening your list of potential CTAs, managed funds, and trading pools, a trading manager can act as an investment counselor, serving as an independent resource who can sift through the jungle of paperwork to help you evaluate CTAs, funds, and managers.

Trading managers collect a fee for doing your legwork, and they get a percentage of your profits, which turns out to be a good incentive for them to find someone who is good for your money. Large investors usually employ trading managers.

Choosing a Broker

If you decide to trade for yourself, you need to choose between a full-service broker and a discount broker. A full-service broker charges you a larger commission but is expected to provide you with good advice about your trades. Some also serve as middlemen between you and CTAs.

Be careful whenever you deal with brokers, CTAs, mutual funds, annuities, and so on because brokers and advisors sometimes earn large incentives for steering you in certain directions, regardless of whether taking those directions with your money is in your best interest.

Look for full access to the following when you open an account:

- **All markets:** Even if you're interested in only a handful of markets right now, you may want to consider expanding your horizons in the future, so choosing a broker who can give you all the choices under one roof is best.

- **Research:** Some brokers offer discounts to newsletters and Web sites, while others offer direct access to their own research departments. Some offer live broadcasts from the trading pits.

- **The full gamut of technical tools:** You really want an opportunity to get as fancy with your trading as you want to in the future, including having the ability to run multiple real-time charts with oscillators and indicators and receive intermarket analysis.

- **Intelligent software:** Some brokers offer you access to software and charting packages that enable you to back test, or review, the results of your trading strategies and indicators.

- **Forward testing your strategy:** Nothing guarantees that you'll match the results predicted by the software, but the ability to forward test your trading strategies is a nice tool to have. Back testing shows you how your trades would have worked based on historical data. Forward testing is based on the probability of certain conditions occurring in the future and is more related to how much money you'd make if certain things happened; however, it's a useful tool only in hypothetical settings.

Follow these suggestions when boiling down your choices between brokers:

- ✔ **Test more than one trading platform.** Most brokers will offer you a trial of their software and trading platforms if you register on their Web sites.

- ✔ **Make sure that the broker offers a 24-hour customer-service line.** This line of communication is crucial if you decide to exit a position overnight in the face of events that are costing you money. If you have to wait until the morning, your losses can be larger than you'd expect. The 24-hour nature of futures trading is another reason to use stop-loss orders.

- ✔ **Make sure that you have the choice of entering trades via the Internet or phone.** If phone lines are busy and you have to make a trade, you want access. If your Internet connection and your backup connection are down, you'd like to have phone access to either check your positions or make trades.

- ✔ **Check all potential trading fees before you sign up and make a trade.** Check all fees, including whether all the trading bells and whistles are included in the commission or whether extra charges or conditions must be met, such as a minimum number of trades to qualify for certain services.

- ✔ **Open an account with a well-known firm.** Going with an established broker can be a good idea, at least when you're getting started. If you try to save a few bucks with a smaller firm, you may be sorry later on, especially if you're concerned about order execution, software glitches, and hidden fees. Large firms are not exempt from fraud but, because of their size, information about their practices is more readily available.

- ✔ **Check for current trading scams:** Look on the CFTC's Web site (`www.cftc.gov`) under the "Consumer Protection" heading for current trading scams and for disciplinary actions taken against firms and brokers. You'll find important bulletins and helpful Web links to important information about general rules and recent enforcement actions. On the National Futures Association's (NFA) Web site (`www.nfa.futures.org/basicnet`), you can search for brokers, trading pools, and CTAs.

Falling in the pit of full service

Some of the same criteria that apply for choosing a CTA can be used for choosing a full-service broker (see the earlier sections on "Reviewing the CTA's track record" and "Other CTA characteristics to watch for"). Especially important is whether you're dealing with an experienced broker, who earns his or her keep.

With brokerage firms, many times you meet the lead guy once, but you never see him again. You're left dealing with underlings, and that can be just like Russian roulette. If you get a good one, you'll be mostly okay, if you can handle the larger fees. Much of the time, especially when you have a smaller account, you're relegated to someone just starting out with the firm, and that may or may not be in your best interest.

Choosing a futures discount broker

Going the route of the discount broker may be a better alternative if you're adventurous and do your homework, which includes practice trading in simulated accounts.

A large number of discount brokers operate in the futures markets, and you can find most of them by using your favorite search engine on the Internet or looking at advertisements in *Futures, Active Trader,* the *Wall Street Journal,* and other publications.

Aside from the important aspects, such as service in general, availability of 24-hour service, commissions, and ease of access to the trading desk, discount brokers offer online trading services. You want to make sure that the trading platform the discount broker provides is easy to use and that the orders you place online are executed in a reasonable amount of time.

Chapter 18

Looking for Balance Between the Sheets

The futures markets are a zero-sum game. Someone always loses, and someone always wins. In other words, any money that you make trading is money that you've taken away from someone else who's also trading.

Put the shoes on your own feet, and you get a better picture of the situation. Yup, out there in cyberworld or in some crazy trading pit, someone is waiting to take your money away from you. So before you decide to start trading, you need to figure out whether you measure up mentally and financially.

I'm not talking about your self-esteem or your intellect here, although good measures of both are required for success in trading. More important, you need to know how much money you have and whether you can manage it well enough for continued success in trading futures — that is, well enough to stay in the game.

In this chapter, I tell you about some basic issues that can help you decide whether you should be a trader or think about doing something else with your money until your finances are in good enough shape to enable you to trade comfortably.

In a sense, you need to keep track of two personal balance sheets: a mental one, from which you figure out why you want to trade, and a financial one, from which you decide whether you have enough money to finance your trading venture. Both are equally important, and ignoring one or the other is a recipe for disaster.

Exploring What's on Your Mental Balance Sheet

Your expectations about futures trading shape the role futures play in your portfolio. As a general rule, futures need to be part of an overall financial plan that includes stocks, bonds, mutual funds, annuities, real estate, and other assets. Although not a mandatory component, futures and commodities in general can be useful in the portfolios of individuals with large net worths, especially as a hedge against risk. However, the central tenet of your mental balance sheet is understanding why trading futures appeals to you.

Why do you want to trade?

Most people look to the excitement often associated with gambling and equate it with trading futures. Unfortunately, trading futures or other assets is not gambling. Trading isn't associated with glitz and shouldn't be associated with liquor or other diversions. In fact, the more aware you are of the current global situation and the current situation in your market, the better off you'll be.

Here's how I answer the question: Trading is a hedge for my life. I have two full-time jobs: my medical practice and my financial business. On occasion, one or the other takes over as a major income producer. When my trading business isn't going well, my medical practice still provides a relatively stable income and vice versa. (I've experienced periods when the opposite has been true.)

I trade for these two reasons:

- ✔ **It's my business.** Trading and the byproducts of trading, such as writing books, selling subscriptions to my Web site, and occasionally providing consulting services, are major contributors to my income. By trading, I'm not only making money, but I'm also testing strategies in real time that I eventually can pass on to my subscribers (www.joe-duarte.com) in the form of recommendations and insights.

- ✔ **Trading provides income diversification and enables me to maximize the total return on my retirement fund.** I add as much to my IRA every year as is legally possible within my means, and I trade the hell out of it. I don't miss an opportunity to contribute to it, no matter what. Most of the time I fund my IRA entirely from the income that trading and related endeavors produce.

For me, trading is an important source of income and income diversification that I derive from a tremendously enjoyable and agreeable mental and intellectual exercise.

When pondering the question that heads up this section, make sure that your answers are truthful. If you're just looking for kicks or you think that trading will fix all your problems, don't fool yourself. Trading is work that requires personal and financial commitment, even if it isn't your primary source of income. If you take it seriously, you need to think about what you expect to get out of it. If you decide not to take it seriously, don't trade.

Trading is a sporadic way to produce income. You can experience long stretches during which no matter how you feel or how accurately you follow your trading plan, you'll still have few opportunities to ply your craft, or you'll end up going through a long and steady string of losses. In a good year, I can make as much or more money by trading than I'm allowed to add to my IRA. By adding money every year, I increase the overall rate of accumulation in the account. But in a bad year, I may have to consider taking out a loan to cover my taxes and to fund my IRA. Fortunately, I haven't had many bad years.

Trading is a serious game that should not be taken lightly. The key to being a successful trader is to be comfortable with yourself, your motivation, and your ability to formulate a plan and put it into action. Before you start trading, it's important that you understand why you want to trade. You need to look at your own life and situation to make a decision that you can live with when it comes to how much time and effort you can devote to trading and whether you're willing to stick to it.

Trading as part of an overall strategy

Trading futures needs to be put into proper perspective. After you've sorted out your mental balance sheet, you can consider where trading fits into your life.

Trading can be a part-time endeavor, or it can be a full-time job. If you're like me, you consider trading as full-time work, but if you do it part time, it can be a useful source of income all the same.

Say, for example, that you're a buy-and-hold investor in stocks, concentrating on income-producing preferred, blue-chip, and utility stocks. Trading futures can add a more aggressive element to your portfolio.

One ideal way for you to trade to your advantage takes place during times when a market is moving sideways, and you can improve your income by writing call options (see Chapter 4 for more about options). Another way is when a market is ready to top out, and you can either sell stock-index futures short or buy put options to protect your stock portfolio.

Trading for a living

On the other hand, when you're trading futures for a living, you may want to consider moving to Chicago or New York and looking for a job in the industry. If that is your goal, it probably will take several years to master the craft and significant amounts of capital, guile, risk taking, and effort may be required on your part to accomplish it.

Regardless of what you decide, you can derive at least some benefit from figuring out your mental balance sheet.

The Financial Balance Sheet

The high-risk world of futures trading requires a higher litmus test of your finances than other forms of investing. In the same way that you took the time to explore the reasons why you want to trade and how trading is going to fit into your life, you now must look at your finances with the least amount of flattery possible.

The big question is whether you have enough money to take risks as a trader. If you're struggling to pay your bills every month and your idea of being solvent is transferring your credit-card balances to a new card every six months to increase your credit line, you're better off not trading futures. On the other hand, if you have enough money, you may want to find someone to do the trading for you. And if you're somewhere in between having no money for trading at all and enough not to worry, you'll probably have to do at least some of the work yourself.

Organizing your financial data

As elementary as it may sound, getting organized is the only place to start. But before you start adding and subtracting, make sure that you have the following matters under control and accounted for within your monthly finances:

- **Your living expenses, especially food, mortgage, rent, and car payments:** If you can't live the way you want to on what you make, looking to the futures markets to save you from your current situation is not prudent. You have to have enough money for the basic necessities, food, transportation, and rent before you do anything else.

✔ **Your life insurance coverage:** The amount here is variable and needs to be based on your family's expected expenses after your death. Some basic life-insurance calculators are available online to help you determine how much you need. I recommend a quick Internet search, using your favorite search engine.

✔ **Your health insurance needs:** Again, the amount of health coverage you have is based on your family and your individual needs. You need to figure in a worst-case scenario, though.

✔ **Your retirement plan:** This aspect of your finances needs to be one of your highest priorities before any kind of investing. Make sure that you establish one and that you fund it as fully as possible before doing any other kind of investing or trading. As I note earlier in this chapter, I trade my retirement account actively and successfully, and I believe that you can do it too if you master the craft well. Just remember, you should not put 100 percent of your retirement money into a futures trading account. Always diversify and time the markets based on your experience and knowledge of trends and indicators.

✔ **Your savings plan, including how you're going to pay for your children's college educations:** Start by calculating your savings rate, which is the percentage of last year's earnings that you didn't spend.

✔ **Your emergency fund:** Set up an emergency fund and don't even think about using it to fund your futures trading. At least three to six months' worth of living expenses is a good start.

When you have the essentials covered, you can turn your sights on reducing or restructuring your debt with a clear and concise endpoint in mind so you can pay it off and start thinking about accumulating money to trade with. One way is to set yourself up with an allowance every month or every paycheck.

If by some miracle you find that you have enough money left over, congratulations! You can consider trading.

A good place to gather information for preparing this kind of a budget is your tax return or any recent loan application you've filed. You can develop a good inventory of your assets and liabilities by reviewing credit-card statements, your checkbook ledger, and your monthly receipts, especially expenses that are recurring every week or month, such as grocery, cellphone, and utility bills, and car and house payments.

Don't forget to include intangibles, such as car repairs and impromptu medical and dental bills, because they can add up in a hurry. Be sure to categorize your expenses according to their similarities, much like when you're preparing your tax return.

Get a second opinion from a financial planner about the state of your finances. Be careful when you do because most will tell you that trading futures is too risky, and some will try to sell you high front-loaded and back-end-loaded mutual funds instead. If you visit a financial advisor or planner, make sure you tell him upfront that you're interested only in him checking your work and your calculations.

Setting realistic goals

Set the bar on your finances high enough that you won't be sorry later. Ideally, you need $100,000 or more as an initial trading stake. If you can't come up with that kind of money, wait until you can at least meet the lowest trading threshold of $25,000. Again, these are guidelines. Stories exist of talented traders who've made millions after starting with as little as five or ten thousand dollars.

When setting your financial goals, consider the following:

- ✔ **Your age:** How old you are is especially important whenever you're not well capitalized. Make sure that you can make your money back if you happen to have a disastrous start or streak.

- ✔ **The size of your family:** As with age, the number of people who rely on you financially is more important when you're not well capitalized. If your income is a significant portion of the family's well-being, then that takes precedence regardless of the circumstances. Never sell your family short.

- ✔ **Job security:** Most traders and would-be traders need a steady infusion of income that's provided by a steady job. If you decide that trading is your job, you still need to find a way to supplement your income during the times when trading won't provide you with enough money.

- ✔ **Your family's attitude toward trading:** If your spouse is going to harass you about trading, or you lose contact with the family because you're up at strange hours trading currencies, you're going to have a major problem at some point.

- ✔ **Your own risk tolerance and emotional status:** If you can't stand the thought of what you'll do if you get a margin call or you get wiped out, find something else to do.

Calculating Your Net Worth

Your net worth can guide you in making your final decision about whether you can actually afford to become a futures trader. The calculation is simple, but it requires attention to detail. Widely used financial computer programs like Quicken can help you do the work. A quick search on your favorite Internet search engine takes you to several Web sites that feature other programs that also can help. You can find a simple free calculator on the Web through a quick search, or ask your bank for a checklist.

You can also do the calculations by hand. If you need a major helping hand with this aspect of getting set up, pick up a copy of Eric Tyson's *Personal Finance For Dummies,* 5th Edition (Wiley).

Figure 18-1 shows you a generic personal balance sheet that's self-explanatory. First, you list your assets and add them all up. Next you do the same with your liabilities. Finally, you subtract the liabilities from the assets, and you get your net worth.

That bottom-line number, your net worth, is the amount you hope that you can get out of all the things you own after you pay off all the debt you owe if for some reason you have to sell everything. And that's the number that can tell you whether trading futures is a good idea.

Pay special attention to the amounts you have in the following:

- ✔ **Cash:** Cash means the amount of money you have in money-market funds, your pocket, and even stashed in your secret hiding place.

- ✔ **Real estate:** Real estate refers to your home and any rental property, second home, or other real property that you may own. As a rule, if you can't sell it tomorrow, it shouldn't count toward this calculation.

- ✔ **Stocks, bonds, and retirement accounts:** Most people hold stocks, bonds, and mutual funds in their retirement accounts, although some also own them outside of their retirement plans. Any money that's in a retirement account will be subject to tax consequences and early withdrawal penalties, so you need to include those amounts in the calculation. However, you also need to be realistic. You're not likely to cash in your IRA or 401(k) plan to go speculate on soybeans. After reading this book, you better not!

- ✔ **Business assets:** Consider how many of your business assets are involved in cash flow and inventory. Be careful not to be too generous in this category.

- ✔ **Credit-card balances**, **second mortgages, and adjustable-rate mortgages:** Pay special attention to these amounts under liabilities, and be sure to include the latest credit-card balance and make sure that the amount includes any big purchases that you've recently made. Don't hesitate to check your account online for the most current, real-time statement on your credit cards.

Cash	15,000
Real Estate	240,000
Car	35,000
Bank Accounts	12,500
Stocks and Bonds	74,000
Mutual Funds	30,000
Retirement Accounts	95,000
Current Values of Businesses	110,000
Others	25,000
Total Assets	636,500
Home Mortgages	200,000
Credit Cards	35,000
Car Loans	28,000
Personal Loans	35,000
Education Loans	12,500
Taxes	13,000
Others	5,000
Total Liabilities	328,500
Net Worth	308,000

Figure 18-1:
A balance
sheet can
calculate
your net
worth.

After you do all the calculations, here's a useful guideline: If your net worth is less than $200,000, you shouldn't be trading at all, much less trading futures.

Differentiating between trading and investing is important. If you have $200,000 or less, investing in mutual funds is perfectly acceptable, perhaps even in a mixture of stocks and funds, as long as you're careful to follow sound money-management and loss-management rules and have a long enough time frame to make it profitable. If you're trading, which by definition means aggressively and actively deploying your money, keep the following in mind as a bare-bones set of criteria.

Never risk more than 10 percent of your net worth as a trading stake unless you have a net worth of at least $500,000 to $1 million or more and you're a well-equipped, stable, and experienced trader. If you are, you may want to risk as much as 20 percent of your net worth to trade, provided your expenses and long-term investments are covered. However, risking more than 25 percent of your net worth in any trading venue is a crapshoot and will likely get you into trouble.

Chapter 19

Developing Strategies Now to Avoid Pain Later

....

In This Chapter

▶ Choosing what to trade and understanding how to trade it

▶ Keeping those profits coming

▶ Checking and practicing trading strategies

▶ Timing your markets for entry and exit points

▶ Checking your trade results and adjusting for success

....

A solid trading plan consists of developing a broad understanding of what you'll be trading, getting a handle on your emotions, finding out about different strategies, and tempering your expectations of and interactions with the market. It also takes in the more methodical nuts and bolts of actually putting together a step-by-step detailed plan in which you microscopically map out your strategies and rules.

In this chapter, I give you the background needed to create a more specific trading plan than you ever imagined.

Deciding What You'll Trade

I have no secret here, no magic rules or revelations. I can tell you only that you need to trade what you like and use what you already know to your advantage as much as possible. So when preparing a trading plan, take the following into account:

▸ **Use your experience.** Use what you know to focus on areas in which you're already an expert, but trade what feels right and what you have success in.

✔ **Get specific and get good by applying and refining your knowledge.**
It's great to be a one-trick pony. Of all the currencies, I prefer the
euro/dollar pairing. I find that for me, it makes sense for two reasons:

- European monetary policy moves at the pace of molasses, and the
European economy usually is slow-moving at best. In other words,
the news from Europe is less likely to move the markets directly.
Instead, the euro is a reactionary currency that tends to move in a
slow, steady, one-directional trend, as opposed to other currencies
that can be more volatile, such as the Japanese yen, the Swiss
franc, and the British pound.

- The dollar, despite the rise of China and other emerging markets,
is still the world's reserve currency. The United States still has the
most transparent markets and the most reliable economic data and
communications infrastructure.

✔ **Study the markets.** See which ones appeal to you the most and make
the most sense. If you enjoy trading stocks, you may do well with stock-
index futures. If you like a particular sector, such as energy, try a few
paper trades (practicing without money) with oil, natural gas, heating
oil, or gasoline.

If you're a political junkie like me, the bond and currency markets may
suit you well because they're the markets that move the most with politics and world crises.

If you're in real estate and construction, consider copper and bond
futures. Interest rates are the fuel for mortgage rates, while copper is
one of the key building materials in home building. If you know one city
or region's real-estate market well enough, consider trading futures for
that market. Real-estate futures and housing futures are now available
also, but may take some time to become mainstream trading vehicles for
the public.

If you own a gas station, you probably have a good understanding of
supply and demand in the energy markets.

If you work in produce, you may have a leg up in grains and seeds.

✔ **Remain flexible.** If you discover that you have a penchant for trading
well in the soybean markets, even though you're not in the business and
you never knew anything about it before, add soybeans to your trading
arsenal.

Adapting to the Markets

A major part of your trading success is your ability to adapt. Even if you're a
specialist trading primarily one or two markets, you still encounter periods
when those markets trade in difficult patterns.

The major point to understand is that no plan works for all situations. However, you can rely on these realities of the markets. They trade in threes:

- **Three market directions:** Up, down, or sideways
- **Three trading styles:** Trading the reversal, momentum trading, and swing trading

You need to be familiar with the three major trading directions and styles. I cover these in the following sections.

Trading the reversal

When trading the reversal, you're looking for the market's turning point, when either a bottom or a top is being made. To find that turning point, you need to keep an eye on the current trend and watch for a significant trend change.

The longer a trend stays in place, the more important the reversal will be, and the longer the new trend is likely to stay in place. Here are some tips for identifying a change in trend:

- Use moving averages, trend lines, and oscillators to predict and pinpoint as precisely as possible the meaningful trend changes. I describe how to use these indicators in Chapter 7, which is about technical analysis, and in the numerous examples of individual trades throughout this book.

- Set your entry points just above the breakout if you're going long, and below the trend breakdown (a switch by the market to a downtrend) if you're going short. See Chapters 7, 8, and 20 for more trading tips. Use a sell stop for long trades and a buy stop to cover your shorts when you're betting on a breakdown.

Trading with momentum

Trading with the trend or with the momentum of the market is a classic style of participating in the markets. In fact, it's something that I always recommend you do. It works the same way in uptrends as it does in downtrends. Just keep the following in mind:

- **If the market is trending up, your position needs to be long.** Even if you're day trading, your primary goal needs to be to look for opportunities to trade when the market is rising.

- **If the market is falling (trending down), you need to be short.**

✔ **As with any other trade, protect yourself by using stops.** Stops are preset instructions that direct your broker to sell your position when a certain price is reached and keep your losses from expanding beyond control (see Chapters, 7, 8, and 20).

✔ **Use the market as your guide in momentum trading.** You need to let the market help you make decisions for buying and selling.

✔ **When you're going long, you need to look for breakouts as entry points.** *Breakouts* are generally signs of market strength.

✔ **When you're going short, you need to look for breakdowns to enter your short position.** *Breakdowns* are generally signs of market weakness.

A rising channel can be used as an opportunity to swing trade or to trade by using momentum strategies. In this case, every pullback to the lower trend line was yet another opportunity to go long, and every tag of the upper trend line was an opportunity to either take profits and watch for what the market would do next or consider a short-term opportunity by short-selling the market. I tell you more about swing trading in the next section.

Swing trading

Swing trading is the best method for trading in markets in which prices are moving sideways, neither going up nor down. For more information about swing trading, see Chapter 8.

Managing Profitable Positions

One of the most important aspects of trading is deciding what to do when you've earned a nice profit, and you're getting antsy about cashing in. This situation may occur during the course of a normal market or one that is reaching the irrational exuberance, or blowoff, stage.

You must watch for several important indicators during a *blowoff,* or in a market that seems unstoppable and experiences short-term corrections. That can mean that sometimes the market sells off in the middle of the day, and buyers are waiting for the market to drop so they can buy at lower prices.

In this kind of market environment, especially when you've earned big profits, taking profits is a good idea whenever the market drops for two consecutive days.

On the other hand, if the market opens down significantly without news, take it as a sign that worse things may be coming. And if the market fails to set a new high after a short-term correction, it's pointing to an important sign that a significant top is developing.

Whenever the market breaks and you don't sell your position in time, use the snap-back rally, which is when the market bounces after an aggressive period of selling that usually develops so you can move out of your position and into the next.

Building yourself a pyramid (Without being a pharaoh)

Futures traders add to profitable positions by *pyramiding,* or adding more contracts to existing profitable positions. When you pyramid a position, you're adding to your existing holdings, not selling your holdings and starting a new position. Check out the example at the end of this section, where I detail how to pyramid a position in which your initial buy is ten contracts.

Never use a reverse or inverted pyramid strategy when trading. By that I mean that the first number of contracts you buy needs to be the guideline for your maximum risk. If, for example, you buy three crude-oil contracts, double your initial investment in the trade, and the market still looks attractive, you can add to your position, but only by a maximum of three contracts each time you add to your pyramid. The goal is to keep adding contracts as long as the market remains in the same trend or until reality sets in and you run out of the money that you'd set aside for this trade.

Use a pyramid strategy only during the early stages of a move, such as the breakout and subsequent early stages of the breakout. If you try it when the market has been moving in one direction for a long time, you're likely to lose money.

Preventing good profits from turning into losses

When you trade and the market turns on you quickly, you obviously have to get out with whatever you have left. But when your positions show nice profits, don't let the market take away your hard-earned gains.

Stay on top of your profits by setting protective sell stops as the market moves. For more details about stops, see the previous section and Chapters 3, 7, 8, and 20. With protective stops, you can (at all costs) make every attempt to at least break even on nice big profits, especially when you're trading markets that move quickly and can change at the drop of a hat if you're not paying attention.

For example, say you establish a position in the euro at 8 a.m., the market rallies, and by 11 a.m. you have a nice profit. In the middle of the day while you take a lunch break away from your trading screen (bad idea), news breaks, and the euro tumbles, taking your profit with it. If you had set a (protective) sell stop and had adjusted it higher as your profits accumulated, you would have gotten stopped out with more money than you started.

Never adding to losing positions

When the market goes against you, it's time to get out. If you *average down*, or add to positions at lower prices in the futures markets, you'll get hurt badly.

Back Testing Your Strategies

Back testing is the practice of using historical data to test how well your indicators work in a particular market. Software programs enable you to look at past markets and test how different methods and indicators have worked in the past, but it's a tricky practice. These capabilities amount to a double-edged sword in a chaotic universe because although your indicators may back test well, you still can get a false sense of security. Similarly, what didn't work in the past may somehow start working.

In other words, no trades ever work exactly the same way twice, so you have to take your back-testing results with a grain of salt. Back testing can, however, help give you a broad feel for how markets behave under certain conditions and help you spot important characteristics of the market, such as the following:

✓ **Seasonal trends:** Seasonal trends work best when trading the energy, grain, seed, and livestock markets, because those markets are dependent on well-established planting and harvesting cycles, as well as the demand for energy during summer and winter. In other markets, such as bonds and currencies, seasonality is often less reliable, except during short periods of time. For example, stock prices tend to rise at the end of every month and the first few trading days of a new month, because institutions put new money to work during that time frame.

✔ **Market tendencies:** The amount of time that a particular market tends to run in a certain direction is a great example. If you look at a long-term chart of the U.S. dollar index, you immediately see that its trend lines tend to last for months to years after they're established (see Chapter 11).

✔ **Indicators:** Use your indicators wisely after you confirm their accuracy by back testing them. Get the big picture. For example, if you're testing a moving average crossover method, remember that the one you're study- ing now may not work as well later. However, if your testing shows that moving average crossovers work in the market you're testing, get a handle on several combinations and then monitor them in the current market to find out which ones work best.

Setting Your Time Frame for Trading

The aspects of trading that are most often mismatched are the trader's personality and the time frame of the trade. Some people are just more patient than others. To be a good trader, you have to find that delicate bal- ance between your level of patience and the reality of the market. If you try to impose your personality on the market, you're going to get hurt. At the same time, you have to let your general tendencies guide you toward your trading style.

Day trading

Day trading is a misunderstood and oft maligned term. Day trading is the practice of holding positions open for short periods of time during the trad- ing day with the goal of accruing small, but numerous, profits. Usually it means that you exit all positions at the end of the trading day and return to the market with a fresh slate the next day. What it doesn't mean is that you trade every day or that you open positions at the open of the trading day no matter what.

When day trading, you still need to keep basic trading principles in mind, such as picking good entry and exit points, placing protective stops, manag- ing your money, and using technical analysis. And you still need to keep an eye on the news and on the overall trends of the markets.

Intermediate-term trading

Traditionally, intermediate-term trading means that you hold a position for several weeks to several months, which ultimately is impractical in the futures markets, where volatility can lead to margin calls and where leverage makes holding positions for extended periods extremely dangerous.

So in the futures markets, intermediate is more likely to mean several days and is more often referred to as *position trading,* where you use a longer-term time frame as your reference point for keeping a position open.

One way to participate in the overall trend of the futures markets for the intermediate term is to use exchange-traded funds. See Chapter 5 for details.

Long-term trading

Long-term trading is impractical in the futures markets, unless you're extremely well capitalized, and you're hedging your business. When that is the case, however, you can use contracts that are several months to even years ahead as your positions as long as you're mindful of expiration dates and other parameters. ETFs can help here as well because they let you trade the trend without worrying about expiration dates and contract rollovers, such as when you're trading straight futures. Don't be fooled, though. ETFs, such as the U.S. Oil Fund (USO) are just as volatile as the market which they mirror. That means that a big loss in oil futures can be a big loss in USO.

Setting Price Targets

Setting price targets is a useful strategy, especially when you're swing trading, which is where you ease into and out of positions by closely watching a market's trading range. Setting targets in momentum markets, however, may do more harm than good because you may sell a potentially huge profitable position too soon.

Adapting your strategy to the market's overall trend is the better approach, but Fibonacci levels and support and resistance levels can help you set targets for taking profits.

Reviewing Your Results

After each trade, finding out why you did well or why you failed is a good idea. Checking your trading data from the time you enter a position to the time you exit it on every single trade can be tedious, but it also can be extremely useful. Here is a fairly good overview of the kinds of information and questions you may want to check and answer after good or bad trades:

✔ **Exit and entry points:** Review your exit and entry points and then ask yourself whether you adapted the right strategy to the right market and whether you used the best possible method to protect yourself.

Did you give yourself enough room to maneuver? For example, was your sell stop too tight? Should you have given the market more room?

✔ **Your charts:** Go back and look at the charts you used to make your trade to find out whether the market you were trading is acting similar to the way history shows it has acted in the past. If it isn't, try to figure out what's different about the market.

✔ **Fundamentals:** Did you really understand what the fundamentals of the market were telling you? Did you understand the nuts and bolts of the industry? For example, did you pay attention to the part of the livestock cycle that the market was in when you traded hogs? Or did you check the weather reports before you shorted soybeans?

✔ **Market suitability:** Are you really suited for trading in a given market? Does it move too fast or too slow for you? If you're trading currencies, for example, can you handle moves that last for several days and keep your positions open overnight? Or does that frighten you and make you lose sleep? If you lose sleep, you'll be flat-footed when you wake up, and you're thus bound to miss something. A 20-minute gap in a chart can be closed in an hour because the bad or good news that moved your currency turned out to be a false alarm, and the market moved briskly beyond (above or below) where it was trading before the news hit.

✔ **Technical analysis:** Did you let your own personal judgment ruin your trade because you thought you knew better than the charts? Always trade what you see and not what you think you know. You may eventually be right, and then you can trade the other way, but in the present, trade with the charts, follow the market's response to the news that hit today, and forget what the talking heads are saying.

✔ **Market volume and sentiment:** Did you consider the market's volume and the overall sentiment before you bought that top and got stopped out in a hurry? Low volume and high levels of pessimism often mean that a market has bottomed, while huge volume and a feeling of invincibility are the hallmark of a pending top.

✔ **Subtleties:** Don't miss the subtle stuff. Did you pay attention to your indicators? Did you look at your RSI and MACD oscillators for signs that the market's bottom that you missed came on a lower low on the charts but a higher low on the indicator?

Remember Your Successes and Manage Your Failures

When things go well, you need to remember the moment in your gut, your mind, and your being. If you fail, do the same. That way, if you're ever faced with a similar set of situations, you have a visceral and mental archive that will let you react in the correct manner.

This strategy is tailor-made for trading. For example, when you make a big profit, you need to sear the particulars of that trade into your mind. Try to remember how you did it, what you saw, what you felt, and what decisions you made along the way.

Following your trading plan all the way down to your checklist always is the better approach to trading, because then you already have a road map with which to evaluate your performance.

When managing your failures, avoiding the markets that you just don't understand is best. For example, I don't trade gold. It just doesn't work for me, so I manage it by avoiding it.

In the rare instances when I do consider trading gold stocks or other gold-related instruments, I always ask myself really tough questions, such as whether I can stand the lack of sleep. The result: I rarely trade gold.

Making the Right Adjustments

After evaluating your successes and your failures, you can make changes that keep you out of trouble by

- ✔ Avoiding markets that you don't understand or that make you uncomfortable.

- ✔ Not adding to positions without planning your strategy before pulling the trigger.

- ✔ Having your road map ready and not deviating from it unless you've previously decided how you'll do it and how far you're willing to go.

- ✔ Not making the same mistake twice. If you get nailed in the oil market, don't trade oil until you've figured out why you got hammered.

Chapter 20

Executing Successful Trades

*T*his chapter is all about putting together the analysis, the execution, and the management of a trade. Although the information throughout this chapter generally is hypothetical, it nevertheless relies on real-life examples of trading. It starts with your pre-trade analysis and then details the actual execution of the trade through a phone conversation with your trading desk, managing the position, and then closing out the trade.

The trade I outline chronologically in this chapter obviously is idealized, but it isn't meant to be a Pollyanna-like exercise. Instead, it's an exercise of discovery that uses a real-life example in an active market — the oil market — during a crucial period of time.

Setting the Stage

Here's the scene: The oil market has been consolidating since October 2007, with prices ranging between $82 and $95. As Figure 20-1 shows, the May contract for crude formed a double bottom between January 11 and February 12, 2008. Note the "W" formation, and also note the clumping of prices around the 20-, 50-, and 200-day moving averages (labeled 20, 50, and 200), as the right portion of the "W" forms.

Figure 20-2, confirms your analysis, as the Bollinger Bands around the 20-day moving average are squeezing the prices. When Bollinger bands squeeze prices and there is consolidation around moving averages or key support or resistance points, such as in these figures, that's known as compression, and it is usually a prelude to a big move. And that's when you should start making plans to trade this market. Three scenarios are possible:

- A move to the up side is possible, which is an opportunity to go long.
- The market might go nowhere, which means that you have to wait some more.
- Or the market is about to fall. In this case, the chart clearly shows that the $85 or better area has held at least two times, as marked by the asterisks.

This kind of chart formation suggests that the market is most likely to rise.

Your three major goals are to

- **Analyze the situation.** Combine your knowledge of technical and funda-mental analyses with the psychology of a market in a multiyear bull market.
- **Design a trading strategy.** Based on your analyses, you must design a well-crafted, step-by-step, careful plan that either makes you some money or gets you out of the position with as little damage as possible (if you're wrong or the market turns against you).
- **Put the plan into action.** Make the trade, establish the position, and then manage it as you take the plunge into chaos.

You wake up, get your coffee ready as your computer boots up, and survey the landscape. As you sip coffee while going through your stretching routine, you scan the latest news on CNBC, in the *Wall Street Journal,* or on Google News or the Dow Jones Newswires. You probably ought to check Reuters and Bloomberg, too. As you scroll through all that information, you have only one goal in mind: watching the different markets as they set up for trading.

What you know for sure is that the date is February 8, 2008, a bull market is raging in oil and has been for several years, and the market is clearly at a crit-ical juncture, because crude oil futures have been consolidating for months and the weekly release of supply data is in about five days — February 13. As you scan the news, you note that there is a big energy conference in Houston next week and that leaks and comments from experts are starting to make the wires.

Most of them are concerned about the effects on the economy of $100 oil, which is still $18 away from the prices you see in electronic trading.

You take another sip of coffee, and scan the markets. The dollar is flat but looking a bit wobbly, and stock-index futures are flat, a couple of days after having gotten hit fairly hard. Bonds are also flat.

That means that you're focused on oil. It's the one market that looks ready to jump and it's the one that suits your style and the one where you've had your share of success.

Getting the Big Picture

As you pour yourself another cup of coffee and grab a roll, you realize that you have some time before heavy trading in crude oil gets going in a couple of hours, but you note that the price has steadily crept higher in the overnight markets. Aside from the news on the upcoming conference in Houston, there is little going on at first glance.

Then the news hits about Exxon Mobil winning a court battle against Venezuela and the price starts to move. Exxon got a court in London to freeze $12 billion worth of assets of Venezuela's state-owned oil company, PDVSA, and the Venezuelan government started making threats about halting oil sales to Exxon. The markets needed a spark, and this seemed to be it.

Viewing the long-term picture of the market

You review your one year chart of crude oil, and the RSI indicator (Figure 20-2). See Chapters 8 and 13 for more about the RSI oscillator.

The RSI oscillator is an important and key indicator that tends to serve as a good early-warning system. Your point of view is now narrowed because you expect that oil will likely bounce, and you're looking for confirmation that the market is oversold enough to carry any bounce for at least a few days.

A perfect example is shown in Figure 20-2. A look at RSI is very encouraging, as it is confirming the "W" bottom on the price. More important, the second bottom in the RSI is higher than the first one, which shows that the selling on the second "V" of the "W" was not as strong as the first "V." This is often an indication that sellers were exhausted during the second bout of selling in "W" formation.

You're all set now. You have the background from which you'll approach your trade. Until proven otherwise, a bottom is in place and this market has to played from the long side.

Doing a little technical analysis

Check out the technical status of the oil market by

- ✔ **Examining the long-term trend:** The crude-oil contract are consolidating just below the 20-, 50-, and 200-day moving averages. The long- and intermediate-term trends clearly are moving sideways, but look ready to turn up. You want to be there when they do. (See Chapter 7 for more about market trends and support.)

- ✔ **Watching the behavior of the market in relationship to the Bollinger bands:** During this consolidation the Bollinger bands — both upper and lower — have served as support and resistance for crude oil (see Figure 20-2). Notice that every time oil prices tag one or the other of the bands, the result usually and eventually leads to a reversal and a tag of the opposite band. Most recently, though, the price of crude came off of the bottom band. This is another clue that a move up is likely.

- ✔ **Noticing that the 20-day moving average also provided fairly good resistance during the recent rally attempt in crude.** You want to make sure that prices stay above that key level before making your move.

- ✔ **Analyzing what the price does above the 50 and 200 day averages:** Figure 20-1, shows all three averages. You decide that you want to make sure that you don't get whipsawed, so you'll put your initial buy point above the 200-day line, at 91.55, just above the 200-day line.

Stalking the Setup

You're now waiting for the setup, or a key set of developments that need to come together almost simultaneously before you pull the trigger and make the trade.

As you wait for these circumstances to occur, run through the following checklist to get ready for the trade:

- ✔ Check the status of your account.
- ✔ Review the key characteristics of your contract.
- ✔ Fine-tune your strategy.
- ✔ Review your plan of attack.

Checking your account

Always know how much money you have in your account. You can check your account status online. Say, for example, that you have $100,000 worth of equity. Your margin check shows that you need an initial margin of $7,763 per May contract and a maintenance margin of $5,750. See Chapters 3 and 4 for details about margins.

You have $100,000 of equity in your account. By consulting the margin requirements for the May contract for crude oil, you quickly calculate that you have enough in your account for going long on one or two contracts because the margin is $7,763 \times 2 = $15,526. Your rule is that you don't want to risk more than 10 percent equity in any one trade, but given the margins, and your analysis, you may want to risk an extra 5 percent in this one. In order to follow your rules closely, though, you decide to only buy one contract during your initial purchase. Let your experience and risk tolerance guide your decision.

You want to figure in how much to limit your losses to, so you have $2,013 per contract that you can play with before you start getting worried about a margin call ($7,763 – $5,750).

Figure 20-1:
Crude oil, moving averages, and buy points.

Reviewing key characteristics of your contract

As you formulate this trade, reviewing the characteristics of the crude-oil futures contract is a good idea. A barrel of oil holds 42 gallons and trades in U.S. dollars per barrel worldwide. The minimum tick of $0.01 (1 cent) is equal to $10 per contract. A single futures contract for light, sweet crude oil is in the amount of 1,000 barrels, or 42,000 gallons of oil.

That means that each penny you gain or lose is $10 worth of gain or loss in the contract, so you figure that $1 in price movement in crude oil is $1,000 worth of gain or loss.

You have $100,000 worth of equity in your account, so you have a good cushion. But you'll get a margin call if your equity drops a little over $2,000. That means that you'll have to work out your sell stop to be somewhere in between those two numbers. You decide that placing your sell stop just above where the margin call would get you is a good idea, so you settle on the initial stop being at $89.05. The margin call would be at $88.53.

See Chapter 17 for the details about trading plan and money-management rules. You need to follow the rules you establish, or else you'll eventually get into trouble.

Regular open-cry trading hours at the NYMEX are from 10 a.m. to 2:30 p.m. (14:30) eastern time. After-hours futures trading takes place electronically via NYMEX ACCESS, an Internet-based trading platform, beginning at 3:15 p.m. Monday through Thursday and concluding at 9:50 a.m. the following day. On Sundays, the session begins at 6 p.m.

Reviewing your plan of attack

After you come up with a plan, review it just to be on the safe side.

Here's what you've accomplished:

- ✔ You were attracted to the oil market (the right one for you) because it's where the action is. You understand the oil market, so it's okay to trade it.
- ✔ You've figured out the technical side of the trade, and you've identified the catalyst for the trade, the news of Venezuela's spat with Exxon Mobil.
- ✔ You've waited patiently for the right setup.
- ✔ You've calculated your risk, and you've decided on your entry point and your sell-stop placement.

CRUDE OIL OCT 2005 . . 30 minute OHLC plot

Prices remained higher overnight.

Put in your trade 15 minutes into the regular season.

Put in second order

Buyers step into the market and drive prices higher.

Raise your stop as the market rallies.

$63-$63.50 is a key short term support level, as prices stopped falling in this area.

Crude oil breaks below $63.50 and finds final support at $62.75 before rallying.

Figure 20-2: A 30-minute chart for crude oil for Aug. 17–19, 2005, zooms in on the action shown in less detail on longer-term charts like Figure 20-1.

Jumping on the Wild Beast: Calling In Your Order

As more traders come in, you see that the action is heating up, so you decide to make your trade because the price is moving swiftly toward your entry point of 90.55.

You have good trading software, but you decide to call your broker because she's been good about giving you good fills, and the guys at the trading desk are good at making sure that you, as a fairly young trader, get the kind of order that you want executed.

So you place the call, using all the correct language. Here's a good template to follow when calling in an order:

1. **Say who you are.**

   "This is Tom Smith."

2. **Say what kind of order you're placing.**

   "This is a futures order."

3. **Give your account number.**

   "My account number is 8648642."

4. **In a clear voice, say what you want done.**

   Buy one October crude oil, $89.05 stop.

5. **Ask for a reading of your order before you agree to have it sent to the floor.**

   The desk usually does this automatically, but it doesn't hurt to remind the person with whom you're working that you need confirmation.

If for any reason you're unsure about your order or unsure whether the desk understood it, make sure that you either cancel it or confirm that the trading desk person knows exactly what you want to do.

You just told the trading desk that you wanted to buy one October crude oil contract at the market price and that you wanted to place a sell stop at $89.05. The desk reads the order back to you, and you agree. The order then gets transmitted to the trading floor, and the desk informs you that you're filled at $90.75 and gives you your order number.

If you had wanted to keep the order active indefinitely, you would have told the trading desk that it was a good-'til-canceled (GTC) order. If you'd wanted to make it a limit order, you would have specified the limit. The fact that you didn't make the order a day order, which would be canceled at the end of the day, makes it a market order, so the point is not that important here. See Chapter 3 for more details about the different types of orders.

When you open an account with a broker, the broker sends you detailed information about how to place orders and what the correct language is. Some have special trading desks for new and inexperienced traders. Most futures brokers are fully aware of the fact that they need your business and will do everything they can to make your life as easy as possible short of guaranteeing that you'll make money.

Riding the Storm

As the day progresses, the market continues to move and it closes at $91.62.

You have some gains after all that waiting — hurrah! And you're still protected by your stop. Now, you raise your stop to $89.92, just slightly below the gains you made,. As the regular trading close nears, the market is rallying even more, so you raise your stop to $65, and you're nicely ahead now, with a guaranteed paper profit of $870 per contract if your stop gets hit without a major catastrophe that knocks prices below your sell stop in a gap. A good rule of thumb in a market that is moving rapidly is to raise your stop by 50 cents for every 50-cent rise in the market. If you make more than 50 cents, you can raise your stop more. Although I'm giving you guidelines here, the more you trade and the more you become familiar with the way each individual market trades, the more likely you'll develop your own guidelines. The message here is that as the market rises, you need to raise your sell stop to lock in gains.

Now you have a decision to make. Your overall profit is $870 at the close on a Friday. Your options prior to the close are

- ✔ **Selling your contract and reentering the market on Monday:** This strategy makes sense because you never know what's going to happen over the weekend.

- ✔ **Tightening your stops:** This strategy can get you stopped out of the market, which means that your sell stop is triggered, your position is closed, and you're out of the market. That would be good if the market crashed or lost ground, and it may cost you some money if you no longer have a position and the market rallies again. Remember, you want to let your profits run.

Knowing If You've Had Enough

Presented with the two trading options in the preceding section, I'd choose to leave the position open and see what happens during the weekend. I'm a cautious trader, and I don't like leaving large positions open during the weekend. But, the rally was very strong, and the Exxon news looked as if it had legs.

By managing my sell stop, I'd accomplish two things. First, I would have locked in my profits on a good trade, and second, I'd leave myself with a reasonable and tolerable risk over the weekend, with the potential to gain more.

By February 19, prices had moved nicely and the price of crude was getting close to $100, a price area that would likely lead to volatility, given the inevitable hype from the media.

On that day, as the price of crude jumped over $4 by the close, there was plenty of opportunity to sell. If you sold somewhere above $99, say $99.25 you bagged $8.50 in profits, or $8,500 minus commissions per contract.

Reviewing Your Trade

After your trade is completed, you need to review what you did right and what you did wrong. One way to conduct such a review is to answer these questions:

- ✔ **Was this market the right one for me to trade?** If you understood the fundamentals and you knew that the action was here, then you traded the right market.

- ✔ **Should you have bought into this market sooner?** More than likely your answer is no. By waiting for the right setup, and managing your sell stops, you had a fantastic trade.

- ✔ **Did you risk the right amount?** You followed your own rules by risking no more than 10 percent of your total equity in one market, and you used the right amount of protection as you set your stops. Best of all, you profited.

- ✔ **Were you patient enough?** Yes, indeed. You didn't jump into the market until you were convinced that the odds of a bounce back to the top of the range were on your side. Then you waited until the trend was clearly established before adding to your position, and you raised your stops at a steady and patient pace.

Mastering the Right Lessons

The trade outlined in this chapter probably is a good prototype for a beginning trader. I tried to make it easy to relate to and used easy-to-follow indicators.

This example is as much about approach as it is about the tools traders use. You can make trading as simple or as sophisticated as you want, but in the end, the only thing that counts is whether you make or lose money by using those tools.

Other books may offer different approaches, and as you gain more and more trading experience, you'll develop your own methods. Nevertheless, at the end of the day, trading is all about knowing your market, setting up your strategy, being patient, executing your trading plan, managing your position properly through vigilance, and following your strategy as well as the market will enable you to.

Finally, remember that a two- or three-day time frame in the futures markets can be a profitable time if you understand how to trade for short periods of time and how to use technical analysis.

Part VI
The Part of Tens

The 5th Wave
By Rich Tennant

I told Julian to take our money to Rappenship's and put it into a good company.

You want to mail your life savings to Procter and Gamble?!

RAPPENSHIP BROKERAGE

Nick's NEWS

WRAP 'N SHIP

In this part . . .

Get ready to put the final touches on your newfound trading abilities. Rules, resources, and strategies are good, but they're a whole lot better when you can use them. That's what this part is all about. I give you a comprehensive and detailed set of concepts and ideas to help you put it all together and fill in any gaps that may have formed. In this part, I take you through ten or so killer rules and must-know hedging strategies with two goals in mind: keeping you solvent and showing you how to survive and thrive as a trader. Don't skip this part!

Chapter 21

Ten Killer Rules to Keep You Sane and Solvent

In This Chapter

▶ Relying on chaos, capital, and patience

▶ Putting your trust in the trends, charts, and diversification

▶ Going small with losses, trades, and expectations

▶ Getting real about trading goals, and knowing your limits

Trading is 90 percent head games and 10 percent money. If your head isn't screwed on straight, you're going to lose a lot of money in a hurry. So in this chapter, I help you keep the old noggin atop your shoulders by providing you with a road map to ten of the best trading rules I've discovered during my 17 years of trading. These rules can help you keep your mind and money where they're supposed to be — between your ears and in your pocket, respectively.

Trust in Chaos

Chaos theory rules the markets. By definition, *chaos* is nonlinear order. In other words, what some describe as random actually is orderly in its own peculiar way. Look at the basic tenets of chaos, and then look at a market chart. It isn't hard to see a connection.

Prices follow a nonlinear order. They tend to stay within defined channels or trading ranges. When they rise above or below the range, they enter an area of disorder, but when they enter a new price range, they go up, down, or sideways, again seeking and eventually finding nonlinear order.

Big money can be made when you figure out how to spot the limits of chaos and the transitions from chaos to disorder and back to chaos. By making this concept the basis of your trading, you'll find that working the market is much easier than buying and holding something forever, hoping its price goes up, and much better than having the market work you or (more precisely) work you over.

When you trade with chaos as your guide, you find it easier to accept that the market will do whatever the market wants to do and that your job is to do your best to be on the profitable side (the right side) of the trade and to correct your mistakes as soon as you can.

Avoid Undercapitalization

If you don't have enough money, don't trade, period. It's as simple as that. Many people open futures trading accounts with $5,000 and lose half of it within a month only to run with their tails between their legs back to something safer. I know. That's what happened to me the first time I tried to trade futures.

How much money do you need? Most pros say that you need $100,000 minimum to open a futures trading account. If you whittle at them long enough, they'll come down to $20,000 to $50,000, but few will tell you that you need anything less than $20,000.

More important is the fact that your $20,000 to $100,000 needs to be money that you can afford to lose.

Why do you need so much money? Bluntly, it needs to last long enough for you to endure all the bad trades until you can finally make a good trade that makes you plenty of money.

Be smart with your money. Don't be one of those fools who maxes out his home equity just to be able to trade oil futures. Sure, you may get lucky and make it work, but the odds truly are against that. You can lose your money, and you'll probably lose your spouse, your family, your home, and your shirt.

Be Patient

The two times when you need patience in the financial markets are when you're becoming a good trader and finding good trades.

The problems with today's markets are that you have access to so much information that you can fool yourself into believing that you must trade all the time. That can get you into big trouble.

In fact, trading for the thrill of it, or because you're bored, is a recipe for disaster. I can remember periods where I didn't trade for days or weeks at a time. These periods of market inactivity occur more often as I develop my trading skills. When I first started, I overtraded, and I paid the price for it. Luckily, I don't make my entire living by trading and can afford to take my time picking and choosing the right times to trade.

Exercising this kind of patience can be to your advantage, too, because you can pick and choose when and how you trade.

Take time to think about your trading life. Some tough choices await you. Here are some important questions to ask before you jump in to the chaotic fray:

- How much of my livelihood do I intend to make by trading futures and options?
- How much time am I willing to put into analyzing the markets to improve my chances of delivering profits consistently?
- How much money am I willing to spend to educate myself and obtain a good trading setup?
- How long will I give myself to fully develop my trading talents?
- When will I trade?

Trade with the Trend

Investors are obsessed with the fundamentals. Futures trading isn't investing; it's speculating, so you need to be interested in technical *and* fundamental analyses. But the key here is that technical analysis tells you the direction in which the market you're trading is headed — how it's trending — and that's something you need to know from the get-go.

When trading futures, the market trend, your time frame, your entry and exit points, and the protection of your capital in between are all that matter. If preservation of your capital jibes with the fundamentals of the market and you make money, you can take a few minutes to celebrate and then go right back to worrying about the following:

- Keeping an eye on your charts
- Following your trading rules

When trading with the trend, never lower your sell stops just because you think the market will turn around and that you were too tight in setting them. Likewise, when selling short, never raise your stops if the market starts going against you.

Believe in the Charts, Not the Talking Heads

The ultimate truth about trading is the price action. Few sources offer a better view of price action than price charts, especially in the fast-moving world of the futures markets.

Opinions are numerous. Some are going to be right; some are going to be wrong. However, the majority of commentators have their own self-interest in mind. In other words, their goal is to look good in front of the camera or in print so they can keep their jobs. If they traded, they wouldn't have time to talk so much or to write reports.

That isn't to say that when I'm on CNBC, I won't be giving you the benefits of my experience, though, or that CNBC and other television channels don't provide access to good guests and good timely information. My point is that you always need to look at all information through the jaded eyes of a trader, and that means looking at the market's response to a story or an opinion and trading on what the market is doing, not on what the story is telling you.

Remember, Diversification Is Protection

In the stock market, diversification means spreading your risk among a large number of stocks and asset classes. Asset allocation models therefore have become quite handy. An asset allocation model is just a way to divide your investment portfolio and is often depicted as a pie chart. A common asset allocation model calls for a 60 percent exposure to stocks, a 35 percent allocation to bonds, and a 5 percent allocation to cash.

In the futures markets, however, diversification is different. It has more to do with how much cash you have on hand and how you allow seasonal tendencies of the market to affect your trading. Futures diversification boils down to your ability to manage your capital, your time, and your experience.

If you have more than one or two positions open at the same time in the futures market, you may find yourself in a dilemma because you have a hard time keeping up with what's happening when the markets move so fast. The way to get around this problem is to limit the number of markets that you trade at any one time. For some of us, it's one, or maybe two. Much depends on which markets you develop a knack for trading as you progress.

Limit Losses

Limiting your losses while trading is a simple rule that should make sense, but it's a rule that bears repeating. The 5 percent rule is commonly used by traders and is easy to see and remember. Don't risk any more than 5 percent of your trading capital on any given position, and limit your losses to 5 percent of the value of any given trade.

Get used to limiting your losses early on in your experience so you become disciplined in your approach to trading.

For a futures trader, a 5 percent loss is probably as much as you'll ever want to handle. If you're day trading, you can use period moving averages to identify where to place your stop-loss orders.

Make it a rule never to get a margin call. You'll sleep better.

Trade Small

Trading small goes along with limiting your losses. But above all else, trade within your means. If you have $5,000 equity, which is way too little to think about trading futures, you should never trade contracts that require a $5,000 margin. A bad day can wipe out your entire equity position, and you'll soon be getting a margin call.

For most beginning traders, trading one or two contracts at a time is a good rule of thumb. If you're trading crude oil, your margin is somewhere near $7,100 per contract, which means that, in a perfect world, you need to have at least $142,000 total equity to be able to trade one contract. See the previous section about how much to risk in any particular market. Your loss limit from that starting point is $355, or 5 percent of $7,100. See the preceding section with regard to limiting losses to 5 percent. (Check out Chapter 3 for more about margins and the futures markets.)

A perfect, or nearly perfect, contract for small accounts is the Chicago Mercantile Exchange (CME) E-mini Eurodollar contract. Margins for the Eurodollar contract tend to be less than $1,500 per contract, so you're thus at least closer to following the 5 percent rule.

Have Low Expectations

Most good traders are right a third of the time on average and half of the time during periods when they're hot. The way you stay in business is to manage your money so that you cut losses short.

Good traders are masters of the low-expectations game. That's where you think that if you come out even or a few bucks short, it's a good day. Pros readily admit they tend to make a lot of trades just on either side of breaking even. Known as *scratch trades,* they're the most common experience that you're likely to have while trading futures.

Having enough money and the sense to be able to continue to trade are key. The longer you stay in the game, the greater your chances of making the occasional big trade.

Set Realistic Goals

After you become well funded, develop a good money-management system, and set your expectations at the right level. The next step is to set realistic goals.

Here are a couple of ideas:

- ✔ **Some pros shoot for a three-to-one reward-to-loss ratio.** If you choose this strategy, that means when things are going well, your goal is to double your money twice over, while (of course) setting prudent stops and managing your money correctly.

- ✔ **Take profits when you've made 20 percent.** I like to take at least partial profits when I make 20 percent on anything. In futures trading, applying this rule is not always possible when you have only one contract, because commissions and fees can eat away at the profit. However, my 20 percent rule works well in the stock market, when I'm trading several hundred shares of stock.

Chapter 22

More Than Ten Additional Resources

In This Chapter

▶ Exploring futures through government and general-information Web sites

▶ Knowing the commodity exchanges

▶ Reading more books about trading

▶ Checking out the newsletters and magazines

*I*f you're going to trade on your own, you need some help, at least in the way of information, so you can apply what you've discovered in this book and in your newfound experiences with trading futures.

Literally hundreds of Web sites and publications deal with trading futures. This chapter lists and describes some of the more reliable information sources. Although the list may not be large, it is full of useful Web sites, books, and other sources of information that can actually help you become a better trader.

Government Web Sites

The Web sites of the Commodity Futures Trading Commission (CFTC — www.cftc.gov), the United States Department of Agriculture (USDA — www.usda.gov), and the Board of Governors of the Federal Reserve System (www.federalreserve.gov) are useful in their own ways. If you're a data hound, there's no better place to look than the St. Louis Fed's Web site (http://stlouisfed.org/default.cfm).

✔ **The CFTC** Web site is a great resource for reviewing trading laws and regulations and finding out what kind of recent advisory rulings have been handed down. When laws and regulations change, your trading can be affected. These changes can affect anything from higher fees to what you can and can't trade under certain circumstances.

✔ **The USDA** Web site runs the gamut from important crop and livestock reports to vital weather information. The USDA site can be of great use to you when you trade commodities.

✔ **The Federal Reserve** Web site offers the Fed Beige Book, a great summary of where the Fed thinks the economy has been and is headed. The Beige Book is the Fed's road map for interest rates, and it sets the stage for much of the action in the bond and stock markets.

✔ **The St. Louis Federal Reserve Bank** Web site is full of charts and statistics that I like to use when I'm doing my history homework, such as when I want to see a chart of interest rates for the last several years. This site is also different from the Fed's main Web site in that it has a more news-oriented, less-academic feel to it.

General Investment Information Web Sites

In this section, I list several important Web sites that can serve as libraries of information about trading futures, options, and other securities and financial instruments. Some of these sites require a fee; others don't. I like them all and visit them regularly.

✔ **The "Economy" section of Wall Street Journal.com:** This section of the Wall Street Journal's Web site is one of my favorites. It's an excellent resource for catching up on the big picture before you trade. The editorial content is first class, but for a futures trader, the best part is the data library, where you can find charts that chronicle the major economic indicators and enable you to perform a good visual inventory of economic activity.

✔ *Investor's Business Daily*'s **"The Big Picture" column:** This is a great resource for getting a fix on the overall trend of the stock market. This column can help your timing of stock index futures as it features clear and easy to understand analysis of when the stock market changes its major trend, up or down. This is a subscription service which has an excellent digital web site (www.investors.com), which I highly recommend and use on a daily basis.

- ✔ **Marketwatch.com's "Commodity Summary"** (marketwatch.com): This summary provides a great overview of the commodities markets, usually with a pretty heavy emphasis on oil. The best part: It's free, but it works better if you register.

- ✔ **Reuters.com** (reuters.com): Another excellent free news site, I especially like to check out Reuters early in the morning because it offers good summaries of the overnight markets.

- ✔ **Barchart.com** (barchart.com): The most complete Web-based charting service specializing in the futures markets, Barchart.com offers real-time data to subscribers, but its delayed data and charting are excellent for beginners who are trying to get a grip on the knowledge part of trading before they move on to the real thing.

- ✔ **CandlesExplained.com** (candlesexplained.com): This free site is from Greg Morris, the author of *Candlestick Charting Explained* (McGraw-Hill). It's a good site for anyone who wants an online review or a quick reference to candlestick charting beyond what's available in this book.

- ✔ **FX-charts.com:** You can find free, real-time, foreign exchange charts at www.fx-charts.com/pgs/toolbox_livecharts.php. This is a great place to get a good feel for real-time charts in the currency market. The charts also have indicators that you choose, including the ability to draw your own trend lines.

- ✔ **Joe-Duarte.com** (www.joe-duarte.com). Sure, this seems like self-promotion, but it's not. If you like what you read in this book, what a better place to get more of the same as well as clarifying any doubts that you may get from time to time. I offer a good deal of market timing information, especially using ETFs for trading energy, stock indexes, and currencies. It is a paid subscription site, but also offers a good deal of free information.

Commodity Exchanges

The Web sites of the Chicago Mercantile Exchange (CME www.cme.com), the Chicago Board of Trade (CBOT www.cbot.com), and the New York Mercantile Exchange (NYMEX www.nymex.com) are excellent resources, especially for beginning traders.

All three exchanges provide excellent overviews of the commodities that trade within their jurisdictions, margin requirements, and delayed charting.

Trading Books

Very few high-quality trading books about the futures markets are available, given the public's major interest in stocks. Here is a good sampling of some of the better books that I've run across:

- *Trading Commodities and Financial Futures* (Financial Times-Prentice Hall, 2005) is written by George Kleinman, an author with a pure trader's mind-set. It offers an excellent step-by-step guide into the analysis and execution of trading.

- *Starting Out in Futures Trading,* 5th Edition, by Mark J. Powers (Probus Publishing, 1993, largely out of print) offers a trader's point of view, moving between an analyst's and an academic's perspective on the futures markets. You can find used copies at very low prices online.

- The Murphy triad: Author John Murphy has compiled and written what some consider a classic trilogy of technical analysis in these three tomes:

  - *Technical Analysis of the Financial Markets: A Comprehensive Guide to Trading Methods and Applications* (New York Institute of Finance, 1999)

  - *Intermarket Analysis: Profiting from Global Market Relationships* (Wiley, 2004)

  - *Technical Analysis of the Futures Markets: A Comprehensive Guide to Trading Methods and Applications* (New York Institute of Finance, 1983)

- *Candlestick Charting Explained* by Gregory L. Morris (McGraw-Hill, 1995) is the easy-to-read-and-use bible for candlestick charting. No trader should be without this one in his or her library.

- *Technical Analysis For Dummies* by Barbara Rockefeller (Wiley, 2004) is a pretty good reference book that can be a companion to *this book*. It offers excellent tutorials for beginners, and it's a great read for building a base for more complex fare, such as Murphy's triad.

- *Currency Trading For Dummies* by Mark Galant and Brian Dolan (Wiley, 2007) is another excellent entry-level book that offers the basic principles of trading, not only in great detail but also in an easy-to-digest style. This book is great for someone who is interested in trading but isn't quite ready to delve into it.

- *Reminiscences of a Stock Operator* by Edwin Lefevre (Fraser Publishing, 1980) is the classic trading book. Although it deals with the stock market during a different era, no other book that I've ever read captures the spirit of speculating better. At the heart of it, this book is about cutting losses at small levels and letting winners run.

Newsletter and Magazine Resources

Many futures publications are available, and many of them can be accessed on the Internet. A few, though, have been around long enough to have become quite reliable, including the following:

- **The Hightower Report (**www.futures-research.com**):** As Fred Sanford of *Sanford & Son* used to say, "This is the big one, Elizabeth." *The Hightower Report* is the most widely circulated futures newsletter in the United States, and it covers the entire futures complex.

- **Consensus National Futures and Financial Weekly (**www.consensus-inc.com**):** This subscriber-supported service, whose major calling card is its weekly sentiment index, provides a poll of bullish and bearish investors on all commodities and futures, from interest rates to energy and livestock.

- **Futures Magazine (**www.futuresmag.com**):** The name says it all; it's the monthly bible of the industry covering all aspects of the trade.

- **Technical Analysis of Stocks & Commodities (**www.traders.com**):** This magazine is written by traders, and it's where I got my start as a writer and an analyst. It's a good resource to scan regularly for good trading ideas.

- **Active Trader: Similar to Technical Analysis of Stocks and Commodities**: This publication tends to offer more about short-term trading.

Index

• **D** •

• P •

• X •

• Y •

BUSINESS, CAREERS & PERSONAL FINANCE

0-7645-9847-3

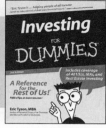

0-7645-2431-3

Also available:

- Business Plans Kit For Dummies
0-7645-9794-9
- Economics For Dummies
0-7645-5726-2
- Grant Writing For Dummies
0-7645-8416-2
- Home Buying For Dummies
0-7645-5331-3
- Managing For Dummies
0-7645-1771-6
- Marketing For Dummies
0-7645-5600-2

- Personal Finance For Dummies
0-7645-2590-5*
- Resumes For Dummies
0-7645-5471-9
- Selling For Dummies
0-7645-5363-1
- Six Sigma For Dummies
0-7645-6798-5
- Small Business Kit For Dummies
0-7645-5984-2
- Starting an eBay Business For Dummies
0-7645-6924-4
- Your Dream Career For Dummies
0-7645-9795-7

HOME & BUSINESS COMPUTER BASICS

0-470-05432-8

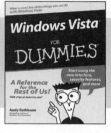

0-471-75421-8

Also available:

- Cleaning Windows Vista For Dummies
0-471-78293-9
- Excel 2007 For Dummies
0-470-03737-7
- Mac OS X Tiger For Dummies
0-7645-7675-5
- MacBook For Dummies
0-470-04859-X
- Macs For Dummies
0-470-04849-2
- Office 2007 For Dummies
0-470-00923-3

- Outlook 2007 For Dummies
0-470-03830-6
- PCs For Dummies
0-7645-8958-X
- Salesforce.com For Dummies
0-470-04893-X
- Upgrading & Fixing Laptops For Dummies
0-7645-8959-8
- Word 2007 For Dummies
0-470-03658-3
- Quicken 2007 For Dummies
0-470-04600-7

FOOD, HOME, GARDEN, HOBBIES, MUSIC & PETS

0-7645-8404-9

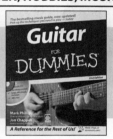

0-7645-9904-6

Also available:

- Candy Making For Dummies
0-7645-9734-5
- Card Games For Dummies
0-7645-9910-0
- Crocheting For Dummies
0-7645-4151-X
- Dog Training For Dummies
0-7645-8418-9
- Healthy Carb Cookbook For Dummies
0-7645-8476-6
- Home Maintenance For Dummies
0-7645-5215-5

- Horses For Dummies
0-7645-9797-3
- Jewelry Making & Beading For Dummies
0-7645-2571-9
- Orchids For Dummies
0-7645-6759-4
- Puppies For Dummies
0-7645-5255-4
- Rock Guitar For Dummies
0-7645-5356-9
- Sewing For Dummies
0-7645-6847-7
- Singing For Dummies
0-7645-2475-5

INTERNET & DIGITAL MEDIA

0-470-04529-9

0-470-04894-8

Also available:

- Blogging For Dummies
0-471-77084-1
- Digital Photography For Dummies
0-7645-9802-3
- Digital Photography All-in-One Desk Reference For Dummies
0-470-03743-1
- Digital SLR Cameras and Photography For Dummies
0-7645-9803-1
- eBay Business All-in-One Desk Reference For Dummies
0-7645-8438-3
- HDTV For Dummies
0-470-09673-X

- Home Entertainment PCs For Dummies
0-470-05523-5
- MySpace For Dummies
0-470-09529-6
- Search Engine Optimization For Dummies
0-471-97998-8
- Skype For Dummies
0-470-04891-3
- The Internet For Dummies
0-7645-8996-2
- Wiring Your Digital Home For Dummies
0-471-91830-X

* Separate Canadian edition also available
† Separate U.K. edition also available

Available wherever books are sold. For more information or to order direct: U.S. customers visit www.dummies.com or call 1-877-762-2974.
U.K. customers visit www.wileyeurope.com or call 0800 243407. Canadian customers visit www.wiley.ca or call 1-800-567-4797.

SPORTS, FITNESS, PARENTING, RELIGION & SPIRITUALITY

0-471-76871-5

0-7645-7841-3

Also available:
- Catholicism For Dummies
  0-7645-5391-7
- Exercise Balls For Dummies
  0-7645-5623-1
- Fitness For Dummies
  0-7645-7851-0
- Football For Dummies
  0-7645-3936-1
- Judaism For Dummies
  0-7645-5299-6
- Potty Training For Dummies
  0-7645-5417-4
- Buddhism For Dummies
  0-7645-5359-3

- Pregnancy For Dummies
  0-7645-4483-7 †
- Ten Minute Tone-Ups For Dummies
  0-7645-7207-5
- NASCAR For Dummies
  0-7645-7681-X
- Religion For Dummies
  0-7645-5264-3
- Soccer For Dummies
  0-7645-5229-5
- Women in the Bible For Dummies
  0-7645-8475-8

TRAVEL

0-7645-7749-2

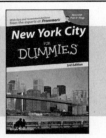

0-7645-6945-7

Also available:
- Alaska For Dummies
  0-7645-7746-8
- Cruise Vacations For Dummies
  0-7645-6941-4
- England For Dummies
  0-7645-4276-1
- Europe For Dummies
  0-7645-7529-5
- Germany For Dummies
  0-7645-7823-5
- Hawaii For Dummies
  0-7645-7402-7

- Italy For Dummies
  0-7645-7386-1
- Las Vegas For Dummies
  0-7645-7382-9
- London For Dummies
  0-7645-4277-X
- Paris For Dummies
  0-7645-7630-5
- RV Vacations For Dummies
  0-7645-4442-X
- Walt Disney World & Orlando
  For Dummies
  0-7645-9660-8

GRAPHICS, DESIGN & WEB DEVELOPMENT

0-7645-8815-X

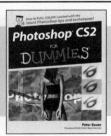

0-7645-9571-7

Also available:
- 3D Game Animation For Dummies
  0-7645-8789-7
- AutoCAD 2006 For Dummies
  0-7645-8925-3
- Building a Web Site For Dummies
  0-7645-7144-3
- Creating Web Pages For Dummies
  0-470-08030-2
- Creating Web Pages All-in-One Desk
  Reference For Dummies
  0-7645-4345-8
- Dreamweaver 8 For Dummies
  0-7645-9649-7

- InDesign CS2 For Dummies
  0-7645-9572-5
- Macromedia Flash 8 For Dummies
  0-7645-9691-8
- Photoshop CS2 and Digital
  Photography For Dummies
  0-7645-9580-6
- Photoshop Elements 4 For Dummies
  0-471-77483-9
- Syndicating Web Sites with RSS Feeds
  For Dummies
  0-7645-8848-6
- Yahoo! SiteBuilder For Dummies
  0-7645-9800-7

NETWORKING, SECURITY, PROGRAMMING & DATABASES

0-7645-7728-X

0-471-74940-0

Also available:
- Access 2007 For Dummies
  0-470-04612-0
- ASP.NET 2 For Dummies
  0-7645-7907-X
- C# 2005 For Dummies
  0-7645-9704-3
- Hacking For Dummies
  0-470-05235-X
- Hacking Wireless Networks
  For Dummies
  0-7645-9730-2
- Java For Dummies
  0-470-08716-1

- Microsoft SQL Server 2005 For Dummies
  0-7645-7755-7
- Networking All-in-One Desk Reference
  For Dummies
  0-7645-9939-9
- Preventing Identity Theft For Dummies
  0-7645-7336-5
- Telecom For Dummies
  0-471-77085-X
- Visual Studio 2005 All-in-One Desk
  Reference For Dummies
  0-7645-9775-2
- XML For Dummies
  0-7645-8845-1